Presenting Women Philosophers

In the series *The New Academy,*
edited by Elizabeth Kamarck Minnich

Presenting Women Philosophers

EDITED BY

Cecile T. Tougas and
Sara Ebenreck

TEMPLE UNIVERSITY PRESS

PHILADELPHIA

Temple University Press, Philadelphia 19122
Copyright © 2000 by Temple University, except Chapter 1 © 2000 by Gerda Lerner,
Chapter 10 © 2000 by Sara Ebenreck, and Chapters 17 and 23 © 2000 by Cecile T.
Tougas.
All rights reserved.
Published 2000
Printed in the United States of America

⊗The paper used in this publication meets the requirements of the American
National Standard for Information Sciences—Permanence of Paper for Printed
Library Materials, ANSI Z39.48–1984

Library of Congress Cataloging-in-Publication Data

Presenting women philosophers / edited by Cecile T. Tougas and Sara Ebenreck.
    p. cm.—(The new academy)
  Includes bibliographical references and index.
  ISBN 1–56639-760-x (alk. paper)—ISBN 1–56639-761-8 (pbk. : alk. paper)
    1. Women philosophers.   I. Tougas, Cecile T. (Cécile Thérèse), 1947– .
  II. Ebenreck, Sara, 1937– .   III. Series.
B105.W6P74   2000
190'.82—dc21

                                                      99–055717

Reprint credits appear on pp. xiii–xiv.

This book is dedicated to

Veda A. Cobb-Stevens,

founder of the

Society for the Study of Women Philosophers

Contents

Series Foreword

Presenting Women Philosophers is that rare thing, an anthology one can sit down and read through—a sustaining, energy-refreshing shared meal, not just an array of appetizers. By gathering essays about philosophizing women, it contributes significantly to the scanty resources yet available for anything like a genuinely inclusive course of readings in philosophy. This would have been enough to recommend it for *The New Academy* series. However, we still need to establish and publish far beyond the academy evidence that, despite all kinds of obstacles, women have always done far more, and done it far better, than the dominant record can report. More specifically, we still need to know that women have been philosophers, which is to know something profoundly and particularly decentering of the dominant culture, driven as it has been by partial yet determinedly universalized and so dangerously falsified notions of Man Who Is Rational. Women philosophers of the past spoke in terms that made sense to them, and that they could hope might be heard, as they took on many of the meanings, and their dangerous implications with practices, of Man Who Is Rational. Their meanings sometimes do, often don't, work smoothly with those we variously find most telling today. *Presenting Women Philosophers* moves into the present, and makes us a present of, thinking women who challenge many molds, including some held by those of us tempted to think that we now know better than our predecessors what needs to be said, to whom, how, and to what ends.

All of this, as I said, would have been enough, but this unusual volume does more. The editors, Sara Ebenreck and Cecile T. Tougas, have taken the wonderful risks of first discerning threads of, and then themselves joining, transhistorical conversations among philosophizing women. Thus, while the words of others are here for us to read and make sense and use of for ourselves, according to our own tastes, needs, and interpretive lenses, we can also follow the story of the intense encounters Cecile and Sara have had with them. These editors have refused discreetly to hide themselves or to play any one role. Here they are, acting as hosts graciously respectful of others' intentions and meaning, concerned with helping us fully prepare to hear each other into speech. And here they are also as philosophers, intensely engaged in their own quests for capacious meaning to sustain lives, and as women, discovering, rejecting, reclaiming, redefining who and what they are, can be, should be, might become with and against offerings and impositions of others. They are here, too, as teachers, providing resources, challenging, questioning, and sometimes going ahead and being open with us about what they think, what troubles or angers or inspires them so they, too, are fully present in the relationship that teaching/learning can be.

A rich brew, this, a feast for those hungering for the sustenance of philosophizing—and still much more, many more are needed to keep philosophizing going as deep and arching as widely as humans, the whole motley lot of us, want and require.

—Elizabeth Kamarck Minnich

Acknowledgments

As editors, we would like to acknowledge our appreciation to the many people who assisted us in the development and preparation of this collection of essays. Elizabeth K. Minnich, editor of the New Academy series at Temple University Press and a founding board member of the Society for the Study of Women Philosophers, helped in multiple ways. She was an active participant in the decision to gather these essays into a book and, at several stages of its process, reviewed it in a creatively critical way. As series editor, she smoothed our path at many points. Charlene Haddock Seigfried, also a board member of the society, provided a careful review of the text, raising questions that helped us better articulate its purposes and limits. Other board members of the Society for the Study of Women Philosophers provided further encouragement, and the society itself supported the effort with funds when necessary. In addition, both Ben Franklin Academy in Atlanta, Georgia, and St. Mary's College of Maryland—home institutions for the editors, respectively—provided technical and other support for the preparation of the manuscript. Linda Vallandingham and Mary Bloomer of St. Mary's College of Maryland entered several articles on computer disks and helped with dozens of other details. Sara Ebenreck wishes to thank both Clyde and Jered Ebenreck for caring support over the long period of work on this book.

We also acknowledge the following permissions:

"Moral Wisdom in the Black Women's Literary Tradition" is reprinted from *Katie's Canon*, by Katie Geneva Cannon. Copyright © 1995 by Katie Geneva Cannon, used by permission of the Continuum Publishing Company.

Veda A. Cobb-Steven's poetry is used by permission of Richard Cobb-Stevens, her husband and estate executor. Copyright 1988 by Veda A. Cobb-Stevens.

Helen J. John's "Hildegard of Bingen: A New Medieval Philosopher?" appeared in an earlier version under the same title in *Tradition and Renewal: The Centennial of Louvain's*

Institute of Philosophy (Leuven: Leuven University Press, 1992) pp. 255–64. The revised version is printed with permission of the publisher.

Elizabeth Minnich's "Hannah Arendt: On the Relation of Thinking and Morality" first appeared as "To Judge in Freedom: Hannah Arendt on the Relation of Thinking and Morality" in *Hannah Arendt: Thinking, Judging, Freedom,* edited by Gisele T. Kaplan and Clive S. Kessler (Sydney: Allen & Unwin, 1989), pp. 133–43. It is reprinted in a slightly revised version by permission of both author and publisher.

Beatrice Nelson's "Susanne K. Langer's Conception of 'Symbol': Making Connections through Ambiguity" appeared in an earlier version under the same title in *The Journal of Speculative Philosophy,* vol. 8, no. 4 (1994), pp. 277–96. Copyright 1994 by The Pennsylvania State University. This modified version is reproduced with the permission of the publisher, The Pennsylvania State University Press, and the author.

Some of the thoughts of Andrea Nye in her essay "Elisabeth, Princess Palatine: Letters to René Descartes" are similar to things discussed at length in her book *The Princess and the Philosopher: Letters of Elisabeth of the Palatine to René Descartes* (Totowa, N.J.: Rowman & Littlefield Publishers, Inc., 1999), although not in the same words. This modified text is used with permission of the publisher.

A portion of Cecile T. Tougas's "Philosophical Friendship, 1996: A Postscript" appeared in *Harvest,* vol. 2, no. 2 (1996), pp. 35–42. Permission for its use has been given by the author. The publisher allows for the author's use of her own material elsewhere at any time.

Mary Ellen Waithe's "Heloise and Abelard" appeared as "Heloise" in vol. 2 of *A History of Women Philosophers* ed. Mary Ellen Waithe (Dordrecht: Kluwer Academic Publishers, 1989), pp. 67–83. It is reprinted here by the kind permission of the publisher and the author.

Mary Helen Washington's "Introduction to *A Voice From the South*" is excerpted from the longer version by the same title, published in *A Voice From the South* by Anna Julia Cooper (New York: Oxford University Press, 1988). It is used by permission of the author, Mary Helen Washington.

Ann Willeford's "A Woman-Centered Philosophy: An Alternative to Enlightenment Thought (1700–1750)" is a translation of "Une alternative à la philosophie des Lumières (1700–1750)" in *Femmes et pouvoirs sous l'ancien régime,* edited by Danielle Haase-Dubosc and Eliane Viennot in the 1991 collection "Rivages/Histoire" directed by Arlette Farge, pp. 223–38. Copyright 1991, Editions Rivages, Paris. It is used by permission of Editions Payot & Rivages, Paris.

Introduction

In the late twentieth century, more and more women are studying and teaching philosophy. Nonacademic women are also concerned with important philosophical questions. Many of us have found that the traditional "canon" of academic philosophy in the West does not satisfy us. In seeking what is missing from it, we—and sometimes our males colleagues, too—have turned to examine the work of women thinkers. In doing so, we wondered if there were women philosophers before the twentieth century whose writing could help fulfill our need for what we felt was missing. We began to seek them and dig their work out of its undeserved obscurity. Slowly we uncovered accounts of experiences and perspectives of great value to us. And we wondered: Why had we known so little about them? Why has so little reference been made to them by the male philosophers whose work comprises the canon? For we were finding that the insights in the work of these earlier women have powerful implications for anyone who asks philosophical questions today.

In 1987, animated by a great desire to uncover the work of women philosophers of the past for their great relevance to our philosophical efforts in the present, Veda A. Cobb-Stevens at the University of Massachusetts Lowell founded the Society for the Study of Women Philosophers. Its purpose was to encourage study of the work of women philosophers by sponsoring sessions on that work during meetings of the American Philosophical Association. In the thirteen years since the society was founded, dozens of papers and discussions have focused attention on the work of women thinkers both past and present. Many essays in this book had their origin in papers given at meetings of the society.

The presentations before this society had the advantage of covering a wide range of Western women—from early thinkers to contemporary ones, from well-known contemporary women like Hannah Arendt or Susanne Langer to little-known women of the past like Ednah Dow Cheney or Madame de Sablé. But the presentations also had the disadvantage of appearing scattered. Each one was interesting, but since each was given without reference to the others, the connections among them were obscured. One might, as Mary Ellen Waithe does so competently in *A History of Women Philosophers* (Kluwer Academic Publishers, 1987, 1989, 1991, and 1994), view these thinkers chronologically. But a new task beckoned: discerning thematic continuity of some sort in this work and finding patterns that would show coherence in the philosophical history of women.

In her essay in the first section of this book—originally an address to our society in 1993—historian Gerda Lerner points out why connection among women thinkers is not easy to discern. She gives historical evidence over many centuries that Western women's intellectual life was "an enforced discontinuity." The few women of earlier times who managed to gain an education and speak and write publicly were not able to learn of one another, for even if they were well-known in their own day, their works were often not reprinted. Rarely was this work welcomed and analyzed by the later—and male-dominated—academic philosophical community. Even worse, this situation existed in sharp contrast to the canonical tradition that most students today meet in colleges and universities under the title "the history of philosophy." In this tradition a continuity of commentary links one male philosopher to another: Hume, for example, comments on Locke, and Kant responds to Hume. But female philosophers did not enjoy such mutual recognition. Christine de Pizan, for instance, does not include the work of the great twelfth-century thinker and mystic Hildegard of Bingen in her fifteenth-century list of the accomplishments of women over the ages. Living in an even more difficult situation, women thinkers who were not white experienced a double exclusion, because of both race and gender; this double exclusion accounts for the tragic loss of still more of women's philosophical work. As the essay on the work of Anna Julia Cooper shows, the articulation of a black feminist philosophy and a written challenge to white women feminists to recognize the voices of black women dates at least as far back as Cooper's publication in 1892 of *A Voice from the South by a Black Woman of the South.*

This book is an attempt to free us from the enforced discontinuity that women intellectuals over the centuries have endured. We present important women philosophers, each the focus of the attention of some current writer. Authors contributing to this book philosophize with earlier women thinkers, thereby establishing community with them. Moreover, when taken together, these contemporary studies of the work of women over many centuries reveal some persistent themes and practices. The naming of reality in nondualistic ways that reflect appreciation for matter, body, and lived experience is one such theme. Another is the practice of philosophizing while trying to be a good friend, which is common to many women. Yet a third theme is emphasis on love and the life of feeling in establishing moral community.

We do not claim, on the one hand, that these are the only themes of women philosophers or that all women thinkers engaged these themes. On the other hand, as editors we did not need to force the connections. The major sections of this book express our happy discovery that many women who did not know one another's work still had similar philosophical concerns and practices. Within each section and in most cases, we ordered the essays chronologically according to the women studied.

This arrangement allows the reader to see how women from quite diverse periods, often without knowledge of one another's work, moved toward common themes as they struggled to articulate philosophies rooted in their experiences. Still, each woman's voice is distinct, and we as editors were not interested in trying to form some generality through which all women might be thought to be understood. Rather, we have respected each woman as in a class by herself, worthy of our full attention. Our aim, then, was to make aspects of one woman's wisdom present in relation to other wisdom expressed in the book. The result is that contributors to our book, in their thoughtful dialogue with previous women philosophers, move towards a genuinely inclusive and varied history of philosophy. Such work is changing the appearance of both philosophy and its history.

In this book we have welcomed reflection on modes of expression that are different from men's conventional modes of writing philosophy. One contributor finds genuine philosophy in the insight of a woman mystic. Another reaches into the oral tradition of black women to analyze the moral values of that community. Still another considers a philosophical statement about the worth of feminine human being as it is spoken in a *dit*, a mid-thirteenth century metrical form used to express personal emotion. Others resurrect philosophy by turning their notice to women's letters, to pages appended to a translation, to novels, to biographical storytelling, or to *maximes*, concise sentences based on ironic observation of manners. Women intellectuals spoke in a variety of ways, not only because men kept them from conventional public expression but also because these particular ways fit what the women had to say. To emphasize the importance of recognizing these alternative ways to express philosophical insight, we have included some poems from our friend, philosopher Veda A. Cobb-Stevens, founder of our society and author of a private collection called *Fifty Forms for Fifty Philosophies* that she gave to a few friends before she died in 1989.

In community of spirit with these alternative ways of approaching philosophy, we close several sections of this book with our personal reflections on what it has meant to each of us to engage in depth the thoughts and questions of our philosophical sisters. In themselves, these editorial essays illustrate both the powerful reverberations and the unique insights that can ensue when someone takes up the work of philosophizing with the texts of women thinkers. Indeed, we hope that we, the editors, lead many readers into extended reflection on how taking these women philosophers seriously affects their own thoughts and practices. Clearly, the book's essays taken as a whole evidence not only the continuities we point to in our sections, but also many of the different perspectives that arise when philosophical queries proceed in deep connection with the life experiences of individuals. It is with delight in the broad range of voices included here that we present these women philosophers.

—Sara Ebenreck and Cecile T. Tougas

Presenting Women Philosophers

I

The Loss and the Recovery of Women's Voices

Sara Ebenreck

Introduction to Part I

The recovery and appreciation of women's philosophical voices requires skills from multiple disciplines: historical skills in locating forgotten texts, literary skills in textual analysis, and philosophical skills in analyzing the insights that are rediscovered. Accordingly, this volume begins with an essay by a feminist historian who has reflected on both the reasons for the loss of women's voices and the importance of recovering them. This broad analysis is followed by an essay from a literary scholar whose evaluation of the historic importance of the work of one early twentieth-century black American feminist provides a powerful instance of the treasures to be regained in the recovery of work by past women thinkers.

With concise directness, historian Gerda Lerner states a central reason for the loss of women's voices in the patriarchal tradition of the European-American West: those with the power to include or to exclude women's voices marginalized women, both within their time and in the studies of history that mark important voices for the attention of later generations. Bereft of the history of women's work and teachings, women thinkers over and over again had to reinvent and defend the most basic of theoretical structures: an argument for their authority to think, speak, and write. When they did write, it was almost always in dialogue with male thinkers of their time rather than by engaging and taking further the insights of previous women thinkers. But today, Lerner writes, we live in a Renaissance time for women, a time when women who experience the painful difference between their life experiences and the values transmitted by patriarchal culture are challenging that culture. As the lengthy list of important earlier women thinkers mentioned in her essay indicates, we must do that challenging, not in a historical vacuum, but rather with conscious awareness of the work of previously unrecognized women who have preceded us.

When race as well as gender contribute to the silencing of a woman's voice, the exclusion is magnified. Mary Helen Washington's commentary on the thought of American black feminist Anna Julia Cooper provides witness to the courageous ways in which one woman surmounted the powerful cultural and institutional obstacles raised against an intellectual who was both female and black. Washington sketches the nature of Cooper's black feminism, including her critique of white feminists who exclude the voices of black women from their considerations. She details the way in which Cooper's education and work as a teacher were made precarious both by the cultural framework in which it took place and by her own nonconformist choices. Yet, as Washington also notes, Cooper herself, to be heard in the larger intellectual world, had to identify herself with "true womanhood" in ways that a contemporary critique may identify as not sufficiently feminist. Washington's evaluation allows us to see the complex facets of Cooper's feminism; in it the reader may recognize the very real difficulties of expressing women's thoughts in a language and intellectual culture so long dominated by men.

Gerda Lerner

1   Why Have There Been So Few Women Philosophers?

My participation in this volume as an outsider to the field of philosophy represents the recognition that feminist scholarship must of necessity be interdisciplinary. I am also very much an insider, not as a philosopher in the narrow sense, but as one engaged in what I take to be our common enterprise: the feminist critique of the foundations of Western civilization, of its leading metaphors, its unspoken patriarchal assumptions, its myths of origin.

As the feminist challenge of traditional interpretations developed, the fields most resistant to the new scholarship have been the sciences, intellectual history, philosophy, and classics. These are the fields within which, from the Middle Ages onward, the educational canon has been defined. Science, the youngest of these fields, has been central to the body of knowledge and tradition only since the end of the nineteenth century, yet from its inception in the academy and outside of it, it has been a predominantly male field. Religion, one of the oldest academic fields, is an interesting exception. Possibly because of the larger numbers of women in the field and because of many reform and renewal movements outside the academy in this century, it has been more receptive to feminist ideas than the other fields. I would suggest that openness to new ideas and structures is generally in reverse ratio to the field's relationship to the core of tradition. The professions can stand reforms, some opening up, some loss of their exclusiveness; but when it comes to challenges to the traditional values by which the field is organized, the defenses go up.

The current, so-called "cultural war" promoted by right wing conservatives has focused predominantly on a defense of the supposedly eternal values represented by the classical canon of academic knowledge. The great philosophers, the great male thinkers, the great classical works represent, according to these defenders of Western civilization, the very essence of its meaning and values. The canon itself has become a metaphor for the intellectual product of Western civilization, which functions like the metaphor of the flag to nationalism—it is supposed to rally us around it, inspire us to battle in its defense and lead us, in unquestioning obedience, to holy war. Academic philosophy, defined in the traditional way, is central to this core metaphor. It is no wonder, then, that feminist philosophers face great resistance on the part of traditionalists.

In my book *The Creation of Patriarchy*, I have traced the social and economic conditions that led to the institutionalization of patriarchy in the Ancient Near East.[1] These conditions were well established at the time philosophy and science were developed in classical Greece. Philosophy, one of the pillars of the edifice of traditional Western civilization, arose in a society in which some men were given the education, leisure and free social space in which to develop systems of ideas and explanations, while their domestic and physical needs were met by the unpaid labor of women and slaves. The educated male elite discovered the power that comes with definition, the power to manipulate symbols, to give form to experience and to offer people explanations for their condition. Because from the start the male system builders were divorced from ordinary life and from the necessities of daily reproduction, they built some conceptual errors into their systems that survive to this day. One of the most serious of these is their claim to universality, their arrogant assumption that they can and are entitled to speak for vast populations that are invisible and silenced—slaves, women, foreigners. By making the term "man" subsume "woman," by making the generic "we" subsume those silenced, men have arrogated to themselves the representation of humanity, even though they are in actuality only half of humanity. I have called this "patriarchal fallacy" an error of vast proportions.[2] By taking the half for the whole, they have not only missed the essence of whatever they are describing, but they have also distorted it in such a fashion that they cannot see it correctly. As long as men believed the earth to be flat they could not understand its reality and its true relationship to other bodies in the universe. As long as men believe their experience, their viewpoint, and their ideas represent all of human thought, they are not only unable to define correctly in the abstract, but they are also unable to see reality accurately.

The fact that the patriarchal system was well established prior to the period when the great philosophical systems were first developed has led the early philosophers to incorporate unexamined and unquestioned patriarchal assumptions into their thinking in such a way as to make them for a long time invisible. Aristotle's argument in his *Politics* is a case in point. At the time this work was written, the moral rightness of slavery was still a questionable and debatable issue. Why should one man rule over another? By what right should one man be master and another slave? Aristotle reasoned, rather lamely, that some men were born to be rulers, others to be ruled. To explain, he used several analogies: the soul being superior to the body, it must rule the body; the rational mind being superior to passion, it must rule over passion. And "the male is by nature superior, and the female inferior; and the one rules and the other is ruled; this principle, of necessity, extends to all mankind."[3] He concluded that "It is clear, then, that some men are by nature free, and others slaves, and that for these latter slavery is both expedient and right."[4]

What is remarkable about this definition is not so much its circuitous logic, as what is assumed and what is deemed in need of explanation. Aristotle conceded that there was some need for justifying the enslavement of people, but he saw no need whatsoever for justifying or explaining the inferiority of women. That was assumed as a given and remained undisputed. Aristotle's misogynist construction became one of the foundation stones of Western civilization, and his assumptions remained unchallenged and endlessly repeated for nearly two thousand years. Thus, from its inception, the power of philosophers to define rested on their power in society and in turn reflected and reinforced that power metaphorically.

The hegemony of patriarchal thought in Western civilization is not due to its superiority over all other thought; it rests upon the systematic silencing of other voices. Women of all classes, men of different races, ethnicities, or religions, and the vast majority of laboring people were kept out of the intellectual discourse. Patriarchal thinkers constructed their edifice the way patriarchal statesmen constructed their archaic states: by defining who was to be kept out. The definition of those to be kept out was usually not even made explicit, for to do so would have meant to acknowledge that there was a process of exclusion going on. They were simply obliterated from sight, marginalized out of existence. Religion, science, philosophy—the three great mental constructs that explain and order the world of Western civilization—were formed and developed without the participation of women. Just as the distribution and allocation of economic resources gives power to the rulers, so does the withholding of information and the denial of explanatory constructs to the oppressed give power to the system builders.

Similarly, when, in the Middle Ages, the great system of European universities made structured learning more widely accessible, the university was so defined as to exclude all women from it.[5] And again, when in the nineteenth century, throughout Europe and in the United States, professions redefined their purposes, restructured their organizations, licensed and upgraded their services, and enhanced their status in the societies in which they operated, this was done on the tacit assumption that women were to be excluded from these professions. It took nearly a hundred years of organized struggle for women to reverse, at least partially, the results of such exclusions. It is no wonder that in our day the defenders of the fortress of tradition see the barbarians at the gate every time we question any aspect of their tradition.

Women, far longer than any other subordinate group, have been kept from the power of definition by a combination of structural and institutional discriminations and by an ideology that denied them their full humanity. The question has plagued all of us modern feminist thinkers: Why have there not been any great women thinkers, no great philosophers, no system builders? The patriarchal answer to the question has always been, because women are mentally inferior. Since the nineteenth century this answer has sometimes been varied by "scientific" explanations as to brain size, hormones, and other biological factors. Obviously, such answers are unacceptable to women. How then can we approach the question?

Historians will start by qualifying it. There have been women philosophers and system builders in the nineteenth and twentieth centuries, and if that is so, why have they not appeared earlier? This was in fact the question I set out to answer in my book, *The Creation of Feminist Consciousness*.[6] The answers I found were contradictory and ambiguous. (1) We can explain why we are not likely to find any great women philosophers; (2) we can resurrect some of them and try to reassess their significance; (3) we can learn to define and recognize the subversive and reconstitutive manner of women's thought and claim its legitimacy. I will briefly attempt to trace these efforts by means of historical evidence.

First of all, we must try to understand the complex effect upon women of material and social restrictions and of ideas that reinforce traditional gender definitions. The principle means of subordinating women has been the systematic educational disadvantaging to which they were subject for nearly two thousand years. In every known society in the Western world women had less access to education than did their brothers; the education they received was inferior and of shorter duration than that of their brothers; and the content of their education was directed toward preparing them for wifely and household duties, while denying them knowledge of more abstract subjects. The exceptions to this rule were the few women of noble, elite families who were expected to accede to political power if there were no men in their families to do so. These "stand-ins" for missing males were excellently educated. Further, all over the world, literacy figures show much greater illiteracy among women than among men, which is another indication of educational deprivation.

Women were forced for hundreds of years not only to argue for their right to equal education but first to prove their capacity to be educated at all. This absorbed the energies of most women of talent and retarded their intellectual growth. Further, up until the end of the nineteenth century in Europe and in the United States, women in order to be educated had to give up their sexual and reproductive lives—they had to choose between wife-and-motherhood on the one hand and education on the other. No group of men in history ever had to make such a choice or pay such a price for intellectual development.

For millennia, women were conditioned to accept the patriarchal definition of their role in society; they have sexually and emotionally serviced men. Their talents were focused on realizing themselves through the development of a man of talent, instead of on self-development. Women were allotted the major responsibility for domestic care and the nurturance of children, which has freed men from the cumbersome details of daily survival activities, while it has disproportionately burdened women with them. Almost universally, men have enjoyed more spare time, and above all more uninterrupted time in which to think, to reflect, and to write than have women. Nurturant support based on intimacy and love has far more readily been available to talented men than to talented women. Had there been a man behind each brilliant woman, there would have been numbers of women of achievement in history equal to the numbers of men of achievement.

Even more devastating than educational deprivation was women's gender indoctrination, which remained unchanged well into the nineteenth century. Women were taught by their parents, by their priests, in school and in church, that they were mentally inferior. It is not surprising that most of them internalized that message and gave up all ambition for achievement. What is surprising is that nevertheless there were in each generation some women who persisted, against all odds, in struggling for self-expression and creative thought.

Those who achieved anything at all were disparaged. Some were accused of having stolen their work from men in their family; others, of having plagiarized it from male sources. Women defended themselves against these accusations as best they could, and for centuries women who did attempt to write and publish also apologized profusely for their daring undertaking.

Such women somehow managed to develop enough feminist consciousness to contradict patriarchal thought that defined them as inferior; they authorized themselves to claim their own thought in public. Still, what they spoke and what they wrote was soon forgotten, even if they had great impact on their contemporaries. Their works were not reprinted; their names, if they were remembered at all, were remembered for the wrong reasons and the significance of their thought was belittled.

"When one reads historical works covering long spans of time there are no more traces of our [women's] names to be found than there are traces to be found of a vessel crossing the ocean," wrote Anna Maria von Schurman, one of the most celebrated learned women of her century, in 1638.[7]

She accurately diagnosed the devastating effect of the absence of women's history on the development of women's thought. Men have developed ideas and systems of thought by absorbing past knowledge, critiquing and superseding it. Women were deprived of knowledge of the works and lives of other women. Therefore, for generations, they struggled to reinvent the wheel, over and over again. I have documented the existence of women's Bible criticism for a period of over one thousand years.[8] This is far longer than anyone has known such criticism to exist. In every century there were numbers of women engaged in this repetitive feminist critique of the biblical texts without knowing that other women before them had already covered the same ground. Their effort did not alter the patriarchal paradigm nor did it propel women's thought in a feminist direction. It helped individual women to authorize themselves and in some cases to create works of lasting impact. What we need to note is the discontinuity in the story of women's intellectual effort. This enforced discontinuity made it impossible for women to do large-scale, system-building work.

To sum up the first answer to our question: we can explain why there have been only a very few great women philosophers until the nineteenth century. It was due to systematic educational disadvantaging of women, due to material constraints on them, and due to the absence of women's history.

Now we will shift ground and argue that indeed there have been great women philosophers; we will resurrect them and reevaluate their work.

The first women in Europe who liberated themselves from the constructs of male thought and from the male claim that women could reach God only through the mediation of the male clergy were mystics. Female mystics strove to establish their full and equal humanity by insisting on their ability to speak to God and to be heard by God. Not only did God speak to them, they made their contemporaries believe that their ecstatic experience was real. Mystical practice and discipline enabled some of these women to proceed to a level of redefinition—in their visions, dreams, and writings they asserted the female component of the Divine.

I will mention only a few examples here. The towering genius among the women mystics is Hildegard of Bingen, a twelfth-century Benedictine nun. She derived her authority entirely from her visions, on the strength of which she managed to create an entirely new role for herself and other women, without ostensibly violating the patriarchal rules of the Church. She was an abbess, a founder and leader of two religious communities, the correspondent and adviser of emperors, kings, popes, abbots, and nuns. She wrote eleven volumes, embodying an encyclopedic knowledge of religion, the natural sciences, folklore and medicine. She composed hymns and choral works, and she inspired the illumination of her visions in works of art executed under her direction. Her works were known during her lifetime and for another century, and were republished during the Renaissance. More important than the range and volume of her work is the subtle feminist revisioning expressed in it. Hildegard's vision of cosmos, nature and humankind is powerful in its holistic approach. Her insistence on the unity of male and female principles in the universe, on earth, and in heaven is another aspect of her highly original philosophy. Her theology breaks sharply with the dichotomized categories of the scholastics and with the patriarchal hierarchies embedded in their thought. Hildegard's vision fuses male and female elements, the physical and the spiritual, the rational-practical and the mystical aspects of existence.

Although she is quite traditional in her use of the masculine designation for God— Father, King, Redeemer—she uses feminine symbols for God throughout her work. In her visions and her narrative, great feminine figures appear repeatedly on a level of equality or predominance. In her theology, the idea of Christ's predestination is preeminently linked with the feminine, and she repeatedly envisions the Church as Mother. Without here being able to do justice to the creativity, complexity, and subtlety of her work, let me observe that she seems to me to qualify in every respect in the categories of a great thinker, a great philosopher and a great theologian.[9]

Among secular women thinkers, the first to come to mind as a woman of great stature is Christine de Pizan (1365–1430). She was the first woman we know to make her living as a writer. She was a poet, an essayist, a historian, and the writer of the first full-length feminist book. While she did not write philosophy in the usual, narrow sense, her insistence on woman's right to judge theory on the basis of her own experience provided a philosophical grounding for a feminist world view. The range and scale of her work qualifies her as a major thinker, and in her feminist ideas she was several centuries ahead of other women.[10] Despite her unquestioned greatness as an intellectual she represents the methodological difficulties we face when we try to find "women philosophers" in the past. They are nearly impossible to find if we apply to them the criteria we apply to male philosophers. Due to the constraints and disadvantages under which thinking women had to live and due to their isolation from institutional recognition, their work and careers look different from those of men. I do not propose to elevate to the level of philosopher any woman who had ideas of any kind or who pursued intellectual interests. But I think we need to be sensitive to the possibility that women's thought, just like women's art, would find different modes of expression than would men's. This brings us to the third part of my argument: we must define and recognize the subversive and reconstitutive thought of women and reclaim its legitimacy.

I consider here only women who tried to construct an alternative to the patriarchal system of ideas and assumptions, even if their efforts did not result in many volumes of work comprehending many fields of knowledge. Seen from this point of view, I would include Emily Dickinson among the women philosophers who created alternative views of the world and who consciously set themselves against traditional patriarchal belief systems. Dickinson, in her several thousand poems, of which only eight were published during her lifetime, dealt with the most fundamental philosophical and theological questions. She did so with the vision of a woman-centered artist whose resistance to patriarchal ideas was in a way more far-reaching and certainly more deeply searching than that of her contemporaries in the woman's rights movement, who defined themselves as feminist.[11]

Yes, there have been great women philosophers, great system builders and questioners, women who resisted patriarchal thought and constructed feminist alternatives. To find them we have to stop looking for women in the male model. We have to be willing to look at small-scale work, at messages delivered "slant," as Emily Dickinson said. We have to look at partial attempts, at aborted insights, at women searching for new forms of expression. We would then include among the women philosophers Mary Astell and Marie le Jars de Gournay; in the nineteenth century Frances Wright, Angelina and Sarah Grimke, Margaret Fuller, Matilda Joslyn Gage, Charlotte Perkins Gilman, Anna Julia Cooper, and Emma Goldman in the United States; Bettina von Brentano, Caroline Guenderrode, and Annette Droste-Huelshoff in Germany; Anna Wheeler, Emma Martin, Harriet Taylor, Virginia Woolf in England.[12] We might also wish to include some of the great novelists, such as the Brontes, George Eliot, and George Sand. What is important is not how many names we can cite, but how to establish the continuity of effort by women to think in terms of larger systems of thought, to study their thought with all of its limitations, to honor it for the way they persisted despite all obstacles. Above all, it is important to understand the conditions necessary for women to develop philosophical thought, large-scale thought. It does not matter how long our list is nor how we define for inclusion—we will have to note that the list of women philosophers is shorter than those of men and we will have to stress that there are good reasons for it.

The ability to "do philosophy," to engage in abstract thought, rests on social conditions more than on the appearance of brilliant minds. For men, it has always rested on education, on having free time, on being relieved of the necessity for daily maintenance through work. It has also rested on the existence of free social spaces in which to pursue such work and on contact with other intellectuals who provide "cultural prodding." All of these conditions have been unavailable to women until late into the nineteenth century and are still unavailable to most women of color or those living in poverty. The most important element in fostering the development of abstract thought has been the existence of an intellectual history of men, which has enabled male thinkers to begin where other men left off, and to argue with the male thinkers before them. This condition has never been available to women and we are barely beginning, through the development of women's history, to make it available today. Educational deprivation and the absence of women's history made it impossible for women to develop consciousness of their own situation, a feminist consciousness.

Without feminist consciousness, without an understanding that their situation is tied to that of other women and can be changed only through the collective efforts of women, individual thinkers could not connect with the women thinkers before them, and had to continue, far longer than was appropriate, to "think like men."

The cruel repetitiousness by which individual women have struggled to a higher level of consciousness, repeating an effort made a number of times by other women in previous centuries, is not only a symbol of women's oppression, but is its actual manifestation. Thus, even the most advanced feminist thinkers up to and including those in the early twentieth century, have been in dialogue with the "great men" before them and have been unable to verify, test and improve their ideas by being in dialogue with the women thinkers before them. Mary Wollstonecraft argued with Burke and Rousseau, when arguing with Makin, Astell and Margaret Fell might have sharpened her thought and radicalized her. Emma Goldman argued for free love and a new sort of communal life against the models of Marx and Bakunin; a dialogue with the Owenite feminists Anna Wheeler and Emma Martin might have redirected her thinking and kept her from inventing "solutions" that had already proven unworkable fifty years earlier. Simone de Beauvoir, in a passionate dialogue with Marx, Freud, Sartre and Camus, could go as far with a feminist critique of patriarchal values and institutions as it was possible to go when the thinker was male-centered. Had she truly engaged with the opus of Mary Wollstonecraft, the works of Mary Astell, the Quaker feminists of the early nineteenth century, the mystical revisioners among the black spiritualists and the feminism of Anna Cooper, her analysis might have become woman-centered and therefore capable of projecting alternatives to the basic mental constructs of patriarchal thought. Her erroneous assertion that, "They [women] have no past, no history, no religion of their own" was not just an oversight and a flaw, but a manifestation of the basic limitations that have for millennia limited the power and effectiveness of women's thought.[13]

Human beings have always used history in order to find their direction toward the future: to repeat the past or to depart from it. Lacking knowledge of their own history, women thinkers did not have the self-knowledge from which to project a desired future. Therefore, women have, up until very recently, not been able to create a social theory appropriate to their needs. Feminist consciousness is a prerequisite for the formulation of the kind of abstract thought needed to conceptualize a society in which differences do not connote dominance.

In order for women to develop feminist consciousness, substantial numbers of women must be able to live in economic independence and see alternatives to marriage as a means of economic security. Only when large groups of single, self-supporting women have existed, have women been able to conceptualize alternatives to the patriarchal state; only under such conditions have they been able to elevate "sisterhood" into a unifying ideal. In order for women to verify the adequacy and power of their own thought, they have needed cultural affirmation, exactly as did men. Mystics and women religious could find such affirmation in their actual or spiritual communities. Secular women sometimes did find it in female networks or clusters, such as the *beguinage* and the intellectual salons of the eighteenth and nineteenth centuries. When printed books and magazines became available, women were able to find it in the response of female readers to their books and articles.

But as long as the vast majority of women depended for their economic existence and that of their children on the support of a man, the formation of such female support networks was the privilege of a tiny minority of upper-class women. Thus, even the intellectually most emancipated women, those hoping to make changes in society, could not conceive of the process other than doing so with the help of powerful men. This fact restrained both their thought and their creativity.

Today, feminist work in philosophy is growing in scope and sophistication. This is so because thinking women, educated in specialized fields, have a deep need to bring their professional knowledge in line with their life experience and their social existence. The gap between who we are and what we have experienced on the one hand, and the transmitted knowledge represented in the patriarchal cultural product on the other hand, is painful and problematic. Ultimately, as thinking women, we must challenge it, and bring our own knowledge and existence to bear on what we think, what we teach, and what we create. Unless we do this, we will continue to "think like men" and thereby undermine our self-esteem, weaken the foundations of our identity as women, and, perhaps worst of all, continue to pass on as universal knowledge a partial and deeply faulty vision of culture.

Women, for millennia denied equal access to education and knowledge, denied a chance to define knowledge, are no longer accepting these restrictions. We are thinking for ourselves, we are bringing our lives into the formation of abstractions, we are insisting on our experiences being considered as valid a test of reality as the experiences of men. A richer, more complex cultural tradition is in the process of formation. It is good to be part of this process, part of this time—the Renaissance for women.

Notes

1. Gerda Lerner, *The Creation of Patriarchy* (New York: Oxford University Press, 1986).

2. Ibid., pp. 220–1. See also Elizabeth Kamarck Minnich, *Transforming Knowledge* (Philadelphia, Pa.: Temple University Press, 1990), pp. 37–40, 71–7.

3. Aristotle, *Politica*, tr. Benjamin Jowett, in W. D. Ross, ed., *The Works of Aristotle* (Oxford: Clarendon Press, 1921), I, 2, 1254b, 4–6, 12–16.

4. Ibid., 1255a, 2–5.

5. The handful of exceptions to this generalization, a few women over the span of seven centuries who had access to university teaching as heirs to their learned fathers, only confirms the rule.

6. Gerda Lerner, *The Creation of Feminist Consciousness: From the Middle Ages to Eighteen-Seventy* (New York: Oxford University Press, 1993).

7. Anna Maria von Schurman to Andre Rivet, as cited in ibid., p. 271. Endnote, p. 329.

8. Ibid., chapter 7.

9. For further reading in English on Hildegard of Bingen see Matthew Fox, ed., *Illumination of Hildegard von Bingen* (Santa Fe, N.M.: Bear & Co., 1985); Barbara Newman, *Sister of Wisdom: St. Hildegard's Theology of the Feminine* (Berkeley, Calif.: University of California Press, 1987). For a fuller bibliography, see Lerner, *Feminist Consciousness*, pp. 351–2.

10. See Christine de Pizan, *The Book of the City of Ladies*, Earl Jeffrey Richards, tr. (New York: Persea Books, 1982); Charity Cannon Willard, *Christine de Pizan: Her Life and Works* (New York: Persea Books, 1984).

11. The original works and letters of Emily Dickinson are readily accessible to the reader. For interesting feminist interpretations of her work, see Paula Bennet, *Emily Dickinson: Woman Poet* (Iowa City: University of Iowa Press, 1990); Suzanne Juhasz, ed. *Feminist Critics Read Emily Dickinson* (Bloomington: Indiana University Press, 1983); Lerner, *Feminist Consciousness*, pp. 181–91, 371.

12. These women are discussed and bibliographical references for them are provided in my book, *Feminist Consciousness*.

13. Simone de Beauvoir, *The Second Sex*, tr. and ed., H. M. Parshley (1952; New York Bantam, 1970) p. xix. For a fuller discussion of this point see Gerda Lerner, "Women and History," in Elaine Marks, ed., *Critical Essays on Simone de Beauvoir* (Boston: G. K. Hall & Co., 1987), pp. 154–67.

The preceding paragraph is taken from my book, *Feminist Consciousness*, p. 281. It expresses exactly what I want to say on the subject and so I see no need to rephrase it.

2   Introduction to *A Voice From the South*

Given Anna Julia Cooper's unparalleled articulation of black feminist thought in her major work, *A Voice From the South by a Black Woman of the South,* published in 1892; given her role as a leading black spokeswoman of her time (she was one of three black women invited to address the World's Congress of Representative Women in 1893 and one of the few women to speak at the 1900 Pan-African Congress Conference in London); given her leadership in women's organizations (she helped start the Colored Women's YWCA in 1905 because of the Jim Crow policies of the white YWCA and in 1912 founded the first chapter of the Y's Camp Fire Girls); and given the fact that her work in educating black students spanned nearly half a century, why is Anna Cooper a neglected figure, far less well known than such distinguished contemporaries as Frances Harper, Ida B. Wells, and Mary Church Terrell? One of her biographers, Dr. Paul Cooke, suggests that Cooper's role as a scholar limited her public profile.

ба   ба

But the exclusion of Cooper from black intellectual history is more than simply disdain for the intellectual. The intellectual discourse of black women of the 1890s, and particularly Cooper's embryonic black feminist analysis, was ignored because it was by and about women and therefore thought not to be as significantly about the race as writings by and about men. . . . Cooper thought differently, maintaining, in fact, that men could not even represent the race. At the heart of Cooper's analysis is her belief that the status of black women is the only true measure of collective racial progress. Because the black woman is the least likely to be among the eminent and the most likely to be responsible for the nurturing of families, it is she, according to Cooper, who represents the entire race:

> Only the BLACK WOMAN can say "when and where I enter, in the quiet, undisputed dignity of my womanhood, without violence and without suing or special patronage, then and there the whole *Negro race enters with me.*"[1]

A Voice From the South begins with this dramatic challenge to the prevailing ideas about black women, and Cooper never softens that uncompromising tone. She criticizes black men for securing higher education for themselves through the avenue of the ministry and for erecting roadblocks to deny women access to those same opportunities.

> While our men seem thoroughly abreast of the times on almost every other subject, when they strike the woman question they drop back into sixteenth century logic. . . . I fear the majority of colored men do not yet think it worth while that women aspire to higher education.[2]

If black men are a "muffled chord," then black women, writes Cooper, are the "mute and voiceless note" of the race, with " *'no language—but a cry.'* "

Cooper is equally critical of the white women's movement for its elitism and provinciality, and she challenges white women to link their cause with that of all the "undefended." Always she measures the ideals and integrity of any group by its treatment of those who suffer the greatest oppression.

ﻭﻭ   ﻭﻭ

Born Annie Julia Haywood in 1858 in Raleigh, North Carolina, Cooper was the child of a slave woman, Hannah Stanley Haywood, and her white master, George Washington Haywood. In a brief autobiographical statement of her early years, Cooper wrote, "My mother was a slave and the finest woman I have ever known. . . . Presumably my father was her master, if so I owe him not a sou & she was always too modest & shamefaced ever to mention him."[3]

ﻭﻭ   ﻭﻭ

When the Episcopal Church opened St. Augustine's Normal School and Collegiate Institute for the newly freed slaves in 1868, Annie Haywood, then about nine and a half years old, was among the first to enter, her admission perhaps reflecting the social and cultural standing of the Haywood family.

As a teenager, Cooper began protesting against sexism when she realized that men, as candidates for the ministry at St. Augustine's, were given preferential treatment, while women were steered away from studying theology and the classics. She complained to the principal that "the only mission open before a girl . . . was to marry one of those candidates." Writing of that experience in *A Voice,* she remembered the difficulties a black girl faced in her struggle for education and how easy the way was made for males:

> A boy, however meager his equipment and shallow his pretensions, had only to declare a floating intention to study theology and he could get all the support, encouragement and stimulus he needed, be absolved from work and invested beforehand with all the dignity of his far away office. While a self-supporting girl had to struggle on by teaching in the summer and working after school hours to keep up with her board bills and actually to fight her way against positive discouragements to the higher education.[4]

In 1877, at the age of nineteen, Cooper did in fact marry one of those candidates for the ministry, George Cooper. His death two years later left her a widow, which ironically allowed her to pursue a career as a teacher, whereas no married woman—black or white—could continue to teach. She began writing letters to Oberlin in 1881 to request free tuition and to apply for employment so that she could earn her room and board. As at St. Augustine's, Cooper rejected the distinctly inferior "Ladies Course" at Oberlin and, like many of the women, chose the "Gentlemen's Course," which she says sarcastically caused no collapse at the college, though the school administrators thought it was a dangerous experiment:

> [It] was adopted with fear and trembling by the good fathers, who looked as if they had been caught secretly mixing explosive compounds and were guiltily expecting every moment to see the foundations under them shaken. . . ."[5]

Cooper attained a B.A. and later an M.A. at Oberlin, and in 1887, as one of the few blacks with a graduate degree, she was recruited by the Superintendent for Colored Schools to teach at Washington's only black high school—first known as the Washington Colored High School, then as M Street High School, and finally as the famous Dunbar High School.[6] For several decades the schools educated the children of the aspiring black middle class and gained a reputation for having both high academic standards and a deep-seated snobbery based on class and color. During her initial tenure at M Street, where she was first a math and science teacher (she later taught Latin) and then the school principal, Cooper was in the midst of a male and racist stronghold that would eventually bring about her humiliating expulsion from the school. According to a former student at the school, Annette Eaton, Cooper might have expected male hostility:

> You must also remember that as far as the Negro population of Washington was concerned, we were still a small southern community where a woman's place was in the home. The idea of a woman principal of a high school must account in some part for any reaction Dr. Cooper felt against her.[7]

Cooper became the principal of M Street in January 1902, when she was forty-four years old. At the time Booker T. Washington's program of vocational and industrial training was emerging as *the* model for black education and consequently was playing into the prejudices of whites who believed in black intellectual inferiority. By contrast, Cooper staunchly maintained M Street's orientation toward preparing black youth for college. In defiance of her white supervisor—Percy Hughes, who told her that colored children should be taught trades—Cooper sent several of her students to prestigious universities, including Harvard, Brown, Oberlin, Yale, Amherst, Dartmouth, and Radcliffe. During her tenure as principal, M Street was accredited for the first time by Harvard. For her intransigence, Cooper became the central figure in the "M Street School Controversy" and was eventually forced to resign. A letter by Annette Eaton testifies to the role of white racism in Cooper's dismissal.

> If you could smell or feel or in any way sense the aura of D.C. in those days, you would know that it only took her daring in having her students accepted and given scholarship

at Ivy League schools to know that the white power structure would be out to get her for any reason or for no reason. It was pure heresy to think that a colored child could do what a white child could.[8]

≥≈   ≥≈

Cooper was brought before the D.C. Board of Education in 1905 and, according to the minutes of the Board meeting, she was charged with the following: (1) refusing to use a textbook authorized by the Board; (2) being too sympathetic to weak and unqualified students; (3) not being able to maintain discipline (two students had been caught drinking); and (4) not maintaining a "proper spirit of unity and loyalty." . . . The dispute dragged on for almost a year until 1906 when the Board voted to dismiss her.[9]

≥≈   ≥≈

In 1910 a new superintendent of M Street summoned Cooper back to resume her position as a Latin teacher. She was fifty-two years old, and the next fifty years of her life (she died at the age of 105 in 1964) were as active as the first. Perhaps to assuage the humiliation of her exile, Cooper began to study for her doctorate at Columbia. Before she could complete Columbia's one-year residency requirement, she adopted, in 1915, five orphaned children, who ranged in age from six months to twelve years and were the grandchildren of her half-brother. She brought all five children from Raleigh to Washington where she had bought a new home "to house their Southern exuberance." As difficult as it was to become the mother of five at age fifty-seven, Cooper tackled it with characteristic resolution and defiance:

> With butter at 75 cents per lb. still soaring, sugar severely rationed at any price and fuel oil obtainable only on affidavit in person at regional centers, the Judge at Children's Court . . . said to me: "My, but you are a brave woman!" Not as brave as you may imagine, was my mental rejoiner—only stubborn, or foolhardy. . . ."[10]

In spite of a newly acquired mortgage, a family of five small children, and a full schedule of teaching, Cooper continued—"for 'Home Work,'" as she called it—to work on her doctorate, this time with the Sorbonne. Once she enrolled the children in boarding schools, she began to study summers in Paris, and in 1924, having requested a sick leave from her teaching job, she went to Paris to fulfill the residency requirements. Apparently the leave had not been granted, and after fifty days in Paris she received this cable from a friend: "Rumored dropped if not returned within 60 days."[11] Not willing to risk the loss of her retirement benefits or income, Cooper returned to her classroom "5 minutes before 9 on the morning of the 60th day of my absence," greeted by the applause of her students. Despite these obstacles from her supervisors at M Street (now Dunbar High), Cooper defended her dissertation in the spring of 1925 and was awarded a doctorate from the University of Paris. At the age of sixty-seven, she was the fourth American black woman to receive a Ph.D.

Cooper continued to write well into the 1940s, but she never again singled out black women as her major subject, nor did she ever again take the explicitly feminist stance that she did in *A Voice*. The critical questions to ask about Anna Cooper's career are these: What happened to her early feminist voice in the years after *A Voice*? What of her steadfast resolve that "there be the same flourish of trumpets and clapping of hands" for the achievement of women as for men?[12]

We can speculate that a life of professional uncertainty and of financial insecurity made it difficult for her to continue her writing. Cooper came of age during a conservative wave in the black community, a period in which Afro-American intellectual and political ideas were dominated by men. In the very year that Cooper published *A Voice From the South*, Frederick Douglas, when asked by historian M. A. Majors to name some black women for inclusion in Major's biographical work on black women, responded: "I have thus far seen no book of importance written by a Negro woman and I know of no one among us who can appropriately be called famous."[13] Five years later in 1897, when leading black intellectuals such as Francis Grimké, W. E. B. Du Bois, and Alexander Crummell formed the prestigious American Negro Academy [ANA] "for the promotion of Literature, Science, and Art," they limited the membership to "men of African descent."[14] Deeply committed to the intellectual and moral goals of the ANA, Cooper reviewed the opening meeting for the February 1898 issue of Southern Workman, in which she noted the exclusion of women with the simple comment, "Its membership is confined to men." She did not comment further, even though she knew that outstanding black women intellectuals were being denied membership. Nor did she comment on the obvious exclusion of women from the masculine imagery of the ANA, which was determined to rescue and elevate "black manhood."

In spite of the reverential way she referred to her male colleagues—Douglas, Du Bois, Grimké, and Crummell in particular—her distinguished counterparts rarely returned the compliment in print. Cooper's relationship with Du Bois underscored how women got left out of black political life. She obviously knew and respected the eminent Dr. Du Bois. She was one of the few black women to address the 1900 Pan-African Congress, which Du Bois helped to organize. She wrote to him at least three times, once in 1936 to ask if he would publish her biographical sketch of her friend Charlotte Grimké. Du Bois said it was too long, although he praised the idea. When she suggested he run it in three serials (probably in the *Crisis*), he neither answered nor returned her notes for the sketch. She wrote to him in 1929, urging him to write a response to *The Tragic Era*, a racist book on Reconstruction by Claude Bowers.

> It seems to me the Tragic Era should be answered—adequately, fully, ably, finally, and again it seems to me *Thou* are the man! Take it up seriously thro the Crisis and let us buy up 10,000 copies to be distributed broadcast thro the land.
> Will you do it?
> Answer
>
> Faithfully,
> Anna J. Cooper

Du Bois' famous book, *Black Reconstruction*, was the result of his response to Cooper's urgings.[15]

ﻬ   ﻬ

I cannot imagine Du Bois being similarly faithful to Anna Cooper, offering to publicize her work, or being willing to hawk ten thousand copies of one of her speeches on women's equality, nor can I imagine that any of the male intelligentsia would have been distraught at not being able to attend the annual meetings of the colored women's clubs. In a compassionate and generally progressive essay called "On the Damnation of Women," Du Bois sympathetically analyzes the oppression of black women, but he makes no effort to draw on the writings of black women intellectuals for their insights into the problems facing black women. In fact, in a remarkable oversight in this essay, Du Bois quotes Cooper's brilliant observation that "only the black woman can say 'when and where I enter' " and attributes the statement not to her but *anonymously* to "one of our women."[16]

Though the embryonic black feminist viewpoint suggested in *A Voice* was never fully developed in any of her subsequent writings, Cooper maintained a natural feminist sensibility that made her—at least occasionally—an outspoken critic of patriarchal politics. Once asked by a white friend why the men of her race seemed to outstrip the women in mental obtainment, Cooper said that men's intellectual superiority was merely an illusion created by their posturing: " ' . . . the women are more quiet. They don't feel called to mount a barrel and harangue by the hour every time they imagine they have produced an idea.' "[17] She instinctively rebelled against the power males exerted over female life even when that male was a trusted friend. In 1936 the Reverend Francis Grimké, one of the most respected men in Washington and a good friend of Cooper's, sent her a copy of a sermon called "Suicide or Self-Murder," which he had preached after the death of a feminist writer, Charlotte Perkins Gilman. The sermon was a judgmental and condemnatory pronouncement of Grimké's deep regret that Gilman had failed to bear her afflictions with Christian courage and patience. Cooper's reply to Grimké's moralism, dated April 9, 1936, shows her unwillingness to have a female life subjugated by a male text. She strongly objected to Grimké's depreciation of Gilman's achievements by focusing only on her death:

> I wish in the leaflet on Frances [*sic*] Perkins Gilman you had given your readers more of
> the life history of your subject. . . . I am sure the facts in that life, leaving out its tragic end,
> would have been full of inspiring interest and stimulating encouragement. But you are
> always the preacher you know and *must* draw your moral for the benefit or the confusion
> of the rest of us poor sinners. I forgive you. . . ."[18]

ﻬ   ﻬ

Everywhere in *A Voice From the South,* Cooper is concerned about the unrestrained power of a dominant majority to crush the lives of the weak and the powerless. As Hazel Carby points out in her essay on black women intellectuals at the turn of the century,[19] Cooper's position was never narrowly confined to the women's issue because she saw this dominance of the strong over the weak as the critical issue, and she saw that tendency to abuse power in the labor and women's movements, both of which were deeply entrenched in "caste prejudice" and hostile to the needs and interest of black women. The sympathy of the labor movement for "working girls" never included black working women who were confined to the most menial and strenuous physical labor:

> One often hears in the North an earnest plea from some lecturer for "our working girls" (of course this means white working girls) . . . how many have ever given a thought to the pinched and down-trodden colored women bending over wash-tubs and ironing boards—with children to feed and house rent to pay, wood to buy, soap and starch to furnish—lugging home weekly great baskets of clothes for families who pay them for a month's laundering barely enough to purchase a substantial pair of shoes![20]

While Cooper believed strongly in the power of the women's movement to challenge patriarchal power, she was not naïve about the capacity of white women to condone and perpetrate race prejudice. Knowing how deeply the South had influenced the women's movement, she devotes an entire chapter in *A Voice* to attacking the white supremacist ideas that had crept into the movement. Women emancipators must first be released from the "paralyzing grip of caste prejudice,"[21] Cooper asserts, and she takes on movement leaders Susan B. Anthony and Ann B. Shaw for their failure to take a strong stand against racism. What precipitated this censure was the refusal of a women's culture club, of which Shaw and Anthony were members, to admit a "cream-colored" applicant to what Cooper called "its immaculate assembly." Cooper felt that as leaders Shaw and Anthony had the power, which they failed to use, to telegraph down the lines of their networks clear disapproval of such attitudes and behavior. She was further troubled by a speech entitled "Woman Versus the Indian," in which Shaw complained that white women were humiliated at being treated less courteously than "Indians in blankets and moccasins." Cooper responded:

> Is not woman's cause broader, and deeper, and grander, than a blue stocking debate or an aristocratic pink tea? Why should woman become plaintiff in a suite versus the Indian, or the Negro or any other race or class who have been crushed under the iron heel of Anglo-Saxon power and selfishness?[22]

For Cooper, the greatest potential of the women's movement lay not with white women but with the women who were "confronted by both a woman questions and a race problem." And it is precisely at this juncture of racial and sexual politics that we would expect Cooper to make her strongest statements in *A Voice*. Her language, when she speaks of the special mission of black women, is beautiful and stirring, almost evangelical: "But to be a woman of the Negro race in America, and to be able to grasp the deep significance of the possibilities of the crisis, is to have a heritage, it seems to me, unique in the ages.[23] "The rhetoric is compelling, but the ideas in this section of *A Voice*, where Cooper tries to connect race and gender issues and to place black women at a pivotal point in that discussion, are disappointing. She is never able to discard totally the ethics of true womanhood, and except for the one passage about black laundry women, she does not imagine ordinary black working women as the basis of her feminist politics. While she admits that black women are an "unacknowledged factor" in both race and gender issues, she insists that their quiet and unobserved presence as they stand "aloof from the heated scramble [of politics]" will eventually make itself felt. Here Cooper is falling back on the true womanhood premise that women need not possess any actual political power in order to effect political change; in true womanly fashion, black women could pressure their husbands to vote the right way by whispering "just the needed suggestion or the almost forgotten truth."[24] The dictates of true womanhood confined women's authority to the domestic realm where they could supposedly derive power from their ability to influence their husbands.[25] Such drawing-room scenarios were hardly relevant to the lives of most black women. Even the examples Cooper gives of black women leaders (Sojourner Truth, Amanda Smith, Charlotte Forten Grimké, Frances Harper) are undermined by the genteel language of true womanhood: They are "pleasing" or "sweet," or "gentle," or "charming," or with a "matchless and irresistible personality."[26]

How did Cooper, a woman who in some ways is so clear-eyed about the need to resist the subordination of women in all its forms, get trapped in the ideological underbrush of true womanhood? As some historians of women's history would claim, many of the tenets of true womanhood did lay the groundwork for a more radical form of feminism, and Cooper obviously expected black women to be at the forefront, if not the helm, of social change. As a middle-class black woman, Cooper, like all of her contemporaries—Fannie Jackson Coppin, Frances Harper, Mary Church Terrell, Ida B. Wells, Josephine St. Pierre Ruffin—had a great stake in the prestige, the respectability, and the gentility guaranteed by the politics of true womanhood. To identify with the issues and interests of poor and uneducated black women entailed a great risk. Cooper and her intellectual contemporaries would have to deal with their own class privilege and would undoubtedly alienate the very white women they felt they needed as allies. Burdened by the race's morality, black women could not be as free as white women or black men to think outside of these boundaries of "uplift"; every choice they made had tremendous repercussions for an entire race of women already under the stigma of inferiority and immorality.

≈ ≈

Cooper and her contemporaries saw themselves in the 1890s, "the Women's Era," as avatars of the progress of black women. As "representative" women, they had dual and conflicting roles: They had to "represent" as advocates that class of American women who were victimized by every social and political policy created by the American power structure, and they had to "represent" the progress that black women were making toward greater refinement, good taste, intelligence, and religious development.[27] And even these efforts were met with contempt and obstructions. Fannie Barrier Williams, in a speech to the 1893 World's Congress of Representative Women, addressed black women's intellectual progress since the Emancipation and declared that every movement of black American women toward intellectual and cultural growth was met with hostility: "If we seek the sanctities of religion, the enlightenment of the university, the honors of politics, and the natural recreations of our common country, the social alarm is instantly given and our aspirations are insulted."[28] Sensing perhaps that she was addressing a sympathetic audience, Cooper also spoke before this same congress and broached a sensitive and potentially damaging subject—the sexual violation of black women. In a speech that could not have taken more than five minutes to deliver, Cooper revealed what is often concealed in *A Voice:* her passionate concern for the poorest black women and her unshakable belief that they were waging a heroic struggle for the necessities of life—for knowledge, for bread, for dignity, and for the simple right of possession of their own bodies.

Without women like Fannie Barrier Williams, Ida B. Wells, Fannie Jackson Coppin, Victoria Earle Matthews, Frances Harper, Mary Church Terrell, and Anna Julia Cooper, we would know very little about the conditions of nineteenth-century black women's lives, and yet the black intellectual tradition, until very recently, has virtually ignored them and devalued their scholarship as clearly subordinate to that produced by black men.[29] These women were activists as well as intellectuals: They worked as teachers, lecturers, social workers, journalists, and in women's clubs. They were more committed to the idea of uplift than to their own personal advancement, partly because they could not isolate themselves from the problems of poor black women. If at times their language betrays their elitism, they were nevertheless forced to given expression to the needs and problems of the least privileged in this society.[30] Cooper wrote in a college questionnaire in 1932 that her chief cultural interest was "the education of the underprivileged," and indeed the fullest expression of her feminism and her intellectual life is to be found in her work as an educator. Still, I do not want to minimize the accomplishment of *A Voice from the South.* It is the most precise, forceful, well-argued statement of black feminist thought to come out of the nineteenth century. Ironically, Cooper and other black women intellectuals were very much like poor black women who were engaged in the most difficult and poorly rewarded physical labor: They did the work that no one else was willing to do.

Notes

1. *A Voice From the South by a Black Woman of the South* (New York: Negro Universities Press, 1969), p. 31. (Originally published in Xenia, Ohio: Aldine Printing House, 1892.)

2. Ibid., p. 75.

3. An undated autobiographical account of her birth by Anna J. Cooper, Courtesy Moorland-Spingarn Research Center, Howard University. Reprinted in Louise D. Hutchinson, *Anna J. Cooper: A Voice From the South* (Washington, D.C.: Smithsonian Press, 1982), p. 4.

4. *A Voice From the South*, p. 77.

5. Ibid., p. 49.

6. Among the distinguished graduates of Dunbar High School were Benjamin O. Davis, the first black U.S. general; Judge William Hastie, a U.S. appeals court judge and the first black governor of the Virgin Islands; Dr. Charles Drew, who devised the method of storing blood plasma in banks; Senator Edward Brooks of Massachusetts, the first black U.S. senator since Reconstruction; Robert Weaver, secretary of the U.S. Department of Housing and Urban

Development under President Kennedy; and Eleanor Holmes Norton, chair of the federal Equal Employment Opportunity Commission under President Carter.

7. Letter from Annette Eaton to Leona C. Gabel, 1977. Smith College Archives.

8. Letter from Annette Eaton to Leona C. Gabel, October 1, 1977, Smith College Archives.

9. Louise D. Hutchinson, *Anna J. Cooper*, pp. 67–84.

10. Anna J. Cooper, *The Third Step*. Anna Julia Cooper papers, courtesy Moorland-Springarn Research Center, Howard University, p. 5.

11. Ibid., p. 6.

12. *A Voice From the South*, pp. 78, 79.

13. Letter from Frederick Douglass to M. A. Majors, August 26, 1892. Reprinted in Dorothy Sterlin, ed., *We Are Your Sisters: Black Women in the Nineteenth Century* (New York: W. W. Norton & Company, 1984), p. 436.

14. Alfred A. Moss, Jr., *The American Negro Academy: Voice of the Talented Tenth* (Baton Rouge: Louisiana State University Press, 1981), p. 38.

15. Letter to W. E. B. Du Bois, 1929. Anna Julia Cooper Papers.

16. W. E. B. Du Bois, "On the Damnation of Women," in *Darkwater: Voices From Within the Veil* (New York: Schocken Books, 1969), p. 173

17. *A Voice From the South*, p. 74.

18. Letter to Francis Grimké, April 9, 1936. Anna Julia Cooper Papers.

19. Hazel Carby, " 'On the Threshold of Woman's Era': Lynching, Empire, and Sexuality in Black Feminist Theory." *Critical Inquiry* 12 (Autumn 1985): 262–77.

20. *A Voice From the South*, pp. 254–5.

21. Ibid., p. 116.

22. Ibid., p. 123.

23. Ibid., p. 144.

24. Ibid., pp. 137–8.

25. For a discussion of the ideology of true womanhood, see Barbara Welter, "The Cult of True Womanhood: 1800–1860," in *Dimity Convictions: The American Woman in the Nineteenth Century* (Athens: Ohio University Press, 1976), pp. 21–41.

26. *A Voice From the South*, p. 141.

27. The list of attributes is suggested by a speech given by Fannie Barrier Williams to the World's Congress of Representative Women in 1893 entitled "The Intellectual Progress of the Colored Women of the United States Since the Emancipation Proclamation," in Loewenberg and Bogin, *Black Women in Nineteenth-Century American Life* (University Park and London: The Pennsylvania University Press, 1976), p. 277.

28. Loewenberg and Bogin, *Black Women in Nineteenth-Century American Life*, p. 277.

29. The first contemporary documentation of the intellectual tradition of nineteenth-century black women was Loewenberg and Bogin's *Black Women in Nineteenth-Century American Life* in 1976.

30. Ibid., p. 21.

II

Naming Reality—
Differently

Sara Ebenreck

Introduction to Part II

Because women were for centuries marginalized in the community of philosophical work, the very categories through which dominant Western culture defined realities philosophically arose primarily from the experience of male thinkers. If philosophy is taken, as it often has been, as an intellectual endeavor whose results are not marked by the gender of the author, this would not be problematic. But, as feminist critiques of Western philosophy have clearly shown, all too often gender does make a significant impact on philosophical work, although it is often a hidden one. To illustrate, one has only to recall Aristotle's paralleling the metaphysical categories of matter and form with the gender categories of female and male. If "female" corresponds to "matter" and "male" to "form," then the social roles of women are seen as passive in comparison to the active roles of men. The full nature of women cannot find expression when constrained by this set of definitions. Alternatively, one can also call to mind the way in which Hildegard of Bingen envisioned mothering qualities in God. Then one can mourn the loss of that vision in the dominant Western image of God the Father as a demanding and justice-oriented judge. Where gender clearly has an impact on thought, it is absolutely important that the work of women as well as men be studied so that the philosophical conversation can be enriched by both truth-seeking perspectives.

It is, of course, still arguable that philosophical reflections of both women and men may at times transcend the shaping influences of gender, reaching toward forms of naming that are simply human, neither female nor male. It is also a fact that some of the women philosophers in this section—Susanne Langer and Hannah Arendt, for example—did not think of themselves as "women philosophers" at all, let alone as feminist philosophers with open attention to the way in which gender might be shaping their thought. Yet, even when questions related directly to gender may not be in focus, it is remarkable how often the insights of such earlier women anticipate later gender-conscious feminist philosophical reflections. For example, Hannah Arendt's incorporation of storytelling in philosophizing anticipates later feminist work on the inclusion of the personal voice as a way to achieve a deeper knowledge in philosophy.

Susanne Langer's concept of "symbol" reaches beyond dualistic categories that many feminists today criticize.

This section of the book contains essays about women thinkers who exercised their power to define the realities they thought about, whether in naming the cosmic process in which we exist, the characteristics of art and symbolism, or a social ethics. Most of these essays also portray issues related to women's exclusion from the task of forming the categories of cultural thought, and they suggest the cultural cost of that exclusion: the ignoring of certain perspectives that are now, in the late twentieth century, seen as having been "before their time." Interestingly, many of these marginalized perspectives have certain patterns in common: an appreciation for body, matter, lived experience, the feminine, diversity, and nondualistic thinking.

Hildegard of Bingen, the twelfth-century mystic, is the focus of the essay by Helen John that opens this section. Hildegard not only envisioned a fundamental equality between men and women but also portrayed Divine Love in womanly form. Moved by a profoundly cosmic vision, she avoided the dualistic bifurcations of spirit and body, and God and world, naming the fundamental power in the universe as God's "greening power," a power that calls up earthy images of growing plants and trees in her rural Rhineland valley. Despite the power and originality of her thought, Hildegard's philosophy was neglected by both subsequent generations of theologians and philosophers studying the contributions of medieval thought to Western culture. In Helen John's assessment, work on the philosophical significance of Hildegard's contributions is only now beginning.

In the late nineteenth century, Ednah Dow Cheney developed a theory of art that Therese Dykeman shows was unique among early American aesthetics. Based on her own experiences with art and artists, and in disagreement with other thinkers, Cheney argued that art is not in itself ethical but rather serves ethics by tending to sensitize the human spirit. Her theory that art is an expression of thought in material form included an emphasis on the complementary nature of these two elements. Her treatment of photography as a form of art anticipates twentieth-century views, as does her theory about women's capacities in art. As Dykeman shows, although Cheney was recognized in her time by the Concord School of Philosophy where she lectured, her theory was neglected, at significant philosophical loss, by both later academic philosophers of aesthetics and historians of American aesthetics.

In the early twentieth century, Jane Addams, founder of Chicago's Hull House, developed a social ethics that is rooted in her experiences of working with poor and marginalized immigrant groups. Marilyn Fischer gives an overview of key themes in that ethic: the vision of society as an organic whole, the fundamental equality of all persons, and an ideal of solidarity in social action. Fischer draws on one of Addams's concerns—the mistreatment of poor young women—to contextualize the theory in ways that show how Addams's social work affected the framing of her ideas. Anticipating contemporary feminist thought, Addams based her sense of human equality in our common experiences of the cycle of life and death rather than in the abstract rationalist arguments common to the masculine philosophy of her period.

Despite the importance and originality of her vision, Addams's work has not been taken seriously by the American philosophical community. Fischer shows why we should reclaim her thought.

In the mid-1960s, Katie Cannon began thinking through the "conspiracy of silence" that had obscured the contributions of blacks to human culture. Her interest in ethics led her to consider how blacks living in a racist society developed a moral wisdom that could not assume the starting point of dominant Western ethics: the perspective of an autonomous moral agent, socially equal to all other humans. In this essay, Cannon works with the black women's literary tradition to describe the moral values embraced by earlier black women in the midst of lives marked by oppression. Such writers, Cannon argues, articulate the values alive in a black oral tradition, establishing community between their work and the vision inherited from black women of the past. While much formal Western ethics concerned itself with articulating the values and principles that, in theory, ought to direct society as a whole, the wisdom of black women living in a racist society had to concern itself with teaching how to survive in a culture designed to denigrate black children, how to ward off attacks on their human dignity, and how to sustain a loving heart in the midst of such persistent attacks. Cannon's essay makes vibrantly clear the philosophical importance of hearing these voices.

Even among women openly recognized as brilliant twentieth-century philosophers, the pattern reappears: the philosophical community fails to recognize the worth of unconventional views. Beatrice Nelson traces Susanne Langer's development of a different and promising concept of "symbol," a concept that was rejected by mainstream philosophers still immersed in the world of symbolic logic. Langer's work rested on her willingness to accept an ambiguous use of the word "symbol" in a way that allowed her to join the uses of that concept in both art and logic. Her approach, moreover, asserted that all our knowledge of the "world" is already in the realm of symbol; that is, what we call "facts" are already "a perspective of an event." Her concept, as Nelson notes, "allows us to face and to transcend the dualisms . . . in our traditional epistemology." Challenging the fundamental Cartesian notion of building philosophical foundations on clear and distinct ideas again had its cost: Langer's work was ignored by mainstream Anglo-American philosophers.

The work of a second well-known philosopher, Hannah Arendt, is the focus of the essay by Elizabeth Minnich, who reflects on the way in which Arendt questioned the dominant Western philosophical assumption about the control we can exercise over our own minds. "Arendt came to believe that thinking is one of our vulnerable . . . abilities," Minnich writes. Arendt's questions about the process of thinking are evident in her approach to writing the life of an earlier Jewish woman, Rahel Varnhagen, as a way to understand the situation of women in an anti-Semitic culture. Arendt sought to understand Varnhagen by a process of identifying with her rather than by taking an "objective" external perspective. In so doing, she was led to the conclusion that what thinking achieves is not primarily a content of knowledge so much as an experience of the mysterious self that thinks and an understanding of the profound subjectivity of other persons. From this perspective, ethical judgment can never proceed simply by rational deductive application of principle to particular case but instead must move back and forth between knowledge of principles and experience of particular individual situations.

Shari Stone-Mediatore's essay begins with a sketch of how scientific rationalism in the West led to a theory of objective history as a disciplined study of data. Approaching Arendt's use of storytelling from a different angle than Minnich's essay, Stone-Mediatore shows how work such as *The Origins of Totalitarianism* uses poetic and emotion-laden descriptions to help readers comprehend the reality of life in Nazi Germany. Stone-Mediatore then shows how feminist writer Susan Griffin takes this method a step further by demonstrating that what has been called "objective data" excludes experiences associated with femininity. In an interesting parallel with the thought of Langer, as traced by Nelson, Stone-Mediatore argues that the achievement of Arendt and Griffin leads one to realize that "objective" history is itself embedded in a particular story that has been presented so abstractly that its story-quality is forgotten. Just as, for Langer, there is no world without symbol-system, so there is no history without story for Arendt, Griffin, and Stone-Mediatore.

Cumulatively, these essays not only show important philosophical contributions of the seven women thinkers but also the fundamental nature of questions that are raised when women address philosophical issues from a perspective that directly involves their own life experiences. Dialogue with their thought, as well as with the thought of their male peers, is essential if we are truly to understand the richness of our Western philosophical heritage. The essay that closes this section reflects on the importance of this inclusion for the editor's own philosophical life.

Helen J. John, S.N.D.

3   Hildegard of Bingen: A New Medieval Philosopher?

When is a person a philosopher?

An easy empirical answer might be: When the person's works are studied in philosophy classes. By this criterion, Kierkegaard and Nietzsche became philosophers shortly after World War II. In my student days at Louvain, we studied Augustine and Aquinas (and their medieval male companions); but their standing *as philosophers* was still up for debate, and study of their work was omitted in many schools of philosophy. Today, the philosophical canonizations of Mary Wollstonecraft and Simone de Beauvoir are still in progress as some of us "mainstream" them into our courses.

Hildegard of Bingen (1098–1179), a twelfth-century Renaissance woman, with her integrated vision of the natural world, of moral experience, and of salvation history, seems a most likely candidate for inclusion among medieval philosophers, yet she has been consistently left out of our histories. I want to examine—and to challenge—the reasons for this omission. Therefore, in what follows, my plan is: (1) to sketch out Hildegard's intellectual achievement, with special attention to her visionary writings; (2) to examine both the intellectual approach used in the visionary writings and Hildegard's own statements about her way of knowing; and (3) to compare these with the approaches of already "canonized" medieval philosophers.

Hildegard's Vision

Hildegard's life and achievements have recently become a focus of lively interdisciplinary interest. Her correspondence is so voluminous that Joan Ferrante has described her as the "Dear Abby" of the twelfth century.[1] Hildegard's medical writings, in *Causae et Curae,* include detailed descriptions of the diverse temperaments of men and women, and how they can best get along with and without each other. Science historian Joan Cadden suggests that this work draws upon the experience of monastic infirmarians, who cared not only for fellow-religious, but for lay people of the neighborhood.[2] Matthew Fox, proponent of creation-centered spirituality, has hailed Hildegard as an early exemplar of environmental mysticism.[3] Hildegard's hymns and her musical mystery play, the *Ordo Virtutum*, have been performed in Europe and the United States and are available on recordings. Peter Dronke, Joan Ferrante, Kent Kraft and Elizabeth Petroff have published literary studies of her writings. Especially significant, for my purposes here, are Barbara Newman's theological study, *Sister of Wisdom: St. Hildegard's Theology of the Feminine*, and the account of Hildegard's theory of sex complementarity in *The Concept of Woman: The Aristotelian Revolution, 750 B.C.— A.D. 1250* by philosopher Prudence Allen, R.S.M.[4]

While Hildegard's correspondence, autobiographical notes, medical writings, and poetry offer important insights into her ways of knowing, it was her vast visionary works that first brought her to public attention, inspired her correspondence, and presented to the world her comprehensive view of God, humanity, and nature. Of these, the first volume, *Scivias* ("Know the Ways [of the Lord]") presents creation and salvation history; the second, *The Book of Life's Merits*, gives an ordered account of the virtues and vices; and the third, *The Book of Divine Works*, portrays each human being as microcosm, a little world, in the great macrocosm of created nature. All three of these works have been translated into German. For the *Scivias* we also have the superb critical edition of the original Latin text prepared by Adelgundis Fuerkoetter and Angela Carlevaris, Benedictine nuns of Hildegard's monastery at Eibingen; and the complete English translation in Paulist Press's Classics of Western Spirituality series. Critical editions of the later visionary works, and of the letters, are now in preparation.

The *Scivias*, when first I encountered it, struck me at once as a kind of audiovisual version of Aquinas' *Summa Theologiae*: an all-encompassing account of divine and created reality, narrating and explaining the whole of the natural world and of salvation history. Like the thirteenth-century schoolmen, Hildegard brings together in her writings the universal concepts of philosophy with the particular details of human experience. The broad design of the *Scivias*, like that of the *Summa*, comes from Pseudo-Dionysius: Creation comes forth from God; humanity, having fallen into sin, is redeemed by Christ; and redeemed humanity, with the whole of created nature, returns to God through the work of the virtues.

The pervasive concepts and themes of Hildegard's vision were deeply rooted in the world of sensuous appearances—the world of created nature and of concrete human experience. Thus, in the *Scivias*, each section begins with a visual image, vividly described, followed by inspired words explaining the vision, and then by detailed interpretation of the symbolism. So essential is the visual imagery to the understanding of Hildegard's thought that her reader (like Dante's) is practically compelled to diagram—on paper or in the mind's eye—in order to grasp the meaning of her text. Accordingly, the visions of the *Scivias* were painted as illuminated minia-tures in her lifetime, and evidently under her direct supervision. These miniatures are beautifully reproduced in the critical edition.[5] At the end of the *Scivias*, after an apocalyptic description of redeemed and condemned humanity, and of the new heaven and earth, Hildegard's vision breaks into song in the *Ordo Virtutum;* hymns in honor of the Blessed Virgin, the choirs of angels, the patriarchs and prophets, and all the saints are followed by the musical drama of the struggling soul who, encouraged by the virtues, overcomes the deceits of the devil.

Scivias is profoundly at home in the spirit of twelfth-century naturalism. Reading it, one breathes in at once the fresh delight in detailed portrayal of nature and the pervasive sense of symbolic meanings that gave birth to the Romanesque and Gothic cathedrals. Hildegard's vision sets forth that total architecture of meaning and design—in the world of created nature, in the pattern of human history, and in the building up of moral character—that led Whitehead to describe medieval thought in terms of the interplay of overarching principles with irreducible and stubborn facts.[6]

To illustrate at close range the intellectual achievements that surely mark Hildegard as a philosopher, I will examine several passages chosen to exemplify the central themes of her thought.

Scivias (Part One, Vision Four) offers us a woman-friendly account of human generation and development. Hildegard beholds both men and women "who have in their bodies human seed" for procreation; she sees the complete form of the human being in the woman's womb, and the soul, like a burning sphere, quickening the child's body.[7]

> ... the soul, burning with a fire of profound knowledge, which discerns whatever is within the circle of its understanding, and, without the form of human members, since it is not corporeal or transitory like a human body, gives strength to the heart and rules the whole body as its foundation, as the firmament of Heaven contains the lower regions and touches the higher. *And* [the fiery globe of the soul] *also touches the person's brain* for in its powers it knows not only earthly but also heavenly things, since it wisely knows God: *and it spreads itself through all the person's members;* for it gives vitality to the marrow and veins and members of the whole body, as the tree from its root gives sap and greenness to all the branches. *But then this human form, in this way vivified, comes forth from the woman's womb....*[8]

The soul here described, like the Aristotelian *enteleche, is* the source of life in the living human organism, integrating its sensuous and spiritual reality. By contrast with Aristotle, however, there is no suggestion of defect in either sex: Hildegard uses *homo* (here translated as "person") for the newborn human being, which further on in the text is clearly portrayed as feminine.

In comparing the new soul to sap from the root of a tree, Hildegard introduces a second favorite and original theme: verdancy (*viriditas*)—the fresh green of new leaves as emblem of new life and energy. She goes on, in the same passage, to relate the unfolding life of the human being to the cycles of life and death, and to the seasons in the world of nature.

> The soul now shows its powers according to the powers of the body, so that in a person's infancy it produces simplicity, in his youth strength, and in adulthood, when all the

person's veins are full, it shows its strongest powers in wisdom; as the tree in its first shoots is tender and then shows that it can bear fruit, and finally, in its full utility, bears it. But then in human old age, when the marrow and veins start to incline in weakness, the soul's powers are gentler, as if from a weariness at human knowledge; as when winter approaches the sap of the tree diminishes in the branches and the leaves, and the tree in its old age begins to bend.[9]

In this whole section, Hildegard stresses at once the integration of body and soul, and the unity and correspondence of each human individual with the vitality and strength, the green freshness, of the natural world.

Viriditas, verdancy, expressed in her central image of the budding green of springtime, becomes for Hildegard the symbolic expression of life and power, truth and beauty, rooted in God and springing forth in human beings and in all created nature. This freshness stands for the actuality and energy of being in everything that is; it becomes what the schoolmen would later call a transcendental attribute of being, a presence of the creator's perfection in every aspect of every creature. In this respect, Hildegard's notion of *viriditas* resembles the "act of existing" in Aquinas' metaphysics, through which each creature participates in divine being; or Duns Scotus' *haecceitas,* the unique and irreplaceable "thisness" of each individual being. Hildegard's thought is distinctive in its emphasis on the ever-new energy and originality, in creator and creatures, that her theme of freshness implies.

A second passage (from Part One, Vision One, Chapter Two, of the *Book of Divine Works*) approaches the same themes from a cosmic perspective, presenting a figure linked at once to Lady Wisdom in the Old Testament and to the Platonic *anima mundi.*[10] Divine Love is here portrayed in womanly human form encompassing and embracing the created universe; she speaks her own praise:

I am the supreme and fiery force who kindled every living spark. . . . And I am the fiery life of the essence of God; I flame above the beauty of the fields; I shine in the waters; I burn in the sun, the moon, and the stars. And, with the airy wind, I quicken all things vitally by an unseen, all-sustaining life. For the air is alive in the verdure and the flowers; the waters flow as if they lived; the sun too lives in its light; and when the moon wanes it is rekindled by the light of the sun, as if it lived anew. Even the stars glisten in their light as if alive. . . . I also am Reason. Mine is the blast of the resounding Word through which all creation came to be, and I quickened all things with my breath so that not one of them is mortal in its kind; for I am Life. Indeed I am Life, whole and undivided—not hewn from any stone, or budded from branches, or rooted in virile strength; but all that lives has its root in me. For Reason is the root whose blossom is the resounding Word. So because God is rational, how could it be possible for him not to work?[11]

In the second vision of the same work, Hildegard recounts the divine plan for the relationship of human beings and the created universe:

God has composed the world from its elements for the glory of his name; he has strengthened it with the winds, bound and illuminated it with the stars, and filled it with the other structures. In it God has surrounded and fortified human beings with all things and steeped them in the greatest power so that all the creatures support humanity in every way, so that people may work with them, since without the other creatures human beings cannot live nor survive.[12]

Central here to Hildegard's thought is the relation of human beings to the natural world, a relation characterized not by mastery and exploitation, but by interdependence and mutual nurturance. Just as she portrayed the infant coming to life as participating in the strength and richness, the *viriditas* of the natural world, so she also sees each woman or man as imaging God in the world through the power of reason and the energy of love.

In the passages cited here, which are broadly typical of her writings, Hildegard exemplifies the profound integration of revealed Christian teaching with human reason and experience that pervaded the cultural climate of medieval Europe—and so characterized the spirit of medieval philosophy.

Hildegard's Way of Knowing

Peter Dronke has especially well described Hildegard's personality as expressed in the originality of her writings:

> Her frankness with people is matched by the way she approaches every field and every problem as if for the first time. While she claims that her learning is rudimentary and her command of language faulty, she writes a Latin that is as forceful and colorful, and at times as subtle and brilliant, as any in the twelfth century; and her learning is often so astounding that (as she gives no source-references) it still sets countless problems to determine all she had read.
>
> While she is clearly of mystical disposition, her sense of the divine presence is the lodestar of her life—she is never in cloudcuckooland. Her medical writings show her attempts, restless yet full of empathy, to understand all ailments, the vagaries of character; so too her letters often show shrewdness, compassion, and helpfulness in practical matters.
>
> There is scarcely a field to which she did not bring her individual contribution. . . . She rediscovers existentially, uninhibitedly.
>
> Her approach to every problem—human, scientific, artistic, or theological—was her own. She took nothing ready-made. Her conviction that she saw the answers to the problems in her waking vision meant that she did not have to defer to established answers.[13]

What Hildegard herself says of her way of knowing presents the tension between her repeated reference to herself as a poor little ignorant woman and the utter assurance with which she asserts what she has seen in and heard from the "living light" of her visions. (An apt comparison would be Socrates' tension between his own ignorance and ineptitude at speaking, and the divine inspiration of his wisdom.) Toward the end of her life, in a noteworthy letter to the monk Guibert of Gembloux, she describes her visions as she has experienced them since infancy. She insists that they come to her with no disturbance of her clear waking consciousness:

But I hear them not with my physical ears, not with my heart's thoughts, nor do I perceive them by bringing any of my five senses to bear—but only in my soul, my physical eyes open, so that I never suffer their failing in loss of consciousness (*extasis*); no, I see these things wakefully, day and night. . . .

Whatever I have seen or learnt in this vision, I retain the memory of it for a long time, in such a way that, because I have at some time seen and heard it, I can remember it; and I see, hear and know simultaneously, and learn what I know as if in a moment. But what I do not see I do not know, for I am not learned. And the things I write are those I see and hear through the vision, nor do I set down words other than those that I hear; I utter them in unpolished Latin, just as I hear them through the vision, for in it I am not taught to write as philosophers write. And the words I see and hear through the vision are not like words that come from human lips, but like a sparkling flame and a cloud moved in pure air. Moreover, I cannot know the form of this brightness in any way, just as I cannot gaze completely at the sphere of the sun.

And in that same brightness I sometimes, not often, see another light, which I call "the living light"; when and how I see it, I cannot express; and for the time I do see it, all sadness and all anguish is taken from me, so that then I have the air of an innocent young girl and not of a little old woman.[14]

Clear as she is in her insistence that her teaching comes from God, Hildegard yet recognizes its connection to the tradition and climate of learning in which she lived. Thus an autobiographical passage from her *Vita* explains:

In that same vision, I understood, without any instruction, the writings of the Prophets, of the Gospels, and of other saints and philosophers, and I explained some of them, although I had hardly any knowledge of letters, since an unlearned woman had been my teacher.[15]

The implication here, and the evidence from her writings generally, is that Hildegard was familiar not only with the Bible, but with the whole religious and secular culture of the twelfth century; her visions drew upon, interpreted and enhanced (rather than substituted for) a grounding in the literary heritage of her time and setting. Thus the editors of the critical edition of *Scivias* note her familiarity with ideas and images from writers from Augustine to her contemporary, Rupert of Deutz.[16]

The Twelfth-Century Context:
Vision, Experience and Philosophical Authority

The brilliance and originality of Hildegard's vision is such that it would seem difficult to study the thought of the twelfth century without considering her work. Indeed, M.-D. Chenu, while he omits *ex professo* consideration of Hildegard from his study of *Nature, Man, and Society in the Twelfth Century*, nonetheless is compelled to mention her in his chapters on "Man [sic] and Nature," "The Symbolist Mentality," and "Theology and the New Awareness of History."[17] Still, it is only in the past decade that Jean Leclercq named her as a necessary addition to the list of twelfth-century monastic theologians.[18] Even less has her work been claimed by the philosophical tradition.

Newman, while she analyzes in some detail Hildegard's use of Philosophia as a parable figure of *intellectua quarens fidem,* holding the crystal of faith, never deals directly with the relation of philosophy to theology in Hildegard's own work.[19]

And so we come back to our original question: When is a person a philosopher?

In the 1950s, when I was studying philosophy at Trinity College, the Catholic University of America, and Louvain, there was a lively discussion in progress as to whether *anyone* in the Christian Middle Ages was a philosopher. The point at issue then was whether the faith commitment of the medieval bishops, monks, friars and clerics so "contaminated" their reasonable reflection upon common human experience as to justify exclusion of their thought from the history of philosophy. The conclusion that ultimately prevailed—if I am not mistaken—was that, although medieval philosophy and theology were intimately connected, their starting points and methods were and are recognizably distinct: Theology begins with the revealed truths of faith, as known through scripture and tradition, and seeks a clearer understanding of these truths; philosophy relies upon human reason and experience in seeking to understand reality. Philosophy may be the handmaid of theology, but she goes out by the day, and has her own house to keep.

Sister Prudence Allen, in the one explicitly philosophical study of Hildegard that I have seen published, draws principally upon the medical writings; she points out that while Aristotle (whose teachings came to dominate the schools) portrayed woman as impotent male, with only a passive role in reproduction and diminished authority in the exercise of reason, Hildegard grounded in her own observation and experience an account of women and men as having equal, and complementary, strengths and responsibilities not only in reproduction, but in the whole range of human activities.[20]

In her focus on Hildegard's medical writings (for which Hildegard lays no claim to visionary inspiration), Allen avoids what to me seems the most serious question about philosophically "canonizing" Hildegard: Is Hildegard's claim to the divine inspiration of her visions compatible with an exercise of philosophical wisdom understood as grounded in natural human reason and common human experience?

Again, we may use criteria that apply to male thinkers to answer our question. When we pick up the standard histories of medieval philosophy (Copleston's and Gilson's are the ones I have on hand), we find the Jewish and Arabic authors, the pioneers of scholasticism (such as Anselm and Abelard), the Platonists, the speculative mystics, and Alan of Lille. Clearly, not all mystics or allegorical writers are excluded. In the work of Alan of Lille, Gilson (a wide-ranging scholar who yet seems to have been ignorant of Hildegard) finds the poetic expression, in the allegorical figure of Nature as inexhaustible fecundity, of the " 'Christian naturalism' of the twelfth century."[21]

It was certainly a commonplace of Christian medieval thought that all wisdom has its source in God, and the overwhelming majority of medieval thinkers were known primarily—and understood themselves—as theologians and mystics. Augustine's *Confessions* was written as a single protracted praise of God. Aquinas, toward the end of his life, laid down his pen, saying that compared with what he had seen in mystical vision, his huge tomes seemed like a handful of straw.

Today it is increasingly clear that women have been left out of intellectual history, not because their achievements were negligible, but because the women themselves, in Aristotle's deplorable phrase, were seen as "without authority." Only recently, in the writings of Newman and Petroff, has it been recognized that visionary insight played an essential role in validating, for the woman herself and for her contemporaries, her authority to speak and act in the medieval world.[22] Hildegard effectively lays claim to authority by appealing to God who raises up the lowly (so that her womanly frailty reinforces her role as God's inspired spokesperson); at the same time, her portrayal of the feminine in God and in creation draws upon and validates her own womanly experience in all its concreteness.[23] To incorporate Hildegard (along with her visionary companions and successors) into the canon of medieval philosophers will require that we look carefully into the criteria by which we recognize in particular authors the authority both of reason and of concrete human experience. This is certainly not a problem unknown to feminist philosophers today.

To situate Hildegard among the medieval philosophers will be, of course, both a theoretical and a practical challenge; like all original thinkers, she raises more questions than she answers. But I would contend that she belongs among the philosophers as a powerful exemplar of the range and the authority of women's vision and experience. Her approach to human generation, her development of the concept of *"viriditas"* and her portrayal of Divine Love in feminine form are strong contributions to the medieval philosophical tradition. The task of finding a place for her will be as rewarding as it is strenuous.

Notes

1. Elizabeth Alvilda Petroff, *Medieval Women's Visionary Literature* (Oxford: Oxford University Press, 1986), p. 139.

2. Joan Cadden, in her presentation to Joan Ferrante's NEH [National Endowment for the Humanities] Summer Seminar on "Medieval Women," Columbia University, 1984.

3. Matthew Fox, *Original Blessing* (Sante Fe, N.M.: Bear & Co., 1983), pp. 68–9.

4. Barbara Newman, *Sister of Wisdom: St. Hildegard's Theology of the Feminine* (Berkeley, Calif.: University of California Press, 1987); Prudence Allen, R.S.M., *The Concept of Woman: The Aristotelian Revolution, 750 b.c.—a.d. 1250* (Montreal: Eden Press, 1985).

5. Hildegard von Bingen, *Scivias*, ed. A. Fuehrkoetter and A. Carlevaris, Corpus Christianorum Continuatio Medievalis 43, 43A (Turnhout, Antwerp, Belgium: Brepols, 1978), vol. 1, xxxiv—xxxv.

6. Alfred North Whitehead, *Science in the Modern World* (New York: McMillan Co., 1925; Free Press edition, 1967), pp. 12–15.

7. *Scivias*, tr. Mother Columba Hart and Jane Bishop, Classics of Western Spirituality (Mahway, N.J.: Paulist Press, 1990), p. 118, c.13; pp. 119–20, c.16.

8. Ibid., p. 120, c.16; words in italics are repeated from the first description of the vision, p. 109.

9. Ibid., pp. 20, c.17.

10. Newman, *Sister of Wisdom*, pp. 64–71.

11. Translation from Newman, *Sister of Wisdom*, pp. 69–70, c.2.

12. Hildegard von Bingen, *Sanctae Hildegardia Abbatissae Opera Ommia,* ed. J. P. Migne, *Patrologia Latina,* vol. 198 (Paris: Garnier Fratres, 1882), p. 755, c.2; my translation.

13. Peter Dronke, *Women Writers of the Middle Ages* (Cambridge: Cambridge University Press, 1984), pp. 200–1.

14. Translation in Dronke, ibid., 167: Latin text, ibid., pp. 250–6.

15. Hildegard, *Sanctae Hildegardis Abbatissae Opera Omnia,* op. cit., p. 104, my translation.

16. *Scivias,* ed. Fuehrkoetter and Carlevaris, Intro. vol. 1, pp. 14–16; cf. Index Auctorum, vol. 11, pp. 652–62.

17. M.-D. Chenu, O.P., *Nature, Man and Society in the Twelfth Century,* ed. and tr. J. Taylor and L. K. Little (Chicago: University of Chicago Press, 1957), pp. 31, 35, 103, 192.

18. Jean Leclercq, "The Renewal of Theology," in *Renaissance and Renewal in the Twelfth Century,* ed. R. L. Benson and C. Constable (Cambridge, Mass.: Harvard University Press, 1982), pp. 68–87.

19. Newman, *Sister of Wisdom,* pp. 83–7.

20. Allen, *The Concept of Woman,* pp. 292–315.

21. Etienne Gilson, *History of Christian Philosophy in the Middle* Ages (New York: Random House, 1955), pp. ix—x and 176.

22. Newman, *Sister of Wisdom,* pp. 34–41; Petroff, *Medieval Women's Visionary Literature,* pp. 5–6.

23. Newman, ibid., pp. 34–41.

Therese B. Dykeman

4   Ednah Dow Cheney's American Aesthetics

At the Concord School of Philosophy in the summer of 1879 it was reported that "Mrs. Cheney . . . talked like a master on aesthetics and the history of art."[1] Phebe A. Hanaford in 1882 wrote that Ednah Dow Cheney was "well known as a lecturer on various themes connected with art . . . adding to the culture of many years of study, the finish of foreign travel and study of art abroad."[2] Yet, Cheney's 1881 book, *Gleanings in the Fields of Art*, which is mainly a compilation of her lectures on art delivered at the Concord School of Philosophy, remains unmentioned in histories of American aesthetics.[3] An examination of Cheney's philosophy of art in the context in which it was written proves that her work should be seen as part of the American aesthetics tradition for three reasons: first, it was among the earliest American aesthetics; second, it was unique; and third, its gender inclusiveness spoke both to her time and to the future century.

Ednah Dow Littlehale Cheney (1824–1904) was a nineteenth-century Renaissance woman. Both a thinker and an activist, she participated in her century by writing, lecturing, and contributing to the setting up of schools, hospitals, and programs to meet the needs of her fellow humans.[4] Although the interests expressed in her writing and in her activity included many beyond aesthetics—for example, abolition, women's advancement, religious freedom, literature, and education—Cheney's belief in the importance of art was deep and sustained throughout her life.

Encounter with art and artists for Cheney came directly. She was personally acquainted with the American painter and art theorist Washington Allston and took lessons from Henri Scheffer, brother of the Dutch artist Ary Scheffer (1795–1858). She accompanied her husband, the noted engraver Seth Cheney, to Europe for the express purpose of meeting with such artists as Ary Scheffer, French miniaturist Savinien E. Dubourjal (1795–1865), and the French painter Jean Francois Millet (1814–1875). Ednah Cheney returned to Europe a number of times (in 1877 with her daughter Margaret) to study art in galleries and museums.

Cheney wrote about art in four books and numerous articles. The sources of Cheney's aesthetics may be found chiefly in her 1881 *Gleanings;* her 1868 article "Art and Religion," published in *The Radical;* and the chapter devoted to art in her 1902 memoirs, *Reminiscences. Gleanings* might possibly have been so named because in the main it is a view of the cosmorama of art throughout history in western Europe and in the United States, from the perspective of Cheney's theory of art, that is set forth in the first chapter. Her theory, developed from "gleanings" of ideas left on the "fields of art," were cast anew from the crucible of her own mind. Cheney wrote the *Life of Christian Daniel Rauch of Berlin* in 1893 because, impressed by his sculptures, she wanted to introduce him to American sculptors. She wrote the memoirs of Seth Cheney in 1881 and of John Cheney, also an important engraver, in 1889 as testaments to their character and artistic productions, and she assisted in the catalogue of their works published in 1891.

Prior to Cheney's writings on art theory, a number of other reflections had been published, the first of which was written by Washington Allston. That book, *Lectures on Art,* published in 1850, made him "the only American theorist on art combining the experience of a creative artist with a philosophical culture. . . . When his *Lectures on Art* came out . . . there was no American tradition of philosophical art criticism to deal with them."[5] In 1872 Henry Day, the rhetorician at Yale University, felt a need to include a history of American aesthetics in his own attempt, *The Science of Aesthetics; or the Nature, Kinds, Laws, and Uses of Beauty.* Here, after remarking that Alexander Gottlieb Baumgarten (1714–1762) in Germany named the science in his two-part "partial and imperfect" works of 1750 and 1758, Day claims that "besides the more formal treatises of Moffatt, Sampson, and Bascom . . . there is no work of commanding interest."[6] He does not list the transcendentalists Peabody, Emerson, and Fuller, with whose work Cheney was closely acquainted.

Few women were writing in the field at that time. In *Gleanings,* Cheney recognized the work of the English art critic and feminist Anna B. Jameson. Twenty years after Cheney's *Gleanings,* Wellesley professor Ethel Puffer published a *psychological* aesthetics influenced by Mary Whiton Calkins, in which Puffer discussed the relation between "excitation" and "repose" in the subjective experience of art (a *physiological* aesthetics, influenced by Herbert Spencer and dedicated to him, had been published by Allen Grant in England in 1877). It appears from a survey of this history that the first American woman to write and lecture on aesthetics was Ednah Dow Cheney.

Despite the 1881 publication of her *Gleanings in the Field of Art,* Ednah Dow Cheney is not acknowledged by Lee Vernon in his 1896 *Art and Life* or mentioned by Raymond in his 1915 *An Art Philosopher's Cabinet* as a different kind of transcendentalist from the Emersonian one he does describe. In effect, Ednah Dow Cheney does not exist in the history of American aesthetics. Hence, to become knowledgeable about what Cheney said about art, in the context in which she said it, is to move aside from the existing history; paradoxically, it is in so doing that she becomes part of history and the American tradition of aesthetics.

Cheney's Aesthetics

In *Gleanings,* Ednah Dow Cheney defines art by first distinguishing it as a discipline from religion and science, and then by distinguishing it from philosophy, natural science, and practical ethics. After the object or aim of art and the derivation of art are identified, she comes to her "first grand principle of art." Finally, Cheney inquires into the relationship of the viewer to the work of art. Cheney rarely uses the word "aesthetics"; rather, she uses the term "art," perhaps because she focused not on music or eloquence but on the visual arts, and also because in aiming at as wide an audience as possible she might have thought the word "art" more accessible. Elizabeth Peabody had used the term "aesthetic" when, a year prior to Allston's *Lectures,* she published one issue of a journal presenting views on philosophy and culture entitled *Aesthetic Papers* (1849). I mention it here because it demonstrates an interest in the concept of aesthetics by a person well known to Ednah Dow Cheney; however, compared to the broad meaning given to "aesthetics" by Peabody, Cheney's concept of art was more narrowly conceived.

Cheney's definition of art is clearly philosophical in what she claims is art's "broadest sense." Art is defined neither in terms of "taste" nor "beauty" but rather as "thought in material form." Art is

> all that which seeks to express thought in a material form, without reference to its use for any material function. It is that human activity which subordinates matter entirely to spirit, but which yet wholly recognizes the function of matter to express spirit, and by that expression to give to spiritual thought its vital force, and put it in human relation.[7]

Compared to Aristotle's definition of art as "a reasoned habit of mind in making," Cheney's definition places less emphasis on "habit" as rational and more on "habit" of thought as human-spirit unity.[8] Perhaps, the difference in emphasis each makes might be apparent in a comparison of the productions of the cerebral "Athena" in the Parthenon and the mortal Copley portraits. Using Santayana's word, I suggest that Cheney defines art as a "comprescience" of matter and spirit.[9] In her chapter "Art" in *Reminiscences,* Cheney explains that the artist gives expression to the "full life of the soul," and she sees art "in true relation to the whole circle of thought and action."[10] If art as "material" stands alone it is "ruined," and if "divorced from nature" it becomes "dead and rigid."[11] Hence, art is "synthetic," "harmonious"; art's "special work" is "in relation."[12]

While philosophy "investigates mental processes," natural science "studies the phenomena of matter," and practical ethics regulate our actions, "art simply seeks to express in outward form, what man can think and feel in his inmost soul."[13] Hence, for Cheney, "art has a distinct province" that "differs from philosophy, natural science, or practical ethics."[14] Cheney distinguished art from religion as well as ethics. Religion controls the "conscience and the will of intelligent beings."[15] Art does not do this; nor is art so simply related to ethics as her contemporary John Bascom had suggested it is. Bascom, like Moffat, endowed the science of beauty with ethics:

It is the vital shaping force of the moral world. . . . art without ethics . . . [is] sorely crippled . . . art, therefore, not only prepares the way for moral culture; it itself is, and demands, as an indispensable antecedent, that culture. . . .[16]

Cheney tells us differently: "To the soul which is not fitted to receive it, Art speaks a dead language."[17] Nonetheless art "serves" ethics

by kindling the imagination, and taking us out of the petty round of self and narrow prejudices—putting that which is noble, pure, and high, before us in a form of beauty which wins our admiration and love, and brings us for the time being into its own pure atmosphere.[18]

But again, only insofar as the observer "welcomes" the service of art can it allow us "the power of going out of ourselves, of imagining the life and needs of others, which enables us to love them and do rightly by them."[19] It is not what art bids us to do, but "what it makes us to be" that is important, and then only when "the whole soul is awakened to its needs."[20] Cheney agreed with Michelangelo's view that art is the "noblest function of man."[21] In "Art and Religion" she argues that art "frees the soul" and as a part of a "free intellectual culture" acts as a corrective to conscience, but "the absolute is not her province."[22] While the purpose of religion is "affirmation," the purpose of art is "expression."[23]

Aesthetics is not ethics for Cheney, but rather aesthetics studies a pre-ethical reality that conditions the human soul by enlarging and deepening the human spirit. Cheney would agree with Iris Murdoch who claims that "aesthetic insight connects with moral insight" and who reiterates Simone Weil's notion that insight comes from "patient attention."[24] In the realm of the practical, Cheney suggests that should one be living in a period of corrupt morals, art will be "no police officer" nor will it teach "a code of morals."[25] Cheney boldly asks that since "We cherish the home today more than the church, why do we not make that also a temple of Art . . . to consecrate it?"[26] Cheney was gratified that the art in her own home pleased the abolitionist Harriet Tubman, and that Tubman was appreciative of art.[27] For Cheney, Michelangelo's art is art not because it decorates the Sistine Chapel, but because "it has soul in it."[28]

Art acts as "corrective" of the extreme tendencies of both religionists and scientists, of spiritualists and materialists.[29] Cheney distinguishes art from science in terms of their ends, subject matter, and means when she claims that although science occupies itself with the "forms and shows of things, with secondary laws, with methods and operations," it "seizes on a mere central truth" when its end becomes as oppressive to the soul as extreme spiritualism.[30] While art presents truth in relation to other truths, science merely presents that truth that is central to it, lacking the synthesizing quality of art.

The content of art is not nature; it does not imitate nature. Yet, it cannot give up nature, for it must study the "surface" of nature rather than its underlying composition.[31] Nor does art have nature's "means" to perfection, so it must emphasize what is important in its own creation. For example, art is not interested in portraying every "twig" and "leaf" of a tree nor "truth to fact," but rather "the truth of relation."[32]

Cheney points out that Etruscan art cannot give us a scientific history, but it can give us the spirit of the Etruscan people. Science isolates the parts; art "knows proportions, but not parts."[33] Unlike science, art's method examines the parts of any reality not in themselves but in relation to a whole: "art must never forget the Unity in the difference"—a statement that Cheney might have made also in reference to her theoretical standing with and standing apart from other philosophers of art.

Cheney differs most completely from the transcendentalists in distinguishing the method of discovering the spirit or human truth in art, that is, in discovering what it means. In method Cheney might be allied more closely with the scientific mode of analysis than the intuitive transcendentalists whom she claims "never entered fully into the great work of modern science" even though science as it appears to be directed "is wholly in harmony with the great truths" held by the transcendentalists.[34] With an artist husband and a scientist daughter, Cheney had the unique opportunity of engaging in an inquiry into both subjects, a position that suited her philosophy.

Cheney does not employ the romantic intuitive method; rather, she analyzes with double vision the "product of the human mind" as "organic creation."[35] Cheney's analytical method is necessitated by her conception of art as "twofold": Art is at once material and spiritual, ideal and real, subjective and objective, of thought and of feeling.[36] Its unity is not oneness but "integrated dualism." The whole is most important to Cheney, not so much as an Emersonian whole—whereby, for example, nature is a symbol for spirit—but rather as an Hegelian whole that considers integration and differentiation at once.[37] But in this she, unlike Hegel, is egalitarian. Her God, her Absolute truth, is dual, equally male and female. Cheney makes it clear early on in her 1868 article, "Art and Religion," that "Art represents . . . the eternal marriage, the masculine divinity, the feminine divinity, God-giving, God-receiving, God-producing. The one, the two, the resulting multiplicity, are all recognized." Its duality makes it subject to analysis; its wholeness allows for aesthetic conception; its oneness and plurality are always in the "consciousness of the manifold."[38]

In contrast to Allston's idealistic "characteristics of art," Cheney concentrates on the "correspondence" of art to life, yet it is necessary in the "correspondence" that it be "fresh and original" and expressive of "organic unity" in accordance with the "truths of relation." Reflecting Emerson's influence, art must be "free and fluent" rather than admitting to an "absolute standard."[39] The ultimate artist is not God, as Cheney claims Allston would have it, but the individual human being. Hence, the "art of humanity," in the words Cheney quotes from Margaret Fuller and applies to art, "accepts the universe" as it encompasses great variety in its "truth," even as its expression includes Absolute truth.[40] Neither idealistic nor realistic, art must be humanistic and pluralistic both in its execution and in what it conveys.

Twenty years after Cheney published *Gleanings*, Professor George Lansing Raymond of Princeton, founder of the Department of Oratory and Aesthetic Criticism, overlooked Cheney in his comments on the transcendentalists as aestheticians. Raymond, who was highly acclaimed by Marion Mills Miller in the introduction of his book as "the author of the only complete system of art-interpretation that has yet been produced in any country,"[41] did not include Cheney by name nor could her theory have fit his conclusions about transcendentalists:

> The transcendentalists of New England who, fifty years ago, were exercising the most pronounced of any effect upon the art and literature of our country were constantly confounding artistic inspiration with religious inspiration.[42]

Had Raymond acknowledged Cheney, he would have found a "transcendentalist" different from his description. Her aesthetics, influenced by yet different from the transcendentalists Allston, Emerson, and Fuller, certainly did not "confound artistic inspiration with religious inspiration."

Cheney claimed that "the history of art follows the development of the history of the nation."[43] While art expresses human soul and truth, it does not escape time. Art arises out of its historical context, for artists execute their studies of nature and their own spiritual awareness through the individuality of their humanity. Their works embody the timeliness of their spatiality. Timeliness is as much a part of art's material-spiritual existence as timelessness. Cheney ever submits the spiritual to the microscope of individuality and the real to the telescope of the ideal. With this method she is able to offer insight in her critique of a portrait of the wife of Dr. C. A. Bartol in her "Art Exhibit by Women": " . . . a stranger asks, 'Why is that almost hazy veiling of the woman's face?' But those who remember it, even as she flitted on her errands of mercy about the streets, recognize it as expressing most fitly the spiritual and poetic atmosphere which always accompanied her."[44]

A measure of Ednah Dow Cheney's consideration of art in the "pragmatic" present was her concern for art as a public experience. She wrote about the relation of education to art and art to education in the classroom, the museum, and the home. For Cheney, studying art as a part of all education has the "power of developing the intellect by quickening perception, and securing accuracy of observation."[45] Cheney was not only involved in the establishment of schools for the study of art as a profession, but in communicating about art by writing newspaper articles on art events. By "education," Cheney meant learning to know one's self as a citizen of the nation of which the self is a part. For her, the aesthetic question is both what art can do for us, and what we can do for art:

> The existence of art rests on the same basis as our political institutions—upon the general intelligence and welfare of the people . . . the atmosphere of freedom, giving an opportunity to genius . . . which affords the true stimulus to art.[46]

Hegelian in scope, this concept of education embraces the individual human being as well as the whole of humanity. The present danger of superficiality in art, Cheney noted, necessitated her writing *Gleanings.* Looking to the future, Cheney optimistically recognized a "new era" in which an awakened interest in art would come to the decadent schools of art with "new power and freedom."[47] Our schools will provide "long and careful training,"[48] and "having been through its primitive stage art will grow."[49]

Cheney emphasized America's "particular works of art, in relation to different media and to the history of art" and, as a forward-looking thinker, considered photography—the newest form of art and new technology. Hence, according to the criteria of twentieth-century historians Elizabeth Flower and Murray Murphey, Cheney is one of the earliest American aestheticians to have had a twentieth-century outlook.[50] For forty years Ednah Dow Cheney followed the successive stages of development of the daguerreotype to photography. She did not see photography as a threat, a replacement of the engravings often then used in ways that photographs came to supplant. Instead, characteristically, she saw photography and other art forms as having limitations, yet remaining valuable. At that time one of photography's limitations was its incapability to move beyond black and white: "The sun, the source of all color, cannot paint its beauties for us on the sensitive plate, and in losing color we lose also the true relations of light and shadow in the picture," but photography could be faithful to "form and shadow."[51]

Cheney's pluralism allowed her to view American art not as "the simple development of one race" but as composed of wide-ranging influences, Native American to a myriad of European.[52] From her perspective as one involved in the world of American art, Cheney noted in her *Reminiscences* that the belief that American art suffered from "cruel neglect and poverty" was practically and theoretically a "shallow view."[53] Still, she believed there was no art—defined as the expression of thought and feeling, with portraiture its highest form—in America until the eighteenth century. She concurred with William Dunlap's history, which claimed the first artist to be the Scotsman John Watson who settled in Perth Amboy, New Jersey, in 1715; the second to be John Smybert in 1728; and following them the early miniaturists Ann Hall of Connecticut and Miss Goodrich. She would not consider legitimate art that was merely decorative or utilitarian and that did not "speak to the mind."[54]

Cheney's inclusive vision could never agree with what Hegel wrote of women and art: "Women . . . are not made for activities which demand a universal faculty such as the more advanced sciences, philosophy and certain forms of artistic production."[55] Such thinking was impossible for Cheney, given her philosophy that the ultimate source of all reality is both male and female. All art and artists by nature are both male and female. But Cheney knew that "without the bracing air of liberal thought, and free activity," women were unable to reach their potential.[56] At a time when women sculptors were questioned as to the propriety of sculpting men's legs,[57] Cheney encouraged women artists. In particular she enthusiastically supported her friend Mary Freeman Clarke, Allston's only pupil; Jane M. Clark, Seth Cheney's student from the Boston School of Design; and Anne Whitney, who sculpted Harriet Martineau for Wellesley College and Samuel Adams for Washington, D.C.[58] As a subject of art, the artist's vision of women, she hoped, would change as the "eternally feminine element of divinity [found] fuller expression in every form of art."[59]

To experience art properly, Cheney suggests that one look to its strengths as opposed to its defects and develop a willingness to "correct" judgments made over the course of time. One's relationship with art develops not as one is educated to standards, but as one becomes educated in general and experiences art directly. This relationship with art is not only intellectual, however, for Cheney makes the point that education and experience are the paths that make the "loving" of art possible.[60] Art, too, she notes, as outward form "loves recognition and sympathy."[61] Hence, Cheney's "loving" of art demands a sensible response to art. With this view, Cheney's aesthetics express the true nature of aesthetics as Baumgarten defined it, "scientia cognitionis sensitive," or as Richard P. McKeon interpreted it, "sensitive cognition."[62]

Conclusion

It is clear, then, that there is a Chenian aesthetics, unacknowledged, but nevertheless a part of the American aesthetics tradition. The contribution Ednah Dow Cheney made to the young discipline of American aesthetics is at once practical and theoretical. Her pluralist, humanist, and feminist understanding of art was wholly American and yet universal. In her theory, art admits of no inner primacy, such as male art over female art, nor is aesthetic truth seen as a prelude to something higher; rather, art correlates to the lived life of the human spirit in all its unique forms of materiality and transcendence. As an American whose point of view was so truly American, steeped in transcendentalism, inspired by Washington Allston, and differentiating her ideas from European predecessors, Cheney can be labeled a "first."

The historians of American philosophy, Flower and Murphey, have suggested that aesthetics has been growing in importance and has been transformed in the past quarter of a century, that is, since mid-century. Aesthetics has now

> moved beyond traditional questions of the nature of the creative process, communication between artist and audience, to the more intensive study of particular works of art, in relation to different media and to the history of the arts, to the interpretation of art as symbolic system, and to comparative studies of the imagination in art and in science.[63]

Now, in the last twenty-five years of the century, the developments of feminist rethinking of aesthetics issues, including the recovery of work by women, can be added to this list. In the case of Ednah Dow Cheney, this recovery discloses an aesthetic that anticipates many of these late twentieth century concerns.

Notes

1. Odel Shepard, *Pedlar's Progress: The Life of Bronson Alcott* (Boston: Little, Brown, 1937), p. 508.
2. Phebe A. Hanaford, *Daughters of America or Women of the Century* (Augusta, Me.: True and Co., 1882), p. 320.
3. Ednah Dow Cheney, *Gleanings in the Fields of Art* (Boston: Lee and Shepard, 1881). In addition to works noted in this text, Cheney's work on art also included the following, listed in chronological order:

"Allston as a Writer," *Commonwealth* (10 February 1866).

"Mr. Morse's Parker," *The Index* (1 January 1874), p. 7.

"Religion in Art," *The Index* (15 October 1874), p. 499.

Untitled, *The Women's Journal* (8 July 1876), p. 217.

"Miss Whitney's Statue of Samuel Adams," *The Index* (2 July 1881).

"The Concord School of Philosophy," *The Index* (2 July 1881).

Ednah Dow Cheney also assisted S. R. Koehler in compiling his 1891 *Catalogue of the Engraved and Lithographed Work of John Cheney and Seth Wells Cheney* (Boston: Lee and Shepard).

4. Having sought advice from Rosa Bonheur (1822–1899), Cheney was instrumental in the creation of The School of Design in Boston.

5. Edgar Preston Richardson, *Washington Allston* (Chicago: University of Chicago Press, 1948), p. 159. In 1846 C. Edward Lestor had acclaimed Allston as the country's best artist (*The Art of America: A Series of Biographical Sketches of American Artists* [New York: Baker and Scribner, 1846], p. 3).

6. Henry N. Day, *The Science of Aesthetics: or The Nature, Kinds, Laws, and Uses of Beauty* (New Haven, Conn.: Chas. Chatfield, 1872), p. 51. Henry Day does list Washington Allston's 1850 *Lectures on Art and Poems*, ed. Richard Henry Dana, Jr. (New York: Baker and Scribner, 1850); along with James Moffat's 1856 *Introduction to the Study of Aesthetics* (Cincinnati: Moore, Wilstack, and Keys, 1856), G. W. Sampson's 1867 *Elements of Art Criticism* (Washington, D.C.: Columbia College), James Jackson Jarves' 1864 *The Art Idea* (New York: Hurd and Houghton, 1864), and John Bascom's *Aesthetics or the Science of Beauty* (New York: G. P. Putnam's Sons, 1871).

7. Ibid., p. 9.

8. George A. Kennedy translates Aristotle's *Nicomachean Ethics* [1140a, 6.4.1] as making the distinction between doing (praxis) and making (poiesis). Kennedy, *Aristotle on Rhetoric: A Theory of Civic Discourse* (New York: Oxford University Press, 1991), p. 20.

9. Noted in Katherine Gilbert, *Studies in Recent Aesthetics* (Chapel Hill: University of North Carolina, 1927) p. 136.

10. *Reminiscences*, p. 128.

11. "Art and Religion," *The Radical* (July 1865), p. 5.

12. Ibid., p. 3.

13. *Gleanings*, p. 10.

14. Ibid., p. 10.

15. Ibid., p. 10.

16. John Bascom, *The Science of Aesthetics*, pp. 5–6.

17. *Gleanings*, p. 16.

18. Ibid., p. 17.

19. Ibid., p. 17.

20. Ibid., pp. 17–18.

21. "The Life and Poems of Michelangelo," *North American Review* (July 1859), p. 29.

22. "Art and Religion," pp. 2–3.

23. Ibid., p. 3.

24. Iris Murdoch, *Metaphysics as a Guide to Morals* (New York: Penguin, 1993), pp. 491–505.

25. *Gleanings*, p. 15.

26. Ibid., p. 14.

27. *Reminiscenses*, p. 82.

28. Ibid., p. 14.

29. "Art and Religion," p. 2.

30. Ibid., p. 2.

31. *Gleanings*, p. 27.

32. Ibid., pp. 29, 30.

33. "Art and Religion," p. 3.

34. *Reminiscences*, p. 189.

35. *Gleanings*, p. 33.

36. "Art and Religion," p. 3.

37. Hegel, often a focus of study at the Concord School of Philosophy, had produced a systematic aesthetics.

38. "Art and Religion," p. 3; p. 1.

39. Ibid., 2–3.

40. Ibid., p. 10; p. 14; p. 3.

41. George Lansing Raymond, *An Art Philosopher's Cabinet* (New York: G. P. Putnam's Sons, 1915).

42. George Lansing Raymond, *The Representative Significance of Form: An Essay in Comparative Aesthetics* (New York: Putnam, 1900), p. iv.

43. *Gleanings*, pp. 17–18.

44. "Art Exhibit by Women," *The Woman's Journal* (18 February 1888), p. 58.

45. *Gleanings*, p. 270.

46. Ibid., p. 307.

47. Reminiscences, p. 185.

48. "Leslie's Handbook of Art," *North American Review* (July 1853), p. 426.

49. *Gleanings*, p. 335.

50. Elizabeth Flower and Murray Murphey, *A History of Philosophy in America* (New York: G. P. Putnam, 1977).

51. Ibid., pp. 270, 29.

52. Ibid., p. 272.

53. *Reminiscences*, p. 129.

54. Ibid., p. 14.

55. From Hegel's *Philosophy of Right*, quoted in Patricia Jagentowicz Mills, "Hegel and the 'Woman Question': Recognition and Intersubjectivity," in *The Sexism of Social and Political Theory: Women and Reproduction from Plato to Nietzsche*, L. Clarke and L. Lange, eds. (Toronto: University of Toronto Press, 1977), p. 94.

56. *Gleanings*, p. 313.

57. Christine Battersby, *Gender and Genius: Toward a Feminist Aesthetics* (Bloomington: Indiana University Press, 1989), p. 103.

58. Jane M. Clark, who sketched the abolitionists Garrison and Phillips, accompanied the Cheneys to Europe. Harriet Martineau's sculpture was burned, but many of her sculptures remain in Boston and environs, and three thousand of her letters are preserved at Wellesley. Among Whitney's sculptures is one of Frances E. Willard.

59. "Art and Religion," p. 14.

60. *Gleanings*, pp. 22–23.

61. "Art and Religion," p. 13.

62. George Kimball Plochmann, *Richard P. McKeon: A Study* (Chicago: University of Chicago Press, 1990), p. 246.

63. Flower and Murphey, *A History of Philosophy in America*, p. 962.

Marilyn Fischer

---

5   Jane Addams's Feminist Ethics

While Jane Addams (1860–1935) is best known as the founder of Hull House, her social activism extended far beyond that. She was a cofounder of the American Civil Liberties Union (ACLU), the National Association for the Advancement of Colored People (NAACP), and the Woman's Peace Party. She worked vigorously for women's suffrage and international peace. In 1931 Addams was awarded the Nobel Peace Prize. She also authored twelve books and hundreds of articles; much of her writing is rich in philosophical content.

Addams's theory of social ethics can be understood in terms of three components: that society is organically interconnected; that all persons are equal; and that ethical action should come through what she calls "associated efforts," rather than individual endeavors. In this paper I will show how Addams, in developing each of these components, anticipates perspectives commonly found in contemporary feminist ethics: the importance of context, with particular attention to women's lives; the inadequacy of the rights approach and the centrality of care and responsibility in ethical theory and response; and the role of emotion in moral understanding and action. Although Addams uses all of these perspectives to develop each of the three components of her theory, in this paper I will pair them and explain, first, how Addams uses context and women's experiences to show society's interconnections; second, how a care and responsibility orientation gives a fuller sense of human equality than does a rights perspective; and, finally, how emotion has a central role in achieving associated efforts.

Society As Organically Interconnected

Addams understands society, and particularly city life, as organically interconnected.[1] Following in the tradition of Auguste Comte, Addams views human history in evolutionary terms: As society becomes increasingly urban, social interconnections become even more complex and penetrating. As social structures change, so ethical ideas should evolve in a corresponding way.[2] Individual morality, appropriate at an earlier age, should be replaced by social morality.

Many writers on feminist ethics stress the importance of context in ethical understanding.[3] Because she lived in the midst of Greek, German, Russian, Italian, Irish, and Polish immigrants, Addams accumulated vast, detailed knowledge of their daily lives. She uses this contextual knowledge repeatedly to show society's organic interconnections. This is particularly clear in *A New Conscience and An Ancient Evil* in which Addams analyzes prostitution, showing how it is linked to an amazing array of larger social issues.[4]

Addams's concern with prostitutes grew out of her own concrete experience. She and the other residents of Hull House had a long, close relationship with the Juvenile Protection Association.[5] In the preface to *A New Conscience* she states, "The reports which its twenty field officers daily brought to its main office adjoining Hull House became to me a revelation of the dangers implicit in city conditions and of the allurements which are designedly placed around many young girls in order to draw them into an evil life."[6] She begins by naming prostitution "this twin of slavery, as old and outrageous as slavery itself, and even more persistent,"[7] and goes on to posit that equivalent efforts will be needed to eradicate it.

Addams begins by analyzing the dynamics of the white slave trade, where women, often quite young, were imported to serve as prostitutes.[8] She tells the story of Marie, a fifteen-year-old French household servant, lured into prostitution and imported to the United States with promises of joining a theatrical troupe. Addams recounts the process by which her spirit, as well as her body, was demoralized.[9]

It was clear to Addams that many dimensions of urban poverty made immigrant girls and women vulnerable to prostitution. Many of her immigrant neighbors worked in factories, spending fourteen hours a day in deadening, often brutal work, for wholly inadequate wages. For many young women, prostitution was the only way to stop hunger pangs in a child or family member.[10] Because of their poverty, immigrant families could often afford housing only in disreputable neighborhoods. Addams tells of two girls, ages eight and twelve, invited by a kindly neighbor to play dress-up with her finery while their mother was away at work. It was some time before their mother learned of her neighbor's occupation, and the true nature of her daughters' visits. Rather than chastise the mother for her inattention, Addams agrees with Wells "that it is a 'monstrous absurdity' that women who are 'discharging their supreme social function, that of rearing children, should do it in their spare time, as it were, while they "earn their living" by contributing some half-mechanical element to some trivial industrial product'."[11]

Her stories continue, showing concretely the links between prostitution and the loneliness of peasant girls transplanted to a confusing city, where the pressures of city life are more than adolescents can bear. Young people need healthy outlets for recreation; the city offered only dance halls attached to saloons where attractive young men acted as procurers.[12] Similarly, Addams tells stories illustrating connections between prostitution and domestic service, racism, military life, police corruption, alcohol, and the lack of vocational training and sex education. She speaks movingly of the tiniest victims—infants born to diseased, prostitute mothers.[13]

With her intimate knowledge of context, and particularly of women's experiences, Addams was able to show the organic interconnections of urban life, linking prostitution to economic conditions, political operations, and lack of civic infrastructure. This enabled her to understand just how far-reaching the solutions would have to be. She hoped that woman's suffrage and women's participation in civic affairs would contribute to undermining urban conditions that permit prostitution to flourish. Even here Addams's use of concrete experience gives her a realistic appreciation of women's potential for ethical action. She thought that, given their long history as nurturers, women "would not brook that men should live upon the wages of captured victims, should openly hire youths to ruin and debase young girls, should be permitted to transmit poison to unborn children."[14] Yet Addams does not approach women's nurturance uncritically. She worries that in public life, women may abandon their "innate concerns" and simply pursue "a masculine policy."[15] As illustrated in her discussion of domestic service, Addams is well aware that women can exploit, as well as nurture, others.[16]

The Equality of All Persons

Human equality for Addams is a rich concept. I will first describe the dimensions of her understanding of human equality, and then show how this understanding is informed by Addams's conviction that a care and responsibility perspective needs to be incorporated into our understanding of justice. For Addams, human equality expresses the following:

a. *Our grounding in nature.* Quoting Delos Wilcox, Addams writes, "Birth, growth, nutrition, reproduction, death, are the great levelers that remind us of the essential equality of human life."[17] It is this connection with nature, rather than the metaphysical equality of eighteenth-century philosophy, that gives the basis for recognizing human equality.

b. *Individual uniqueness and creativity.* Addams believes that each person is capable of making valuable and unique contributions to society. Each person is a source of dynamic power and energy that, with appropriate education, can be released. Again, she links individual uniqueness with social well-being, illustrating organic interconnections.[18]

c. *Sentiment of universal brotherhood.* Addams was influenced by Tolstoy and by her own understanding of early Christianity. She writes that we have an almost primordial longing for shared humanity, and that love is a "creative force" that binds us together and, through our interdependence, makes us human.[19]

d. *Solidarity.* Speaking of the settlement movement, Addams writes, "It must be grounded in a philosophy whose foundation is on the solidarity of the human race, a philosophy which will not waver when the race happens to be represented by a drunken woman or an idiot boy."[20] This sense of solidarity is not just a premise for how to think of people, but also a realization that good is accomplished only when it is secured for all.[21]

This complex understanding of equality underlies Addams's theory of social democracy. Encompassing far more than constitutional guarantees or governmental procedures, democracy is realized when all persons can develop and contribute their unique capacities and can participate fully in all areas of life—economic, political, social, and cultural.[22]

While Addams does not use the vocabulary of the justice-care debate, many concerns of contemporary feminists are present in her writings. Much contemporary work on justice derives from enlightenment traditions—for example, Nozick's indebtedness to Locke, and Rawls's to Kant—and feminist critiques often focus on the inadequacies of those traditions to give a full understanding of morality. Addams is penetrating in her criticisms of what she called "eighteenth-century philosophy," writing that "That old Frankenstein, the ideal man of the eighteenth century, is still haunting us, although he never existed save in the brain of the doctrinaire."[23] Again, concrete experience is crucial. Rights are not inborn and inalienable, but rather are "hard-won in the tragic process of experience" and easily lost.[24] Addams saw the failure of American commitment to equality in criminally unsafe factories, inadequate wages, and the simple refusal of the well-to-do to associate in friendship and fellowship with the poor.[25]

Thus, our ideals must be tested and interpreted by actual experience; eighteenth-century abstractions of justice and equality fail this test.[26] Addams writes, "We conscientiously followed the gift of the ballot hard upon the gift of freedom to the negro, but we are quite unmoved by the fact that he lives among us in a practical social ostracism. We hasten to give the franchise to the immigrant from a sense of justice, from a tradition that he ought to have it, while we dub him with epithets deriding his past life, or present occupation, and feel no duty to invite him to our houses."[27] That prostitution flourished in Chicago amply illustrated how "the great principle of liberty has been translated . . . into the unlovely doctrine of commercial competition."[28]

In Addams's discussions of achieving equality—meeting biologically-based needs, developing creative capacities, and working toward universal brotherhood and solidarity—perspectives of care and responsibility are apparent. This is illustrated in the reasons she gives for woman's suffrage. (Addams served for several years as vice president of the National American Woman's Suffrage Association.[29]) Quite simply, women needed the vote to fulfill their obligations to their children and families. How can women keep their children healthy when garbage is not picked up, sewers are not connected, and milk is contaminated? Women need to vote so they can care effectively; they need to participate in municipal affairs because so much of public life is in fact "municipal housekeeping."[30]

Here Addams's evolutionary understanding of history and her organic view of urban life come into play. Historically, caretaking in the domestic sphere encompassed economic production, education, health care, and many political and legal functions. In the modern city, many of these functions have moved out of the home and are carried out in factories, schools, hospitals, and political and legal arenas.[31] If women in the city are to carry out their historic caretaking responsibilities, they must be able to participate in civic life. Not only would the civic arena benefit from women's experience, but women themselves would experience the educative effects of such participation.[32]

In Addams's discussion of women's suffrage there is no mention of women's rights to an abstract equality. Her advocacy is based on conditions required for women to carry out their caretaking responsibilities and to develop their own creative capacities.

Role of Emotion in Associated Efforts

The third component of Addams's ethical theory is that change—or "ethical action"— should be carried out through "associated effort" rather than through individual effort. To reflect the organic interconnections of an urban, industrial society, ethical action should come through widespread, cooperative, highly participatory efforts, rather than through individually directed activities. The latter may appear more effective, but they are more apt to be based on an inaccurate assessment of needs, and less apt to develop the skills, talents, and social responsiveness of those being helped.[33]

Contrasting associated effort with individual effort, Addams writes, "He [the person working through associated effort] has to discover what people really want, and then 'provide the channels in which the growing moral force of their lives shall flow.' What he does attain, however, is not the result of his individual striving, as a solitary mountain-climber beyond that of the valley multitude, but it is sustained and upheld by the sentiments and aspirations of many others. Progress has been slower perpendicularly, but incomparably greater because lateral."[34]

Addams's discussions of associated effort reveal the role she sees for emotion in ethics. Her accounts share much with those of her more contemporary sisters.[35] She gives countless examples of how appealing to and cultivating emotions is critical for ethical change. In *The Spirit of Youth and the City Streets,* she tells of a boy growing up without parents, without love. He ran away and worked for years as a dock laborer, during which time he befriended a little disabled boy. Addams comments that it was the pull on his sympathies that turned him around; abstract moral appeals would have been useless.[36] Her point is that intellect alone is inadequate for moral action.

In her 1915 Presidential Address to the International Congress of Women at the Hague, Addams criticized Kant's writings on peace as focused too exclusively on reason, stating, "Reason is only a part of the human endowment; emotion and deep-set radical impulses must be utilized as well, those primitive human urgings to foster life and to protect the helpless of which women were the earliest custodians, and even the social and gregarious instincts that we share with the animals themselves. These universal desires must be given opportunities to expand and the most highly trained intellects must serve them rather than the technique of war and diplomacy."[37]

Addams often refers to such "primitive human urgings" and to people's "impulses for goodness."[38] The earliest moral codes grew out of feelings of emotional solidarity. She claims that these impulses have been carried through social evolution, and can be valuable, as "a state of emotion is invariably the organic preparation for action."[39]

In her analyses of social problems, Addams repeatedly stresses how emotions are the starting point for ethical change. But emotions need to be cultivated and guided by experience and reason. In addressing social problems, Hull House residents first gathered statistics and empirical data,[40] but then interpreted the data in light of their direct experience as neighbors of the poor. Together this would give "sympathetic knowledge," which Addams calls "the only way of approach to any human problem."[41] Sympathetic knowledge—combining emotional impulses, reason, and the understanding gained by concrete experience—would reveal the ultimate futility of individual efforts, no matter how philanthropically motivated, and give the solidarity for effective, associated action.

Thus, in both method and content Addams's theory of social ethics gives central attention to context, women's experiences, care and responsibility, and the emotions. The ethical perspectives of contemporary feminists have a past; for us, an exciting task is to uncover and reconstruct that history. Jane Addams's life and writings stand strongly in our lineage.

Notes

1. J. Addams et al., *Philanthropy and Social Progress* (1893 reprint ed., Montclair, N.J.: Patterson Smith, 1970), p. 23.

2. J. Addams, *Twenty Years at Hull House* (New York: Macmillan, 1912), pp. 81–82.

3. See M. Friedman, *What Are Friends For?* (Ithaca, N.Y.: Cornell University Press, 1993), pp. 91–116; and M. Walker, "Moral Understandings: Alternative 'Epistemology' for a Feminist Ethics" in E. B. Cole and S. Coultrap-McQuin, eds., *Explorations in Feminist Ethics* (Bloomington: Indiana University Press, 1992), pp. 165–75.

4. J. Addams, *A New Conscience and An Ancient Evil* (New York: Macmillan, 1912).

5. *Twenty Years*, pp. 323–4.

6. *A New Conscience*, p. ix.

7. Ibid., p. 4.

8. For a lengthy analysis of the white slave trade see V. Bullough and B. Bullough, *Women and Prostitution: A Social History* (Buffalo, N.Y.: Prometheus Books, 1987), pp. 259–90.

9. *A New Conscience*, pp. 17–22.

10. Ibid., pp. 60–1.

11. Ibid., p. 115.

12. Ibid., pp. 49–50.

13. Ibid., p. 132.

14. Ibid., p. 192.

15. J. Addams, *Second Twenty Years at Hull House* (New York: Macmillan, 1930), p. 110.

16. J. Addams, *Democracy and Social Ethics* (1907, reprint ed. Cambridge, Mass.: Harvard University Press, 1964), chap. 4.

17. J. Addams, *Newer Ideals of Peace* (New York: Macmillan, 1906), p. 117.

18. *Democracy and Social Ethics*, pp. 178–9.

19. *Philanthropy and Social Progress,* pp. 10–11, 19–20.

20. Ibid., p. 23.

21. Ibid., p. 7.

22. *Twenty Years,* pp. 116, 452–3.

23. *Newer Ideals of Peace,* p. 60.

24. Ibid., p. 33.

25. *Philanthropy and Social Progress,* p. 3.

26. *Newer Ideals of Peace,* p. 41.

27. *Philanthropy and Social Progress,* p. 3.

28. *A New Conscience,* p. 206.

29. *Second Twenty Years,* p. 84.

30. *Newer Ideals of Peace,* pp. 182–3.

31. Ibid., pp. 188–208.

32. Ibid., p. 184.

33. *Democracy and Social Ethics,* pp. 153–5.

34. Ibid., p. 152.

35. See Virginia Held, *Feminist Morality* (Chicago: University of Chicago Press, 1993), chap. 2.

36. J. Addams, *The Spirit of Youth and the City Streets* (1909, reprint ed., Urbana: University of Illinois Press, 1972), p. 155.

37. Addams, J., "Presidential Address," *Report of the International Congress of Women at The Hague,* reprinted in Allen Davis, ed., *Jane Addams on Peace, War, and International Understanding: 1899–1932* (New York: Garland, 1976), pp. 67–71.

38. *Newer Ideals of Peace,* p. 21.

39. *A New Conscience,* p. 11.

40. *Twenty Years,* p. 129.

41. *A New Conscience,* p. 11.

Katie Geneva Cannon

---

6 Moral Wisdom in the Black Women's Literary Tradition

Origins

I first began pondering the relationship between faith and ethics as a schoolgirl while listening to my grandmother teach the central affirmations of Christianity within the context of a racially segregated society. My community of faith taught me the principles of God's universal parenthood, which engendered a social, intellectual, and cultural ethos embracing the equal humanity of all people. Yet my city, state, and nation declared it a punishable offense against the laws and mores for Blacks and Whites "to travel, eat, defecate, wait, be buried, make love, play, relax and even speak together, except in the stereotyped context of master and servant interaction."[1]

My religious quest tried to relate the Christian doctrines preached in the Black church to the suffering, oppression, and exploitation of Black people in the society. How could Christians who were White flatly and openly refuse to treat as fellow human beings Christians who had African ancestry? Inasmuch as the Black church expressed the inner ethical life of the people, was there any way to reconcile the inherent contradictions in Christianity as practiced by Whites with the radical indictments of and challenges for social amelioration and economic development in the Black religious heritage? How long would the White church continue to be the ominous symbol of White dominance, sanctioning and assimilating the propagation of racism in the mundane interests of the ruling group?

In the 1960s my quest for the integration of faith and ethics was influenced by scholars in various fields who surfaced the legitimate contributions of Afro-Americans that had been historically distorted and denied. Avidly I read the analysis exposing the assumptions and dogmas that made Blacks a negligible factor in the thought of the world. For more than three and a half centuries a "conspiracy of silence" rendered invisible the outstanding contributions of Blacks to the culture of humankind. From cradle to grave the people in the United States were taught the alleged inferiority of Blacks in every place in society.

When I turned specifically to readings in theological ethics, I discovered that the assumptions of the dominant ethical systems implied that the doing of Christian ethics in the Black community was either immoral or amoral. The cherished ethical ideas predicated upon the existence of freedom and a wide range of choices proved null and void in situations of oppression. The real-lived texture of Black life requires moral agency that may run contrary to the ethical boundaries of mainline Protestantism. Blacks may use action guides that have never been considered within the scope of traditional codes of faithful living. Racism, gender discrimination, and economic exploitation, as inherited, age-long complexes, require the Black community to create and cultivate values and virtues in their own terms so that they prevail against the odds with moral integrity.

For example, dominant ethics makes a virtue of qualities that lead to economic success—self-reliance, frugality, and industry. These qualities are based on an assumption that success is possible for anyone who tries. Developing confidence in one's own abilities, resources, and judgments amid a careful use of money and goods in order to exhibit assiduity in the pursuit of upward mobility have proven to be positive values for Whites. But when the oligarchic economic powers and the consequent political power they generate own and control capital and distribute credit as part of a legitimating system to justify the supposed inherent inferiority of Blacks, these same values prove to be ineffectual. Racism does not allow most Black women and Black men to labor habitually in beneficial work with the hope of saving expenses by avoiding waste so that they can develop a standard of living that is congruent with the American ideal.

Work may be a "moral essential," but Black women are still the last hired to do the work that White men, White women, and men of color refuse to do, and at a wage that men and White women refuse to accept. Black women, placed in jobs that have proven to be detrimental to their health, are doing the most menial, tedious, and by far the most underpaid work, if they manage to get a job at all.

Dominant ethics also assumes that a moral agent is to a considerable degree free and self-directing. Each person possesses self-determining power. For instance, one is free to choose whether he or she wants to suffer and make sacrifices as a principle of action or as a voluntary vocational pledge of crossbearing. In dominant ethics a person is free to make suffering a desirable moral norm. This is not so for Blacks. For the masses of Black people, suffering is the normal state of affairs. Mental anguish, physical abuse, and emotional agony are all part of the lived truth of Black people's straitened circumstances. Due to the extraneous forces and the entrenched bulwark of White supremacy and male superiority that pervade this society, Blacks and Whites, women and men are forced to live with very different ranges of freedom. As long as the White-male experience continues as the ethical norm, Black women, Black men, and others will suffer unequivocal oppression. The range of freedom has been restricted by those who cannot hear and will not hear voices expressing pleasure and pain, joy and rage as others experience them.

In the Black community, the aggregate of the qualities that determine desirable ethical values, uprightness of character, and soundness of moral conduct must always take into account the circumstances, the paradoxes, and the dilemmas that constrict Blacks to the lowest rungs of the social, political, and economic hierarchy. Black existence is deliberately and openly controlled: "how we travel and where, what work we do, what income we receive, what we eat, where we sleep, with whom we talk, where we recreate, where we study, what we write, what we publish."[2] The vast majority of Blacks suffer every conceivable form of denigration. Their lives are named, defined, and circumscribed by Whites.

The moral wisdom that exists in the Black community is extremely useful in defying oppressive rules or standards of "law and order" that unjustly degrade Blacks in the society. It helps Blacks purge themselves of self-hate, thus asserting their own validity. But the salient point here is that the ethical values that the Black community has fashioned for itself are not identical with the body of obligations and duties that Anglo-Protestant American society requires of its members. Nor can the ethical assumptions be the same, as long as powerful Whites who control the wealth, the systems, and the institutions in this society continue to perpetuate brutality and criminality against Blacks.

Method

The method used in this study departs from most work in Christian and secular ethics. The body of data is drawn from less conventional sources and probes more intimate and private aspects of Black life. The Black women's literary tradition has not previously been used to interpret and explain the community's sociocultural patterns from which ethical values can be gleaned. I have found that this literary tradition is the nexus between the real-lived texture of Black life and the oral-aural cultural values implicitly passed on and received from one generation to the next.

Black women are the most vulnerable and the most exploited members of the American society. The structure of the capitalist political economy in which Black people are commodities, combined with patriarchal contempt for women, has caused the Black woman to experience oppression that knows no ethical or physical bounds.

> As a black, she has had to endure all the horrors of slavery and living in a racist society; as a worker, she has been the object of continual exploitation, occupying the lowest place on the wage scale and restricted to the most demeaning and uncreative jobs; as a woman she has seen her physical image defamed and been the object of the white master's uncontrollable lust and subjected to all the ideals of white womanhood as a model to which she should aspire; as a mother, she has seen her children torn from her breast and sold into slavery, she has seen them left at home without attention while she attended to the needs of the offspring of the ruling class.[3]

The focus of this essay is to show how Black women live out a moral wisdom in their real-lived context that does not appeal to the fixed rules or absolute principles of the White-oriented, male-structured society. Black women's analysis and appraisal of what is right or wrong and good or bad develop out of the various coping mechanisms related to the conditions of their own cultural circumstances. In the face of this, Black women have justly regarded survival against tyrannical systems of triple oppression as a true sphere of moral life.

Black women are taught what is to be endured and how to endure the harsh, cruel, inhumane exigencies of life. The moral wisdom does not rescue Black women from the bewildering pressures and perplexities of institutionalized social evils; rather, it exposes those ethical assumptions that are inimical to the ongoing survival of Black womanhood. The moral counsel of Black women captures the ethical qualities of what is real and what is of value to women in the Black world.

Black women writers function as continuing symbolic conveyors and transformers of the values acknowledged by the female members of the Black community. In the quest for appreciating Black women's experience, nothing surpasses the Black women's literary tradition. It cryptically records the specificity of the Afro-American life.

My goal is not to arrive at any prescriptive or normative ethic. Rather, what I am pursuing is an investigation (1) that will help Black women, and others who care, to understand and to appreciate the richness of their own moral struggle through the life of the common people and the oral tradition, and (2) to further understanding of some of the differences between ethics of life under oppression and established moral approaches that take for granted freedom and a wide range of choices. I am being suggestive of one possible ethical approach, not exhaustive.

I make no apologies for the fact that this study is a partisan one. However, it is not merely a glorification of the Black female community, but rather an attempt to add to the far too few positive records concerning the Black woman as moral agent. For too long the Black community's theological and ethical understandings have been written from a decidedly male bias. The particular usefulness of this method should enable us to use the lives and literature of Black women to recognize through them the contribution to the field of ethics that Black women have made. One test will be whether those who know this literary tradition find that I have done justice to its depth and richness. The second test is whether Black women recognize the moral wisdom they utilize. The third test is whether Black feminists who have given up on the community of faith will gain new insights concerning the reasonableness of theological ethics in deepening the Black woman's character, consciousness, and capacity in the ongoing struggle for survival. If these criteria are met, I will have reached my objective.

It is my thesis that the Black women's literary tradition is the best available literary repository for understanding the ethical values Black women have created and cultivated in their participation in this society. To prevail against the odds with integrity, Black women must assess their moral agency within the social conditions of the community. Locked out of the real dynamics of human freedom in America, they implicitly pass on moral formulas for survival that allow them to stand over against the perversion of ethics and morality imposed on them by Whites and males who support racial imperialism in a patriarchal social order.

Findings

The story of the Afro-American has been told quite coherently but has repeatedly left out the Black woman in significant ways. Seldom in history has a group of women been so directly responsible for exerting indispensable efforts to insure the well-being of both their own families and those of their oppressors. At the same time the Black woman is placed in such a sharply disadvantaged position that she must accept obligingly the recording of her own story by the very ones who systematically leave her out. But, the work of Black women writers can be trusted as seriously mirroring Black reality. Their writings are important chronicles of the Black woman's survival.

Despite their tragic omission by the literary establishment, Black women have been expressing ideas, feelings, and interpretations about the Black experience since the early days of the eighteenth century. Throughout the various periods of their history in the United States, Black women have used their creativity to carve out "living space." From the beginning, they had to contend with the ethical ambiguity of racism, sexism, and other sources of fragmentation in this land acclaimed to be of freedom, justice, and equality. The Black women's literary tradition delineates the many ways that ordinary Black women have fashioned value patterns and ethical procedures in their own terms, as well as mastering, transcending, radicalizing, and sometimes destroying pervasive, negative orientations imposed by the mores of the larger society.

Toni Morrison describes the moral agency of old Black women reared in the South in this way:

> Edging into life from the back door. Becoming. Everybody in the world was in a position to give them orders. White women said, "Do this." White children said, "Give me that." White men said, "Come here." Black men said, "Lay down." The only people they need not take orders from were black children and each other. But they took all of that and recreated it in their own image. They ran the houses of white people, and knew it. When white men beat their men, they cleaned up the blood and went home to receive abuse from the victim. They beat their children with one hand and stole for them with the other. The hands that felled trees also cut umbilical cords; the hands that wrung the necks of chickens and butchered hogs also nudged African violets into bloom; the arms that loaded sheaves, bales and sacks rocked babies to sleep. They patted biscuits into flaky ovals of innocence— and shrouded the dead. They plowed all day and came home to nestle like plums under the limbs of their men. The legs that straddled a mule's back were the same ones that straddled their men's hips. And the difference was all the difference there was.[4]

The bittersweet irony of the Afro-American experience forces Black women to examine critically the conventional, often pretentious, morality of middle-class American ideals.

The Black women's literary tradition provides a rich resource and a coherent commentary that brings into sharp focus the Black community's central values, which in turn frees Black folks from the often deadly grasp of parochial stereotypes. The observations, descriptions, and interpretations in Black literature are largely reflective of cultural experiences. They identify the frame of social contradiction in which Black people live, move, and have their being. The derogatory caricatures and stereotypes ascribed to Black people are explicitly rejected. Instead, writings by Blacks capture the magnitude of the Black personality. Spanning the antebellum period to today's complex technological society, Black women writers authenticate, in an economy of expression, how Black people creatively strain against the external limits in their lives, how they affirm their humanity by inverting assumptions, and how they balance the continual struggle and interplay of paradoxes.

The Black Women's Literary Tradition Parallels Black History

The Black women's literary tradition is a source in the study of ethics relative to the Black community because the development of the Black women's historical and literary legacy is tied to the origin of Black people in America. Most of the writing by Black women captures the values of the Black community within a specific location, time, and historical context. The literary tradition is not centered automatically upon the will and whims of what an individual writer thinks is right or obligatory, nor even upon whatever she personally believes to be true for her own localized consciousness. The majority of Black women who engage in literary compositions hold themselves accountable to the collective values that underlie Black history and culture. Dexter Fisher makes the point this way:

> To be totally centered on the self would be to forget one's history, the kinship of a shared community of experience, the crucial continuity between past and present that must be maintained in order to insure the future.[5]

As creators of literature these women are not formally historians, sociologists, or theologians, but the patterns and themes in their writings are reflective of historical facts, sociological realities, and religious convictions that lie behind the ethos and ethics of the Black community. As recorders of the Black experience, Black women writers convey the community's consciousness of values that enables them to find meaning in spite of social degradation, economic exploitation, and political oppression. They record what is valued or regarded as good in the Black community. Seldom, if ever, is their work art-for-art's-sake. "Whatever else may be said of it, Black American writing in the United States has been first and last, as Saunders Redding once observed, a 'literature of necessity.' "[6]

> The appeal of a basically utilitarian literature written to meet the exigencies of a specific historical occasion usually declines after the occasion has passed. That this is much less

true of Black literature is due to constant factors in Afro-American history—the Black presence and white racism.[7]

The Black Women's Literary Tradition Uses the Oral Narrative Devices of the Black Community

The irresistible power in the Black women's literary tradition is its power to convey the values of the Black community's oral tradition in its grasp for meaning. The suppression of book learning and the mental anguish of intellectual deprivation obliged the Black tradition to be expressed mainly in oral form. What is critical for my purpose is that these women reveal in their novels, short stories, love lyrics, folktales, fables, drama, and nonfiction a psychic connection with the cultural tradition transmitted by the oral mode from one general to the next. As serious writers who have mastered in varying degrees the technique of their craft, Black women find themselves causally dependent on the ethics of the Black masses. Black women writers draw heavily upon the Black oral culture.

The folk tales, song (especially the blues), sermons, the dozens, and the rap are all expressions of creativity that provide Black writers with the figurative language and connotations of dim hallways and dank smells, caged birds and flowers that won't sprout, curdled milk and rusty razors, of general stores and beauty parlors, nappy edges and sheened legs. The social and cultural forces within the Black oral tradition form the milieu out of which Black writers create.

Black women writers document the attitudes and morality of women, men, girls, and boys who chafe at and defy the restrictions imposed by the dominant White capitalist value system. They delineate in varying artistic terms the folk treasury of the Black community: ways to deal with poverty and the ramifications of power, sex as an act of love and terror, the depersonalization that accompanies violence, the acquisition of property, the drudgery of a workday, the inconsistencies of chameleon-like racism, teenage mothers, charlatan sorcerers, swinging churches, stoic endurance, and stifled creativity. Out of this storehouse of Black experience comes a vitally rich, ancient continuum of Black wisdom.

This capacity to catch the oral tradition also means an ability to portray the sense of community. Barbara Christian recognizes this unique characteristic common to Black women's literature as the "literary counterpart of their communities' oral tradition."

> The history of these communities, seldom related in textbooks, is incorporated into the tales that emphasize the marvelous, sometimes the outrageous, as a means of teaching a lesson. In concert with their African ancestors, these storytellers, both oral and literary, transform gossip, happenings, into composites of factual events, images, fantasies and fables.[8]

This important characteristic of Black women's writing is increasingly recognized by literary interpreters. Jeanne Noble says, "We would be scripted in history with little true human understanding without the black writer telling it like it is."[9] Mary Helen Washington says that this deeper-than-surface knowledge of and fondness for the verbal tradition is a truth that is shared by the majority of Black women writers:

> This remembrance of things past is not simply self-indulgent nostalgia. It is essential to her vision to establish connections with the values that nourish and strengthen her.[10]

Verta Mae Grosvenor captures the essence of the oral tradition at the very outset of her book *Vibration Cooking:*

> Dedicated to my mama and my grandmothers and my sisters in appreciation of the years that they have worked in miss ann's kitchen and then came home to TCB in spite of slavery and the moynihan report.[11]

Marcia Gillespie, in the May 1975 editorial of *Essence Magazine,* concludes that recording the oral tradition is a way of releasing the memories of mamas and grand-mamas:

> . . . the race memory of our women who, though burdened, neither broke nor faltered in their faith in a better world for us all.[12]

Black women's combination of the Western literate form with their unique sensibility to the oral narrative devices expresses with authority, power, and eloquence the insidious effects of racism, sexism, and class elitism on members of their communities. By not abandoning the deeply ingrained traditions of the Black community, these writers are able to utilize common sources that illustrate common values that exist within the collective vision of Black life in America.

The Black Women's Literary Tradition Capsulizes the Insularity of the Black Community

Black female writers, as participant-observers, capsulize on a myriad of levels the insularity of their home communities. Due to systemic, institutionalized manifestations of racism in America, the Black community tends to be situated as marginated islands within the larger society. The perpetual powers of White supremacy continue to drop down on the inhabitants of the Black community like a bell jar—surrounding the whole, while separating the Black community's customs, mores, opinions, and system of values from those in other communities. Black female authors emphasize life within the community, not the conflict with outside forces. In order to give faithful pictures of important and comprehensive segments of Black life, these writers tie their characters' stories to the aesthetic, emotional, and intellectual values of the Black community.

For instance, Ann Petry's *The Street* (1946) depicts the inevitability of crime for Black mothers who provide for their families against all odds in hostile urban environments:

A lifetime of pent-up resentments went into the blows. Even after he lay motionless, she kept striking him, not thinking about him, not even seeing him. First she was venting her rage against the dirty, crowded street. She saw the rows of dilapidated old houses; the small dark rooms; the long steep flight of stairs; the narrow dingy hallways; the little lost girls in Mrs. Hedges' apartment, the smashed homes where the women did drudgery because their men had deserted them. She saw all of these things and struck them.

Then the limp figure on the sofa became in turn Jim and the slender girl she'd found him with; became the insult in the moist-eyed glances of white men on the subway; became the greasy, lecherous man at the Crosse School for Singers; became the gaunt Super pulling her down into the basement.

Finally, and the blows were heavier, faster, now, she was striking at the white world which thrust black people into a walled enclosure from which there was no escape; and at the turn of events which had forced her to leave Bub alone while she was working so that he now faced reform school, now had a police record.

She saw the face and the head of the man on the sofa through waves of anger in which he represented all these things and she was destroying them.[13]

Again, for instance, Gwendolyn Brooks's novel *Maud Martha* (1953) focuses on the coming of age for the Black woman-child who has a dark complexion and untamable hair and must learn how to ward off assaults to her human dignity.

I am what he would call sweet. But I am certainly not what he would call pretty. Even with all this hair (which I have just assured him, in response to his question, is not "natural," is not good grade or anything like good grade) even with whatever I have that puts a dimple in his heart, even with these nice ears, I am still definitely not what he can call pretty if he remains true to what his idea of pretty has always been. Pretty would be a little cream-colored thing with curly hair. Or at the very lowest pretty would be a little curly-haired thing the color of cocoa with a lot of milk in it. Whereas, I am the color of cocoa straight, if you can be even that "kind" to me.[14]

And, still again, Margaret Walker's *Jubilee* (1966) captures the richness of Black folk culture: the songs, sayings, customs, food, medicinal remedies, and language. This historical novel portrays the character of Vyry's movement from slavery to freedom.

I wants you to bear witness and God knows I tells the truth, I couldn't tell you the name of the man what whipped me, and if I could it wouldn't make no difference. I honestly believes that if airy one of them peoples what treated me like dirt when I was a slave would come to my door in the morning hungry, I would feed 'em. God knows I ain't got no hate in my heart for nobody. If I is and doesn't know it, I prays to God to take it out. I ain't got no time to be hating. I believes in God and I believes in trying to love and help everybody, and I knows that humble is the way. I doesn't care what you calls me, that's my doctrine and I'm gwine preach it to my childrens, every living one I got or ever hopes to have.[15]

Black women writers find value consciousness in their home communities, which serve as the framework for their literary structure. They transform the passions and sympathies, the desires and hurts, the joys and defeats, the praises and pressures, the richness and diversity of real-lived community into the stuff for art through the medium of literature. As insiders, Black women writers venture into all strata of Black life.

Using the subject matter close to the heart of Black America, the Black women's literary tradition shows how the slavery and its consequences forced the Black woman into a position of cultural custodian. Black female protagonists are women with hard-boiled honesty and down-to-earth thinking, the ones who are forced to see through the shallowness, hypocrisy, and phoniness in their continual struggle for survival. Alice Childress paints the picture in this manner.

> The emancipated Negro woman of America did the only thing she could do. She earned a pittance by washing, ironing, cooking, cleaning, and picking cotton. She helped her man, and if she often stood in the front line, it was to shield him from the mob of men organized and dedicated to bring about his destruction.

The Negro mother has had the bitter job of teaching her children the difference between the White and the Colored signs before they were old enough to attend school. She had to train her sons and daughters to say "Sir" and "Ma'am" to those who were their sworn enemies.

She couldn't tell her husband "a white man whistled at me," not unless she wanted him to lay down his life before organized killers who strike only in anonymous numbers. Or worse, perhaps to see him helpless and ashamed before her.

Because he could offer no protection or security, the Negro woman has worked with and for her family. She built churches, schools, homes, temples and college educations out of soapsuds and muscles.[16]

Conclusion

The work of Black women writers can be trusted as seriously mirroring Black reality. Their writings are chronicles of Black survival. In their plots, actions, and depictions of characters, Black women writers flesh out the positive attributes of Black folks who are "hidden beneath the ordinariness of everyday life." They also plumb their own imaginations in order to crack the invidiousness of worn-out stereotypes. Their ideas, themes, and situations provide truthful interpretations of every possible shade and nuance of Black life.

Black women writers partially, and often deliberately, embrace the moral actions, religious values, and rules of conduct handed down by word of mouth in the folk culture. They then proceed in accordance with their tradition to transform the cultural limitations and unnatural restrictions in the community's move toward self-authenticity.

The special distinctiveness of most Black women writers is their knack of keeping their work intriguing and refreshing without diminishing its instructiveness. They know how to lift the imagination as they inform, how to touch emotions as they record, how to delineate specifics so that they are applicable to oppressed humanity everywhere. In essence, there is no better source for comprehending the "real-lived" texture of Black experience and the meaning of the moral life in the Black context than the Black women's literary tradition. Black women's literature offers the sharpest available view of the Black community's soul.

Notes

1. Pierre L. Van Der Berghe, *Race and Racism: A Comparative Perspective* (New York: Wiley, 1967), p. 77.

2. W. E. B. Du Bois, *Dusk at Dawn* (New York: Harcourt Brace and Co., 1940).

3. Frances M. Beal, "Slave of a Slave No More: Black Women in Struggle," *The Black Scholar* 12 (November/December 1981): pp. 16–17; reprinted from vol. 6 (March 1975).

4. Toni Morrison, *The Bluest Eye* (New York: Holt, Rinehart and Winston, 1970), pp. 109–10.

5. Dexter Fisher, ed., *The Third Woman: Minority Women Writers of the United States* (Boston: Houghton Mifflin Co., 1980), p. 148.

6. Quoted in Arna Bontemps, "The Black Contribution to American Letters: Part I," in Mable M. Staythe, ed., *The Black American Reference Book* (Englewood Cliffs, N.J.: Prentice-Hall, 1976), p. 752.

7. Richard K. Barksdale and Kenneth Kinnamon, eds., *Black Writers in America: A Comprehensive Anthology* (New York: Macmillan Co., 1972), p. 59.

8. Barbara Christian, *Black Women Novelists: The Development of a Tradition, 1892–1976* (Westport, Conn.: Greenwood Press, 1980), p. 239.

9. Jeanne Noble, *Beautiful, Also, Are the Souls of My Sisters: A History of the Black Women in America* (Englewood Cliffs, N.J.: Prentice-Hall, 1978), p. 63.

10. Mary Helen Washington, *Midnight Birds: Stories of Contemporary Black Women Writers* (Garden City, N.Y.: Doubleday & Co., 1979), pp. 95–6.

11. Verta Mae Grosvenor, *Vibration Cooking* (New York: Doubleday & Co., l970).

12. Marcia Gillespie, Editorial, *Essence Magazine*, May 1975, p. 39.

13. Ann Petry, *The Street* (Boston: Houghton Mifflin, 1946; reprint, New York: Pyramid Books, 1961), p. 266.

14. Gwendolyn Brooks, "Maud Martha," in *The World of Gwendolyn Brooks* (New York: Harper and Row, 1971), pp. 178–9.

15. Margaret Walker, *Jubilee* (Boston: Houghton Mifflin Co., 1966; reprint, New York: Bantam Books, 1981), p. 406.

16. Alice Childress, "The Negro Woman in American Literature," in Pat Crutchfield Exum, ed., *Keeping the Faith: Writings by Contemporary Black Women* (Greenwich, Conn.: Fawcett Publications, 1974), p. 32.

7 Susanne K. Langer's Conception of "Symbol": Making Connections through Ambiguity

I

The term "symbol" changes meaning in different discourses (the discourse of logic and the discourse of art, for instance) and in her philosophic work Susanne Langer (1895–1985) preserves this ambiguity. Langer's philosophy forms a bridge between the older analytic philosophies and the newer constructive philosophies, and in so doing challenges logical and ontological commitments in both traditions. It asks philosophy to rethink its scope and to rework its boundaries. Yet her philosophy, which may be among the most important of the century and which addresses in new and promising ways many of our most recalcitrant philosophical questions, is hardly recognized by philosophers as philosophy. Her contributions to the fields of anthropology and aesthetics have been noted, but her work is largely absent from the mainstream of Western Anglo-American philosophy. A clue both to her contribution and to why her philosophy has been overlooked lies in her use of the term "symbol."

Commentary on Langer's work has deflected the challenge that her work offers philosophy by questioning and rejecting her use or definition of the term "symbol." Ernest Nagel's review[1] of *Philosophy in a New Key*, published over fifty years ago, helped to shape the climate within which Langer's work has been seen as peripheral to mainstream Anglo-American philosophy. In that review, Nagel rejected her attempt to provide a careful logic of symbol that might tie together its various uses and meanings. As we shall see below, he remained committed to a positivist epistemology in the context of which her attempt to construe a symbol as something that did not refer to anything other than itself was untenable. Writing twenty years after the publication of *Philosophy in a New Key*, Berel Lang reiterates Nagel's criticism, calling Langer's formulation "the collapse of the symbol."[2]

Oddly, other commentators on Langer's work have repeatedly misconstrued her work in another way, thinking that she herself is committed to a positivist or "Tractarian" epistemology.[3] To positivists her constructivist epistemology seems untenable; to others committed to a more constructive epistemology her work seems bound within positivist discourse.[4] The aim of this paper is to understand how her notion of "symbol" allows a new epistemology that situates mind within the world and reforms the very dualisms from which her commentators view her work.

II

Langer began her philosophical career in the company of Whitehead and the logician Henry Sheffer and published early articles that contributed to the logical positivist discussion. Langer saw in her neo-Kantian heritage a way of making a contribution to the thinking of such mathematical logics as Wittgenstein's *Tractatus* and Whitehead and Russell's *Principia Mathematica*. Langer's first two published philosophical articles, "Confusion of Symbols and Confusion of Logical Types"[5] and "Form and Content: A Study in Paradox,"[6] both published in 1926, deal with questions of denotation and abstraction of logical symbols. In her third published article, "Facts: The Logical Perspectives of the World,"[7] she outlines a proposal for construing the relationship of propositions and reality and argues that denotational symbols cannot refer to the world *simpliciter*, but must refer to the world as already construed in a symbol system. The three articles develop a view of symbols and of their operation in human intelligence that is at the core of Langer's later work.

The "problem" of form and content is related to the problem of abstraction and reality. A positivist reading wants to retain a pre-symbolic or pre-linguistic access to reality (content) and to construe symbols (abstractions, forms) as referring to that reality. "One problem seems yet to reduce even 'scientific philosophers,' i.e., logicians, to a sort of mysticism: that is the problem of relating the abstract form of anything to its specific content," Langer tells us in "Form." (References in this paragraph are to "Form," pp. 436–8.) The source of this problem is a paradox that is generated when we try to express the relationship of form to content as R(f,c): "thereby we have transformed our empirical content into a term of the formal structure, i.e., we have formalized it, and are no longer dealing with the non-logical content." She seeks to defuse this paradox by claiming that "a logical form is always relative to a system," and ultimately by concluding that "if 'form' always means *a* form, then content always means *a* content [i.e., a particular form, a particular content], because content is relative to form; content means 'that which is not given as part of this logical structure.' "

Langer tells us that "if there is more to 'content' than just this penumbra of extraneous and irrelevant other structure, that more is not communicable and not cognizable" ("Form," p. 438). This view of the relationship of form and content might have taken Langer away from content into a kind of Platonism. Instead we find this very distinction at the base of her later account of the symbolic process in which the presentational symbol takes on the job of presenting "content" to our understanding.

In "Facts: The Logical Perspectives of the World" Langer again takes up the question of how what is being talked about, i.e., content, can enter the conversation. She concludes by saying "the structure of propositions really is analogous to the structure of facts—I think Mr. Wittgenstein's analysis of meaning, expressed in the words: 'We make ourselves pictures of facts,' etc., is probably correct. But it is only with reference to what he himself would call a 'projection' that we could say, 'The world is everything that is the case,' for only with such reference can there be any 'case'" ("Facts," p. 187).[8] Langer is not propounding a Tractarian relationship between our words and the world. Before we can even think of "world" there must be some mental activity, activity that she will later, following Cassirer's lead, call "symbolization."

In this essay Langer considers "the relation that holds between symbols (such as propositions) and the facts they represent" ("Facts," p. 178). She criticizes the assumption that she calls "the credo of all rationalistic metaphysics," exemplified by Spinoza's claim that "the order and connection of ideas is the same as the order and connection of things" (Spinoza, *Ethics*, II, 7). She notes further that as soon as it is outgrown in one form, it is replaced by another more refined form. This *credo* underlies Nagel's epistemology, and Wittgenstein's in the *Tractatus*, as well as current forms such as foundationalism and physicalism.[9] The same assumption exists in much of our thinking in a form that Owen Barfield called RUP, or Residual Unresolved Positivism, and as an assumption rather than a *credo* it may be harder to root out because we do not want to be accused of holding it.[10]

The problem that Langer uncovers in this essay is a persistent tendency on the part of philosophers to believe that what they would call "a complete analysis is always exhaustive of the possibilities of analysis in its object" ("Facts," p. 181). This is not the case, she maintains, because analysis cannot apply to reality directly, but only to "conceptual constructions" or "forms of realities." She draws an analogy to the werewolf, which "could appear as wolf or woman or other living creature, and remain the same 'Werwolf,' but there was no form that was its 'real' embodiment; similarly, a proposition expresses a true and sufficient formulation of an actual event, but it is an analysis of form, and therefore of a perspective only" ("Facts," p. 184). We see that her rejection of the possibility of our construing some content apart from some particular logical form continues in this essay. Facts, in both philosophical and ordinary discourse, have seemed to tie our statements about the world to the world itself. But Langer clearly rejects this positivist position. It is not the case that "facts are both the actual constituents of reality, and the content of propositions" ("Facts," p. 184). "A fact is that which is expressible in a proposition, and is a perspective of an event" ("Facts," p. 185).[11]

III

Langer's account of symbol, developed in *Philosophy in a New Key*, applied to art in *Feeling and Form*,[12] and made the basis for a theory of mind in *Mind: an Essay on Human Feeling*,[13] addresses the perplexities she uncovers in the three early articles. How can we account for the way in which our symbol system makes the world available to us, that is to say formulates the events and experiences in ways that are cognizable, and for the way in which we can manipulate the world so understood? Her intention was to develop a notion of symbol that could withstand the rigors of logical analysis and yet not be restricted to what philosophers tend to allow into the field of the rational. She criticizes the positivists, who limit "the knowable" to "a clearly defined field, governed by the requirement of discursive projectability," and asserts that "there is an unexplored possibility of genuine semantic beyond the limits of discursive language."

> But intelligence is a slippery customer; if one door is closed to it, it finds, or breaks, another entrance to the world. If one symbolism is inadequate, it seizes another; there is no eternal decree over its means and symbols.[14]

"Genuine semantic beyond the limits of discursive language" is what Langer is proposing in her investigation of presentational, in addition to discursive, symbols.

In theoretical discourse the term "symbol" is used in many ways. It is used to mean something that refers to, represents, or stands for something else. It is also used, for instance in art, to refer to such things as the art work's "unified complexity, or self-contained wholeness," or it suggests some meaning that is embodied by the work of art, or sometimes "the symbol . . . is the 'image' which presents the only way through to the 'truth' which lies 'beyond' it."[15]

The term's ambiguity in theoretical discourse has been exploited, for example by Freud, who refers to the symbolism of the dream, and thus posits at one stroke a kind of mystic revelation (symbol as "the 'image' which presents the only way through to the 'truth' which lies 'beyond' it") and an intimate connection with the waking life of the dreamer (symbol as something that refers to, represents, or stands for something else). This ambiguity gives potency to our interpretation of dreams, of poetry, of art, for it links what is presented in the symbol (*qua* art or dream) to our discursive or referential world.

Langer, however, exploits this ambiguity in a different way. The ambiguity of "symbol" contributes to the power of Freud's work, but it does not disturb our epistemological or ontological categories. In Langer's hands, the ambiguity calls into question the assumptions and presuppositions that tie our words and our worlds together and push us towards an epistemological "paradigm shift." The ambiguity of the concept forms a bridge between competing referential systems.[16]

Langer tells us, in *Philosophy in a New Key*, that a study of symbolism must have a clear logical basis, for without that "the whole argument would remain intangible, unfounded, and would probably appear more fantastic than cogent." (References in this paragraph are from *Philosophy in a New Key*, pp. 51–52.) The study, she suggests, will demonstrate that "symbolization is both an end and an instrument" and will "relate these two distinct conceptions of symbolism, and exhibit the respective parts they play in that general human response we call a *life*" (emphasis hers). The accomplishment of this account requires, as its foundation, an alteration of our notions of symbol in which "these two distinct conceptions of symbolism"—that "typified by mathematical expressions" and that typified "by swastikas or genuflexions"—can be related.

Langer calls these two distinct conceptions of symbol "discursive" and "presentational." Discursive symbols lend themselves to combinatory, linear, one-after-the-other use; they are susceptible to translation and paraphrase; they tend to have little or no interest beyond directing us to whatever it is they symbolize (Langer speaks of the "transparency" of discursive symbols). Presentational symbols, on the other hand, are not combinable or separable; they do not yield to paraphrase or translation; they are grasped all at once; and they do not refer to anything beyond themselves. We might take as an example of a discursive symbol the word "water," and imagine a Turner painting as an example of a presentational symbol. The word "water" can be used in many different sentences; it is easily translated; it hardly holds our attention in itself but handily denotes its object ("Give me a glass of water"; "The water is beautiful today"; and so on). Turner's painting, in contrast, is an art symbol, a presentational symbol, "a single, organic composition . . . which formulates and objectifies experience for direct intellectual perception" (*Problems of Art*, pp. 134, 139).

Although it is possible to exemplify the contrast between the discursive and the presentational symbol, the contrast is best made as a distinction of analysis. The word "water" can serve as a presentational symbol (say as a part of a poem or painting); and Turner's painting can serve as a discursive symbol (say as a place holder in a conversation: "We'll include this kind of thing [pointing to the Turner painting] in our next exhibit"). It would be precisely contrary to Langer's whole analysis to suppose that there might be discursive symbols *simpliciter* and presentational symbols *simpliciter*. Symbols can be seen as, analyzed as, used as discursive or presentational, and they will be recognized by their use or in their context.

Much philosophical work on language and symbol seeks to reduce or eliminate ambiguities. Langer not only preserves the ambiguity of "symbol"; she makes this ambiguous concept a cornerstone of her philosophy. This is no careless ambiguity; it is a systematic ambiguity, to use a distinction of Quine's,[17] and it is a systematic ambiguity that Langer is using in order to achieve a philosophical goal.

Ambiguity, or susceptibility to more than one interpretation, can serve a valuable role in philosophy as it does in poetry, bringing together what would otherwise be separate. Ambiguity is also no bar to the specification in formal contexts that Langer seeks. It is possible to achieve domain-specific formulations while seeking metalogical formulations that allow for connections to be made between or among domains. The issue may come to this: having specified or unambiguously defined the term in various contexts, must we then invent new symbols to designate these different uses? Must we speak of Symbol(A) and Symbol(B)? Langer argued for the preservation of the ambiguous term so that the meanings of symbol would not "diverge until the word has two unrelated meanings."[18] Such synthetically ambiguous terminology points towards reconstruction of the current debate between traditional and constructivist epistemologies and transcends the dualisms that are both implicit and explicit in such epistemology. Langer's concept of symbol provides an articulated logical landscape on which to build a new epistemology. And precisely at this point, where her work might have been most serviceable, she has been overlooked and misconstrued.

IV

Ernest Nagel's review of *Philosophy in a New Key* was reprinted in his book of essays entitled *Logic Without Metaphysics* (1956). In an earlier essay included in that book ("Symbolism and Science") he provides us with what we might now call a semiotic analysis of "symbol." He tells us that "by symbol I understand any occurrence (or type of occurrence), usually linguistic in status, which is taken to signify something else by way of tacit or explicit conventions or rules of usage."[19] Nagel concedes that "the word 'symbol' is employed in the current literature in a wide variety of senses," and adds that "I do not wish to suggest that senses of these words other than those I associate with these latter are illegitimate."[20] Despite his disclaimer, Nagel's criticism of *Philosophy in a New Key* is based on Langer's having redefined "symbol" in a way that does not consistently accord with his own definition.[21]

Nagel's preferred sense of "symbol" accords with Langer's characterization of a discursive symbol as a quadratic relationship. As Langer puts it in *Philosophy in a New Key*, "The relation between a symbol and an object, usually expressed by 'S denotes O,' is not a simple two-termed relation which S has to O; it is a complex affair: S is coupled, for a certain subject, with a conception which fits O, i.e., with a notion which O satisfies."[22] For Langer as for Nagel, the symbolic relationship is one that consists of a symbol, an object to which the symbol refers, a subject for whom the symbol symbolizes the object, and a conception or rule that links the object with the symbol. This is Langer's formulation of the discursive symbol.

This analysis of "symbol" addresses the formal and semantic aspects of the term. But Langer is concerned with questions that transcend the purely formal or semantic. Langer's account of "symbol" quite clearly includes elements of a pragmatic nature. "The proof of a pudding is in the eating" she tells us in "On a New Definition of Symbol."[23] The utility of concepts is a philosophical touchstone for Langer throughout her career.[24]

> It was in reflecting on the nature of art that I came on a conception of the symbol relation quite distinct from the one I had formed in connection with all my earlier studies, which had centered around symbolic logic. . . . In many years of work on the fundamental problems of art I have found it indispensable; it served as a key to the most involved questions.[25]

This different conception was the conception of the presentational symbol, which at the most elemental level is found in the way in which "we promptly and unconsciously abstract a form from each sensory experience, and use this form to conceive the experience as a whole, as a 'thing.'"[26]

In *Feeling and Form*, and in two subsequent essays on art, Langer returns to the question of the definition of symbol. She credits her critics (among them Nagel) with bringing home to her "the nature and extent of the difference between the function of a genuine symbol and a work of art." She adds that "the difference is greater than I had realized before," and she retreats from her position in *Philosophy in a New Key*, conceding that what the art symbol expresses "is not 'meaning' in any of the precise senses known to semanticists."[27] But in "On a New Definition of 'Symbol'" Langer returns to her insistence that the application of the concept "symbol" is wider than that which is countenanced by the scientific philosophers.

In "On a New Definition of Symbol" Langer applies notions similar to those developed in "Facts" to account for the diverse and yet linked conceptions of "symbol." "In any given context," she tells us, "some of its functions are likely to be more important or more obvious than others, and the concept . . . will be defined with reference to its relevant properties." If the definition of symbol is restricted to those properties that are seen as relevant to semanticists, it may be "incapable of yielding any derivative concepts that might serve other interests." These "other interests" are "less obvious, but perhaps . . . equally important—the formulation of experience by the process of symbolization."[28] If we seek an account of symbol that can include the scientific/semantic uses of "symbol" as well as the uses found in such domains as art, myth, and psychology, we will demand "a basic concept elastic enough to allow the widely diverse definitions we want to derive, in essential relation to each other."[29]

Presentational symbols in particular are linked to the way in which we think: we abstract what occurs to our senses so that what we see, hear, touch, etc., becomes a world about which we can think. "No matter what heights the human mind may attain," Langer tells us, "it can only work with the organs it has and the functions peculiar to them."[30] Symbolic abstraction is how we think of or see something: we see this as that because the presentational symbol presents it as that. It is through the office of the presentational symbol that the world is present to us as something other than James's "blooming, buzzing confusion."

> An object is not a datum, but a form construed by the sensitive and intelligent organ, a form which is at once an experienced individual thing and a symbol for the concept of it, for this sort of thing.[31]

Symbolic expression is particular to the sensing and abstracting organ: "the eye and the ear make their own abstractions, and consequently dictate their own peculiar forms of conception."[32]

Nagel's account assumes a world that, according to Langer, must already have been symbolized. What she contributes to such accounts is the presentational symbol, for it is the office of symbolization that the presentational symbol performs.

V

Langer makes it clear, throughout her writings, that symbols have two functions, play two roles in our mental life, and these can be related to the logical or discursive and to the aesthetic or creative. There are no naturally occurring symbols, however, that we can label "discursive" or "presentational." The label in any given case will depend on our analysis, and any analysis will be a perspective, never a complete analysis, and ultimately must be pragmatic or context-based.

Bound together as the concept of symbol must be in practice, it performs for Langer the job of holding together two apparently disparate systems, for "no symbol is exempt from the office of logical formulation, of conceptualizing what it conveys."[33] In *Feeling and Form* Langer tells us that "the prime function of symbols" is to "make the first abstractions . . . for our intellectual intuitions. . . . Their second function is to allow us to manipulate the concepts we have achieved."[34] The power of her work derives from her refusal to let go of either end of this polarity, and so to allow the term "symbol" to bring together, in vital juxtaposition, two philosophical currents.

Notes

1. Reprinted in *Logic Without Metaphysics* (Glencoe, IL: The Free Press, 1956). Hereafter *Logic*.

2. Lang ("Langer's Arabesque and the Collapse of the Symbol," *Review of Metaphysics*, 1962, 16:349–65), quotes Langer in *Problems of Art: Ten Philosophical Lectures* (New York: Charles Scribner's Sons, 1957); Hereafter, *Problems of Art*:

> But a work of art does not point us to a meaning beyond its own presence. What is expressed cannot be grasped apart from the sensuous or poetic form that expresses it. In a work of art we have the direct presentation of a feeling, not a sign that points to it. (*Problems of Art*, 133–4; quoted in Lang, 363)

Lang takes this to be the collapse of the symbol, and this collapse ought, Lang feels, to have produced a crisis in Langer's thought, but "the threat . . . does not produce the repercussions . . . which might be anticipated" (Lang, 362). Why it does not, on account of the enlargement of the concept "symbol" in Langer's hands, is the topic of this essay.

3. One persistent misreading of Langer identifies her philosophy, and in particular her theory of symbols, with early positivism and with the theories espoused by Wittgenstein in the *Tractatus*. Garry Hagberg, in "Art and the Unsayable: Langer's Tractarian Aesthetics" (*British Journal of Aesthetics*, 1984, 24:325–40), claims that Langer's conception of meaning is modelled on Wittgenstein's theory in the *Tractatus* and that in this theory "the word . . . must get its life by reaching out to another thing, its meaning." Richard Hart, "Langer's Aesthetics of Poetry" (paper read at the Retrospective Celebrating the Centenary of the Birth of Susanne K. Langer, Society for the Advancement of American Philosophy, APA Central Division Meeting, April 27, 1995) concludes that "in the end, however, one cannot help but question whether her early positivistic tendencies came to pervade and structure her outlook on art."

4. See James Campbell, "Langer's Understanding of Philosophy" (APA Retrospective, April 27, 1995): "The undervaluing of Langer's work results, I think, from the initial inaccessibility of her overall perspective. Unfamiliar readers are thrown off by her simultaneous maintaining of two apparently conflicting components. . . . Readers who value [her broad conception of the richness of human experience] are puzzled by her inclination towards analogies from physics and her trumpeting of logic; readers who value the latter are puzzled by her stubborn inclusion of the analytically unwieldy material from art and psychology and anthropology."

Campbell suggests that "we will have to balance the two [components] better if we are to understand and evaluate her philosophical work," and he sets philosophers a charge: "with Langer we philosophers must pursue the clarification of discursive meaning without ever forgetting the fullness of life that discourse [i.e., language] cannot grasp."

5. *Mind*, 1926, 35:222–9. Hereafter "Types."

6. *The Journal of Philosophy*, 1926, 23:435–8. Hereafter "Form."

7. *The Journal of Philosophy*, 1933, 30:178–87. Hereafter "Facts."

8. See also p. 82, *Philosophy in a New Key: A Study in the Symbolism of Reason, Rite, and Art* (Cambridge, Mass.: Harvard University Press, 1942; references in this essay are from 1974, 3d ed.). Hereafter *Philosophy*.

9. See, for instance, Tim Crane and D. H. Mellor, "There Is No Question of Physicalism" *(Mind*, 1990, 99:185–206) who assert that "physicalism is now almost orthodox in much philosophy, notably in much recent philosophy of mind," and Tim Triplett, "Recent Work on Foundationalism" (*American Philosophical Quarterly*, 1990, 27:93–116) who concludes that foundationalism is alive and well.

10. I heard about "RUP" from Ann Berthoff, and think that whether apocryphal or true it bears repeating.

11. This notion of perspective is continued in her later accounts of symbolic abstraction and is picked up by Nelson Goodman in *Languages of Art: An Approach to a Theory of Symbols* (Hackett Publishing Company, Inc., 2d ed., 1976): "For an aspect is not just the object-from-a-given-distance-and-angle-and-in-a-given-light; it is the object as we look upon or conceive it, a version or construal of the object. In representing an object, we do not copy such a construal or interpretation—we achieve it" (p. 9).

12. *Feeling and Form: A Theory of Art* (New York: Charles Scribner's Sons, 1953); hereafter *Feeling and Form*.

13. *Mind: An Essay on Human Feelings* (Baltimore: Johns Hopkins Press, 1967 [Vol. I], 1972 [Vol. II], 1982 [Vol. III]); hereafter *Mind* I, II, or III.

14. *Philosophy*, p. 86.

15. These characterizations are given by Sonia Greger, "Presentational Theories Need Unpacking," *British Journal of Aesthetics*, 1969, 9:157–70.

16. See Jaakko and Merrill Hintikka, "How Can Language Be Sexist?" (in Sandra Harding and Merrill Hintikka, eds., *Discovering Reality*, Reidel, 1983) for an illuminating distinction between what they call "the referential system" and "the structural system." They tell us that it is the referential system that plots our assumptions about word to world relationships, but that as long as it works ("By 'working,' we mean here sufficing as the sole or main input into the structural system" [p. 141]) it is hardly ever called into question.

17. See Willard Van Orman Quine, *Methods of Logic* (New York: Holt, Rinehart and Winston, Inc., 3d ed., 1972), p. 1.

18. "On a New Definition of Symbol," p. 60, (*Philosophical Sketches*, Baltimore: Johns Hopkins Press, 1962). References in this essay are from the 1979 reprint edition by Arno Press Inc., New York. Hereafter "New Definition."

19. *Logic*, p. 109.

20. *Logic*, p. 103.

21. Langer notes this inconsistency of Nagel's in "New Definition," p. 60.

22. *Philosophy*, p. 64.

23. "New Definition," p. 58.

24. See for instance the introduction to *Mind* I: "The value of a philosophical outlook does not rest on its sole possibility, but on its serviceability" (p. xxiii).

25. "New Definition," p. 58.

26. *Philosophy*, p. 90, emphasis hers.

27. *Problems of Art*, pp. 126–7.
28. "New Definition," p. 62, emphasis hers.
29. "New Definition," p. 65.
30. *Philosophy*, p. 90.
31. *Philosophy*, p. 89.
32. *Philosophy*, p. 91.
33. *Philosophy*, p. 97, emphasis hers.
34. *Feeling and Form*, p. 128.

Elizabeth K. Minnich

8   Hannah Arendt: On the Relation of Thinking and Morality

> *I will admit that I am, of course, primarily interested in understanding. This is absolutely true. And I will admit that there are other people who are primarily interested in doing something. I am not. I can very well live without doing anything. But I cannot live without trying at least to understand what happens.*
> ——Hannah Arendt, "On Hannah Arendt (A Conversation)"

Hannah Arendt (1906–1975) spent her life trying to understand what was happening, but her intense involvement with the problems posed by the dangerous and dramatic times in which she lived was not the result of any original taste for politics. As a student, she planned to lead the exalted life of the mind that, following the dominant Western tradition, she understood to be quite separate from the sordidness of action. But the dark times in which she lived would not allow her to remain in the ivory tower. She chose to try "at least to understand." Despite the mildness of that phrase, it names a passionate choice, a deep commitment.

With that choice, she expressed her difference from, and profound disillusionment with, those "professional thinkers"[1] who refused to face what was happening as Hitler came to power—with those who retreated into the academic version of the "inner emigration"[2] of many Germans of the time as well as with those who, horrifyingly, turned into apologists and even collaborators. Watching friends, students, professors fail to comprehend what was happening, she learnt in no uncertain terms that the academic life of the mind, as she said later, is no protection against culpable political stupidity.[3]

Later in her life, in a similarly quiet statement, she noted that "it may even be nice that we lost the monopoly of what Kant once very ironically called the professional thinkers. We can start worrying about what thinking means for the activity of acting."[4] And that, indeed, is what she 'worried' about for the rest of her life. The question that was basic to Hannah Arendt's work came into being then, and remained. She set out to discover if there is a life of the mind that does not unsuit us for good political judgement, if in thinking itself there might be a basis for a morality adequate to action.

As a contemporary of the creation of totalitarianism (about which she wrote her classic study), Arendt came to believe that thinking is one of our most vulnerable, not one of our most persistent, abilities. It is not only true, she decided, that freedom requires thought: thought also requires freedom. She would say, with a sigh, that Spinoza's belief in the freedom of the mind was possible to him as a thinker only because totalitarianism had not yet been invented. Totalitarianism proved, to her, that few can go on thinking when all around them have ceased to do so.

In an utterly characteristic move, she turned upside down the centuries-old assumption that the one thing over which we do have complete control is our own minds. She considered that the human mind requires publicness, hence the freedom of public communication. In emphasizing publicness, as in so many things, she learnt from or found corroboration in Kant, in this case in his political writings where he argues for the essential nature of freedom of the pen.[5] But Arendt, having faced totalitarianism, pressed this insight much farther. She made it basic to all her thought and so also articulated its complexities as perhaps no other philosopher has.

It is important to notice here, from the beginning, that freedom is a critical consideration. As Arendt thought about thinking and whether it provides a basis for a morality adequate to action, she was thinking about freedom. As part of that emphasis on freedom, she early thought about how to *comprehend* reality—not how to know it, not how to explain it, but how to remain, as a thinker, open to it.

In *Rahel Varnhagen: The Life of a Jewish Woman* (written in 1933, published first only in 1957), Hannah Arendt created an unusual biography that suggests, at least, the kind of understanding she continued to seek. She set out to find a way to uncover the meaning of Varnhagen's life, not the truth about it. She writes of her method:

> [I do not use] interpretations according to the psychological standards and categories that the author introduces from the outside; nor about her position in Romanticism and the effect of the Goethe cult in Berlin, of which she was actually the originator; nor about the significance of her salon for the social history of the period; nor about her ideas and her "weltanschauung" [world view], in so far as these can be reconstructed from her letters. *What interested me solely was to narrate the story of Rahel's life as she herself might have told it.*[6]

Arendt wanted to understand from within, not to know about. She stood within the center of the circle with her subject, rejecting all the viewing posts around the perimeter from which the experts might have claimed to speak knowingly about the gazed-on subject. Arendt sought some act of mind that could move her both in and out of Varnhagen's life in a way that neither Rahel, caught within her own story, nor others, standing outside of it, could achieve. She decided to think *with* Rahel Varnhagen, and neither *as* nor *about* her.

She chose not to think *about* Rahel, because of her conviction that to turn a subject, an individual, into an object violates the freedom that only makes sense for subjects— for people, not things—and, at the same time, falsifies reality. People are not simply things. Arendt held it to be a given about human beings that "nothing entitles us to assume that [humans have][7] a nature or essence in the same sense as other things."[8] To know our own individual or collective nature or essence would be a trick akin to "jumping over our own shadows"[9]; only some sort of god could know us as we know things. For Arendt, humans are subjects always, and must not be understood as objects—not, that is, if we value freedom.

Hannah Arendt used to say that the real problem with strict behaviorism (or any social 'science' that mimics knowledge about things) is not that it is not accurate but that it could become so. She would then note that those who take the proof of their theories to lie in their ability to predict human behavior have a very dangerous stake in increasing predictability—that is, in reducing freedom—in the real world.[10]

The idea that knowledge needs to be 'above' change, to be of the realm of Being rather than that of Becoming (as Plato put it in *The Republic*), is, Arendt said, one of the basic reasons why "political philosophy" would have seemed to the ancients to be a contradiction in terms.[11] The turn to thinking rather than to knowing when she set out to write about Rahel Varnhagen was Arendt's early way of working through such problems. In this biography she was beginning to rethink thinking, to break loose from the notion that thinking has its end, its termination or purpose or justification, in knowing. After all, insofar as knowledge is made up of answers to questions, it is not appropriate to humans who are, as Arendt liked to say (paraphrasing Augustine), questions to themselves.[12]

That we cannot know ourselves was, according to Arendt, no cause for despair; quite the contrary. This realization frees us to consider what it means that we can *think*. Arendt's work on thinking is most evidently engaged in conversations with Kant—whose "maxims of common human understanding" in *The Critique of Judgement*[13] include "putting ourselves in the position of everyone else," as Arendt tried to do with Rahel—and with Socrates, whose metaphors for the thinker (midwife, electric fish, gadfly) and for thinking (a wind that blows everything down, a conversation between me and myself) recur throughout her writings.

Thinking stings us awake—as Socrates, the Athenian gadfly, stung with his questions anyone who claimed to know something about humans and how we ought to be. When we are stung into thought, we awake from the bemusement of our certainties and are thus thrown back into the world, back into genuine, open converse with others. We no longer have anything to teach; we have only the kind of questions Socrates learned to ask from his brilliant teacher, Diotima (whom he credits in the "the Symposium"). The Diotemic method uses questions motivated by Eros, the yearning for that which we do not and cannot possess. Thinking, like love, effects a kind of propulsion out of ourselves toward others. This is one way in which it is related to the political.

However, while thinking is related to the political, it is not sufficiently so. It does throw us out into the public and require our engagement with others, but it also requires that we have solitude (even in the midst of others). When we are actually caught up in thinking, we pursue our own internal conversation. The wind of thought can throw us suddenly out of the very public realm into which it has propelled us. Socrates, we remember, was renowned not only for his presence in the market place but also for the trances to which he was subject. Sometimes, he would stand absolutely still for great stretches of time, oblivious to all around him. Thinking is like a wind that blows everything down, a stinging fly that wakes us up—but it is also, Socrates was careful to tell us, like an electric fish that paralyses.

"Stop and think," Arendt often said, with delight at the aptness of the cliché. Furthermore, when we have stopped to think and so removed ourselves from those around us, we also "move among invisibles," as Arendt liked to put it.[14] With the use of memory that "makes present what is absent"[15] and imagination that can change what is really unchangeable, we leap above the stubborn here/now/thisness of this world.

Is thinking, then, finally non- or even anti-political, despite the fact that it propels us into the company of others and prepares us to comprehend them? The answer to this for Arendt is no: in thinking lies the basis for political virtue.

Arendt wrote:

> Reason itself, the thinking ability which we have, has a need to actualize itself. . . . We have forgotten that every human being has a need to think, not to think abstractly, not to answer the ultimate questions of God, immortality, and freedom, nothing but to think while . . . living.[16]

Thinking is a basis of human being, a common virtue. It is not an ability belonging only to the few; it belongs to us all. It is, then, a basis for our being "political animals," creatures who live together, even though it also throws us out of company when we actually do it. It is from thinking that we develop that critical political virtue, common sense.[17]

In addition to grounding our commonality with others such that we can, if we will, develop common sense, thinking also relates us to reality, the realm of action. Arendt wrote: "The task of the mind is to understand what happened, and this understanding, according to Hegel, is [the human] way of reconciling . . . with reality; its actual end is to be at peace with the world."[18] Understanding, emerging from thinking not as a product, not as knowledge, but as reconciliation with reality, expresses not just the ability and the need of all human beings to think but the link between thinking and reality. For Arendt, thinking is an antidote not just to a notion of the life of the mind that scorns the messiness of reality, not just to the whatness of knowledge, but to the despair of those for whom reality has been more than they can bear. It is a faculty we need if we are to be able to live with others, with ourselves in our real world.

In 1944 in her essay "The Jew as Pariah" she wrote: "A true human life cannot be led by people who feel themselves detached from the basic and simple rules of humanity nor by those who elect to live in a vacuum, even if they be led to do so by persecution. [People's] lives must be nominal, not exceptional." And she goes on to note that for Kafka, whom she greatly admired, his

> whole genius, his whole expression of the modern spirit, lay precisely in the fact that what he sought was to be a human being, a normal member of human society. It was not his

fault that this society had ceased to be human, and that, trapped within its meshes, those of its members who were really [people] of goodwill were forced to function within it as something exceptional and abnormal—saints or madmen.[19]

In such a world, to seek to be normal is, like the effort to understand, a terrible struggle. We remain beings who can think but that does not mean that we will do so, or that we will do so well. Our ability to think does not deny us the capacity to lie to ourselves. We are many within ourselves. Our thinking actualizes the split between "me" and "myself" and invokes the voices of others within us with whom we think. In so doing, it creates conscience from consciousness[20]—but we are always free to choose to silence those voices that say what we do not want to hear.

Indeed, Hannah Arendt worried that "thoughtlessness—the heedless recklessness or hopeless confusion or complacent repetition of 'truths' which have become trivial and empty"—is "among the outstanding characteristics of our time."[21] And, as she saw it, such thoughtlessness is an aspect of, or makes possible, human evil. That, too, marks thinking as a basis for political virtue: it gives us our commonality and common sense, calls us to think and so speak together, awakens conscience from consciousness, allows us to reconcile ourselves with reality, and so, when we turn from it, allows us to be politically very dangerous indeed.

It was while covering the Eichmann trail in Jerusalem that she "found herself with a concept," as she liked to say—that of "the banality of evil."[22] Eichmann, the consummate bureaucrat who was as well-behaved a prisoner as he had been a Nazi, stood before her as the incarnation of the evil of thoughtlessness. Arendt found herself with the question that is basic to all her work now crystallized:

> Could the activity of thinking as such, the habit of examining and reflecting upon whatever happens to come to pass, regardless of the specific content and quite independent of results, could this activity be of such a nature that it "conditions" [humans] against evil-doing?[23]

The negative phenomenon of Eichmann, as well as the other aspects of thinking we have noted, might well suggest that this is the case. But being "conditioned" against evil-doing does not guarantee anything at all about being able to do good. We have not yet answered her question.

Arendt summed up the problem along with her main propositions as follows:

> *First,* if such a connection [between the ability or inability to think and the problem of evil] exists at all, then the faculty of thinking as distinguished from the search for knowledge, must be ascribed to everybody; it cannot be a privilege of the few.

We have seen that she assented to this proposition, and why. She held that all humans have the ability to think and a need to do so. Not all will develop that ability, but that does not change its givenness.

> *Second,* if Kant is right and the faculty of thought has a "natural aversion" against accepting its own results as "solid axioms," then we cannot expect any moral propositions or commandments, no final code of conduct from the thinking activity, least of all a new and now allegedly final definition of what is good and what is evil.

This, too, she accepted. Thinking, in actualizing the split between me and myself and drawing in all the others with whom we have thought, is resultless. There is always another perspective, another question. The wind of thought blows everything down.

> *Third,* if it is true that thinking deals with invisibles, it follows that it is out of order because we normally move in a world of appearances in which the most radical experience of *dis*appearance is death . . . hence, *the question is unavoidable: How can anything relevant for the world we live in arise out of so resultless an enterprise?*[24]

This, then, is the problem: our ability and need to think make it possible for us to prepare for moral action and yet give us no positive guidance on what to do. But that does not mean that thinking changes nothing. It actualizes and develops certain basic human abilities—it has, not results-as-products, but effects. What, then, are the effects of thinking? From the perspective of the person, the particular "who" that thinks, the "who" that lies at the heart of all human beings, the effect is far from negative. Thinking opens us to the unmediated experience of the subject. And that, the experience of being human in the essential mystery of the unknowable subject-self, is in itself moral. It is an experience Eichmann did not have. Eichmann needed to know the rules to know himself, and from a self so constituted, monstrous deeds—far beyond his own limited capacity to conceive, to intend, to feel—were possible. Eichmann killed indirectly, just as he lived, and finally died, indirectly—playing a role, not enacting himself. He did not actualize himself through thinking; he did not realize his own common humanity; and so he could not comprehend that of others. They were "whats," not "whos," to him.

In a culture that has held up to us as models of courage those willing to be martyred—and far too often, to kill—for their certainties, it is worth comparing Eichmann and Socrates. Socrates, the thinker, died rather than renounce his uncertainties, his need to talk with others because he himself did not know anything. On his death bed, after refusing an offer to help him escape, Socrates discussed with his friends his utter lack of fear of death, which sprang not from his certainties but from his uncertainty as to whether death should be feared or desired. In our frustration that thinking prepares us for morality without giving us positive guidance on what we should do, we should not overlook the critical effects it does have: it undoes certainties that are inappropriate and so threatening to action, and it actualizes a self that is able freely to act well with others understood to be subject-selves.

Still, if we have no rules, no principles, no maxims to apply, are we not left vulnerable to the worst sort of relativism, the kind that slides quickly into nihilism, or utter egocentricity, or unaccountable particularity of the most eccentric sort?

It is here that Arendt turned to the human faculty of judgement. She writes: "The purging element in thinking, Socrates' midwifery, that brings out the implications of unexamined opinions and thereby destroys them—values, doctrines, theories, and even convictions—is political by implication." We have seen some of the reasons she had for so saying, but in this late essay on "Thinking and Moral Considerations" she is ready to add something important:

For this destruction has a liberating effect on another human faculty, the faculty of judgement, which one may call, with some justification, the most political of [our] mental abilities. It is the faculty to judge *particulars* without subsuming them under those general rules which can be taught and learned until they grow into habits.[25]

Thinking, then, does not give us directions on what to do. It prepares us for, precisely as it makes us aware that we need to turn to, a different faculty—judgement.

Arendt drew on Kant's *Critique of Judgement* to explore the faculty that enables us to change realms, as it were, to move from principle to particular—from thought to world and back, not deductively and not inductively, but as thinkers.

Deduction asks us to apply principles to the world without taking the world into account: what is right is right, regardless of circumstance, of history, of motive. Induction takes the world into account without regard for principle: what is right is what I have learned I need to do in many here and now experiences. A purely inductive judge is like the Queen in Alice in Wonderland, making up rules only from and for occasions.

But a thinker, having found that all principles can be questioned and that particular situations can be comprehended if we think them through—think *with* them—is free to bring non- determinate judgement to bear, to ask which principle might illuminate this situation, to see how this situation illuminates that principle.[26]

The thinker understands that, in the realm of human action in which freedom is fundamental, neither the tyranny of principle nor the tyranny of random individual experience or will is acceptable. S/he is like the (rare and wonderful) judge who is able to honor both principle and individual, struggling to bring them together such that neither is violated but both are illuminated, both are better understood.

What we need to exercise good judgement is knowledge of relevant principles or laws; an understanding of what we know; experience that can give us a sense of what knowledge, which principles, rules, laws, might be relevant and helpful—and the ability to see, to hear, to comprehend the individual or particular situation as Arendt tried to understand Rahel Varnhagen. Judgement does not stand alone, or enter as a kind of mental *deus ex machina*. What it does is move between what we know and understand and what, in the moment, we comprehend as *this* that is before us.

But how are we to learn judgement? Arendt accepts from Kant that judgement emerges as a "peculiar talent which can be practiced only and cannot be taught" because "judgement deals with particulars, and when the thinking ego moving among generalities emerges from its withdrawal and returns to the world of particular appearances, it turns out that the mind needs a new 'gift' to deal with them."[27]

How then is it done, the movement from principle to particular, from rule to person, such that both are comprehended and taken equally into account? We have arrived at the key, and the trick, question: "How is it done?" sounds as if it is a question to be responded to with directions, with a method codified and so reproducible. For Arendt, the correct response is: "It is done in freedom." That is essential, for as soon as it is not done freely, judgement has become something else, has been collapsed back into deduction or induction.

We cannot be taught how to think or exercise good judgement, but that does not mean that we cannot learn. If we are thinkers, we are developing a self capable of being good in action among others. Then, to develop the capacity to judge well so that we may make sound moral judgements about what we should do in the realm of action, or praxis, we must *practice*. No code, no principles, no training will suffice or substitute for practice, which must then be thought through, learned *with*. To practice living well, it is necessary to exercise all of our human faculties within our particular reality, comprehended insofar as we are able so that we may be reconciled to it and will not be tempted to flee it, to except ourselves from the great struggle to understand what happens. We must think as ourselves, with others, in an effort to think what we are doing, as Arendt put it in the Prologue to *The Human Condition*.[28]

Finally, Arendt's question "Is there a ground for morality adequate for action in thinking itself?" has to be answered. In any ordinary sense the answer is no. But in the sense that the life of thought prepares us for judgement that gives us guidance without allowing us to give up freedom, the answer is yes. Thinking, and all it actualizes in us, not only liberates us from dogmatism but develops in us the common sense on which judgement relies as the ground on which to bring together principle and individual in the real world we share.

As we practice thinking, judging, and acting, we become who we are. If we do so well, we remain our own friends, we achieve reconciliation with ourselves, the others we think with, and with reality. On this Arendt agreed with Plato: the just person, the one who makes good judgements, is one who acts so as to be able to go on being her/his own friend. When we fail, we fail in reconciliation with others, with the world we share with them, and in so doing we fail ourselves. For Arendt, finally, the life of the mind of the thinker in itself constitutes a reason for caring about the life of action.

Notes

1. "Hannah Arendt: On Hannah Arendt," in M. A. Hill, ed., *Hannah Arendt: The Recovery of the Public World* (New York: St. Martin's Press, 1979), p. 303. Hereafter, *Hannah Arendt*.

2. The phrase "inner emigration" was used often by Hannah Arendt in her lectures and conversation. For an instance of its usage in print, see Arendt "On Humanity in Dark Times: Thoughts about Lessing," in *Men in Dark Times* (New York: Harcourt Brace Jovanovich, 1968), p. 19.

3. Throughout this paper, I am drawing not only on Hannah Arendt's published works but on my recollections of our conversations and the courses I took with her when I was a graduate student and her teaching assistant at the Graduate Faculty of The New School for Social Research.

4. *Hannah Arendt*, p. 303.

5. See Hans Reiss, ed., *Kant's Political Writings*, tr. H. B. Nisbet (London: Cambridge University Press, 1970).

6. Hannah Arendt, *Rahel Varnhagen: The Life of a Jewish Women* rev. ed., tr. R. and C. Winston (New York and London: Harcourt Brace Jovanovich, 1974), p. xv; emphasis added.

7. I have substituted the parenthetical "[humans have]" in this line to avoid the distraction of Arendt's use of "man," as I have changed her use of "he" and "mankind" elsewhere in

the paper. In general, I consider correcting authors' usage of exclusive language a very tricky business, and never do so without considerable care and thought. In many cases, changing "mankind" to "humankind," for example, succeeds only in hiding the genuine exclusiveness of the text: its author may actually have intended to refer only to males, and often only to a particular group of males, such as literate upper-class Western males at that. To change the language of such a text so that it appears that its author was being inclusive when such was not the case only further mystifies the tradition within which the exclusion of some human subjects was so fully accepted that it passed without notice. In this case, however, I have corrected Hannah Arendt's language for several reasons. She genuinely intended to be inclusive when she spoke on a general level about humankind. That her language, and more importantly the dominant tradition within which she was educated and lived, may sometimes have betrayed her intention may also be true—but that is another story.

8. Hannah Arendt, *The Human Condition* (Chicago: University of Chicago Press, 1958), p. 10.

9. Ibid.

10. I am here recalling comments she made to me in conversation that are, I believe, borne out by her written work: cf. her essay on Lessing in *Men in Dark Times*, pp. 3–31.

11. This is a comment with which she liked to begin her lectures at the Graduate Faculty of The New School for Social Research.

12. See, for example, her comment in *The Human Condition*, p. 10.

13. Immanuel Kant, *Critique of Judgement*, Hafner Library of Classics (New York: Hafner Publishing Co., 1964), p. 136.

14. Hannah Arendt, "Thinking and moral considerations: a lecture," *Social Research*, 38, 1971; pp. 417–46.

15. I am paraphrasing a comment that Arendt made frequently in her lectures and seminars; cf. her lecture on "Thinking and moral considerations," as well as her discussion in *The Life of the Mind* (New York: Harcourt Brace Jovanovich, 1978), I: esp. pp. 85, 133, and 201.

16. *Hannah Arendt*, p. 303.

17. This is a critical notion that has been given far less than due consideration in this paper. For some of its background in Arendt, see the lecture on "Thinking and moral considerations," p. 425; "Willing," in the appendix on "Judging" in *The Life of the Mind*, II: pp. 267–71; and, of course, Arendt's source, Kant's *Critique of Judgement*, para. 40, "Of taste as a kind of sensus communis."

18. Hannah Arendt, *Between Past and Future* (London: Faber and Faber, 1961), p. 8.

19. Hannah Arendt, "The Jew as Pariah: A Hidden Tradition," reprinted in Arendt, *The Jew as Pariah*, ed. by R. H. Feldman (New York: Grove Press, 1978), p. 89.

20. This is also an important notion that begs further elaboration. For some of its background in Arendt, see *The Life of the Mind*, I: p. 190. and "Thinking and moral considerations," pp. 418 and 442.

21. Hannah Arendt, *The Human Condition*, p. 5.

22. Hannah Arendt, "Thinking and moral considerations," p. 419.

23. Hannah Arendt, "Thinking and moral considerations," p. 418.

24. Ibid., pp. 425–6 (emphasis added).

25. Ibid., p. 446.

26. Obviously, I am not here following Kant's definitions of the different forms of judgement closely, but trying to suggest what I take to be an understanding closer to Arendt's.

27. Hannah Arendt, *The Life of the Mind*, Vol. I, *Thinking* (New York: Harcourt Brace Jovanovich, 1978), p. 215.

28. Hannah Arendt, *The Human Condition*, p. 5. The preceding points in the sentence are paraphrases of two of Kant's "Maxims of common human understanding" in his *Critique of Judgment*, para. 40.

9 Hannah Arendt and Susan Griffin: Toward a Feminist Metahistory

Although writers are increasingly challenging the division between history and story, efforts to introduce storytelling into historiography have sparked intense debate.[1] The question of whether creative and highly subjective stories have a place in historiography is of particular interest to women. At issue here is the status of epistemological approaches that have been associated with women and that have recently been reappropriated by feminist epistemologists, approaches that include a concretely situated perspective, emotional engagement, focus on particulars, and the use of figurative language. Moreover, writing that identifies itself as storytelling has been vital to bringing public attention to the experiences of groups regularly excluded from orthodox historiography. Women clearly have a stake in defending storytelling against charges that it is nothing more than what Frank Kermode calls the "politically correct" distortion of "historically correct" historiography.[2] Yet, at the same time, we cannot ignore that stories inevitably serve particular interests—and not always feminist ones.

Feminists can meaningfully defend the role of storytelling in historiography only by challenging the division between the two, that is, by showing that all historiography is necessarily a kind of storytelling. In this light, the question becomes one of *what kind of stories* are most valuable to us. To treat this question, we need a metahistory that articulates how stories are related to the very structure of historical understanding and that makes explicit the goals of this understanding. Such a "feminist metahistory" can be drawn from the work of Hannah Arendt (1906–1975) and Susan Griffin (1943–), two women who saw that we can make sense of historical reality only through telling stories. By building on their analyses, I present a case for stories that make explicit their creative, engaged, open-ended character. I argue that such stories are not only necessary to understand historical events, but can also help us to challenge deeply-rooted patriarchal values and work toward less violent futures.

The End of Storytelling

The radical import of Arendt's and Griffin's affirmations of storytelling is apparent in light of the origins of academic historiography in the United States. Before its disciplinization, historiography had been mainly a leisure-time activity of independently wealthy men. These "patrician historians" often had distinguished ancestral ties and took personal pride in glorifying particular figures. Turn-of-the-century professional historians sought to differentiate their work from that of these dilettantes by establishing a methodologically regulated, "objective" history. Although motivated by an admirable concern to hold history accountable to community standards, they found these standards in an untenable notion of "scientific history." Scientific history was born of the belief that disciplined study of historical data could yield knowledge of the past more reliable than that based on memory, more factual than that conveyed through poetic language, more balanced than that influenced by concerns of the present, and more universal than tales of particular individuals. In effect, historical objectivity was constructed by opposing history to storytelling.[3]

Skeptics have criticized scientific history since its inception. Most recently, scholars including Roland Barthes, Louis Mink, and Hayden White have demonstrated that historical documents are themselves social constructions and that historical "facts" are constituted by historical discourse.[4] Yet, even while the idea of scientific history has been discredited, its characterization of historiography's task—to objectively represent an independently existing historical reality—continues to influence the writing of many histories. For instance, many histories use a detached, authoritative voice to name actions and characters as if these terms (e.g., "defense" or "America") corresponded to ontological units. Histories often present data without questioning why these data exist while other phenomena are denied this form of representation. Also common is the reduction of documents to an homogenized narrative, as if they fit naturally into a single plot. References to the author's work of producing the text may appear in the preface but are usually absent from the main text.

The result of this attempt to eradicate storytelling from history proper is not only the naive and untenable positivism that the aforementioned theorists have criticized. It is also the impoverishment of "the past," rendering it abstract, fixed, and dehumanized. Consequently, many histories have seemed remote from experience and have failed to help people understand their world. As an alternative, some ethnographers, sociologists, and historians have begun to treat their material by telling stories. This revival of storytelling is just as significant as the epistemological critiques of scientific history; it reminds us that, in spite of the impossibility of objective historical representation, we nonetheless need stories of the past if we are to experience our world in all of its richness and complexity of meaning.

At the same time, lest we condone every story, we cannot forget scientific history's legitimate concern for critical standards. If not objective representation, then what sort of standards are appropriate to historiography *qua* storytelling? To address this, we must rethink "historical truth" in light of the insight that it is conveyed, not by scientific facts or laws, but by stories. Such a project was initiated by Hannah Arendt, the first modern philosopher who dared call herself a storyteller.

Arendt's Revaluing of Storytelling

In calling her work storytelling, instead of the more rarified-sounding "historical narration," Arendt announced that her work participates in the same historical world that it studies. Given her familiarity with Benjamin's essay "The Storyteller," she was well aware that her term evoked the image of someone who recollects rather than merely repeats information, who leaves her own imprints on her material, and who shapes it in view of the practical concerns of a specific audience.[5]

Arendt first turned to storytelling in her efforts to come to terms with Nazism. After witnessing the Nazis' ability to defy Enlightenment principles of respect and responsibility and to actually reconstruct reality on their own terms, she realized that appeals to facts and principles had little power to inspire resistance against Nazism. Moreover, when we judge Nazism with our "universal" norms, we assume a stance outside Nazism and cannot learn from it lessons for our own world. Arendt therefore sought an approach that compelled a moral and emotional response, yet did not depend on transcendent principles. She sought to treat the strangeness and the horror of events, yet to do so in a way that did not simply label the events as alien but confronted them as human phenomena and as part of our heritage. "Storytelling" was Arendt's answer to this dilemma.[6]

Arendt's *The Origins of Totalitarianism* is a story in that it does not trace Nazism to previously known causes, but rather to historically specific and essentially subjective "elements." These elements include a political life reduced to a process of accumulating power, biologically defined conceptions of identity and community, and masses of people made superfluous in their capacity as creative and moral actors. Arendt does not describe these phenomena in conventional categories of analysis, but in the poetic and engaged descriptions that she deemed appropriate to the unpredictable character and the moral and emotional content of human phenomena. For instance: the disempowered individual of the imperialist state is "a cog in the power-accumulating machine"; racism creates a conception of identity in which "peoples are transformed into animal species"; and conditions in which hundreds of thousands of people are homeless and millions economically superfluous is the "preparation of living corpses."[7] By thus drawing on familiar images but pushing these beyond accustomed usage, she invites readers to imagine the affairs narrated without covering over the difficulty of such imaginative work. Moreover, by tracing Nazism to imperialist politics, race-thinking, and world-alienation, her story interweaves Nazism's story with stories of our own globalized network of nation-states. *Origins* has been criticized as lacking principled judgment, theoretical distance, solid theoretical grounding and standard scientific categories.[8] Such criticisms, however, overlook Arendt's argument that these conventions are futile for overcoming Nazism's own internally consistent system and, moreover, that they impede comprehension of the human experiences that made widespread compliance with Nazism possible.

Storytelling as Story Making

Arendt was more concerned to narrate world events than to theorize her method. Yet we can articulate the structure of storytelling if we pursue the implications of Arendt's notion of story *making*. Arendt suggests this notion when she says that, even though historical events are inherently storylike, "it is not the actor but the storyteller who perceives and 'makes' the story."[9] This is significant because "making" has a precise meaning in her analysis of the *vita activa:* making is the activity of *work*, i.e., the use of human-made materials to produce something new.[10]

As a kind of work, storytelling relies on already processed materials. Arendt's discussion of remembrance suggests that memories are the storyteller's "materials."[11] This is a radical suggestion, as scientific history dismisses memories as parochial and unreliable. Scientific history's claim that history can be written without recourse to memory seems plausible, for historians critically evaluate the reliability of documents, often testing these against statistics and artifacts that exist independently of anyone's memory. Arendt reminds us, however, that historical reality is not a mere collection of data but a story; only in a story do facts "acquire some humanly comprehensible meaning."[12] And yet a story is never empirically given. The story that is "invisible," but that somehow bears the meaning of the past event, is manifested, she says, through *remembrance*. What she calls remembrance does not merely retrieve stored information, but "straighten[s] out the stories and put[s] them into words," showing how a panoply of incidents "fit together and produce a harmony."[13] This remembrance-given whole, or what I will call a *narrative matrix*, is presupposed by historiography because it provides the context in which factual data have significance. In suggesting that storytelling relies on remembrance, Arendt in effect tells us that storytelling's "materials" are an endless chain of stories.

Storytelling for Arendt also adds something "new" to the world: it not only draws on previous stories but freshly articulates and elaborates upon them. Arendt considers this creative work to be essential to storytelling's capacity to offer understanding of an event. A political event's essence, a collection of lived deeds and sufferings, is meaningful only when one confronts those deeds and sufferings as part of one's own world and when one has a sense of what it would be like to endure the basic sort of experiences (e.g., basic relations to others, to one's labor, to the common world, to truth, and to oneself) that those deeds and sufferings entailed. Therefore, if a historian is to offer understanding of an event, she must create a narrative framework that shows how past elements figure in stories of a specific present, and she must create images that give contemporary resonance to the past event's lived aspects.

Storytelling is also "productive" in a second sense: stories can bring otherwise privately endured, "uncertain, shadowy" phenomena into public light, thereby adding to the world of things publicly acknowledged and spoken about. In describing storytelling as the means to endowing a phenomenon with "publicity," Arendt suggests an alternative to the rigid division between public and private that she describes elsewhere (a division much criticized by feminists); here she indicates that a phenomenon's public status depends on whether or not it has been narrated.[14]

If storytelling is a kind of making that draws on and adds to a community's stock of stories, and that in so doing brings phenomena into public discussion, then the aim of storytelling cannot be to present the definitive account of a dead past. The aim of storytelling is rather to open the space "between past and future," that is, to invigorate a community's creative relation to its past by offering new ways of articulating past incidents. Such storytelling continually tests our culture's stories, broadens the realm of phenomena that public debate must consider, and thus sustains what Arendt calls "public life"[15] wherein we exchange perspectives and orient ourselves to a world shared with others.

Limits of Arendt's Theory

This account of storytelling as story *making*, or the creative rewriting of memories that then informs subsequent storytelling, begins to account for the role of historiography *qua* stories in our understanding of historical events. But it also underscores the problem of bias in these stories. Despite her emphasis on the storyteller's creative work, Arendt did not pursue the problem of adjudicating among competing stories. Nor did she address how specific kinds of stories support and are supported by specific kinds of social arrangements, although her concern in *Origins* to situate race-thinking historically presupposes such a connection between a community's stories of itself and its social and political practices.

Arendt's failure to address fully the political role of the historian as a story maker can be traced to her reliance on Kant's notion of reflective judgment to explicate the historian's method. She turned to Kant because he describes a judgment that is accountable to the community yet is, nonetheless, based on one's experience of the phenomenon and does not require an *a priori* standard. According to Kant, such a judgment can be achieved by means of *enlarged thought*: one tests one's judgment against the imagined "possible" judgment of others and, upon this testing, "disregards the subjective private conditions" that affect one's judgment. Kant's notion of enlarged thought allows Arendt to explain how she can judge a political phenomenon in such a way that her judgment is agreeable and communicable to the human community.[16] Insofar as Arendt accepts Kant's particular approach to enlarged thought, however, she loses sight of historically- and communally-situated storytelling and replaces it with the imagination of an isolated mind.

For instance, though likely not Arendt's intent (given her high regard for public debate and given her intense engagement with personal stories in *Origins*), when she turns to Kant's model of imaginary dialogue with hypothetical others, she discounts the practical task of actually listening to specific others (or perusing others' testimony, letters, etc.). Further, when she follows Kant's approach to "putting [oneself] in the place of any other man,"[17] she abstracts from the other's particular social identity. Whatever the utility of this approach for judging an artwork, it is inappropriate for determining the meaning of a political phenomenon; for, when someone experiences a political phenomenon, her particular social location is integral to her experience. This is evident in Arendt's own example of the slum dwelling. She proposes to judge a slum dwelling by imagining "how I would feel if I had to live there" and concludes that the slum exhibits "poverty and misery."[18] Yet Arendt's conclusion overlooks the more nuanced and specific meanings that the slum has for persons whose social identities differ from hers. For instance, an Afro-American male or a Mexican-American woman living in a slum each face specific sorts of dangers and responsibilities, specific sorts of encounters with employment agencies and police officers, and specific sorts of media images of themselves, each of which contribute to their basic experience of self and world. These variations in experience are essential to the meaning of living in a slum, for they arise from social and political institutions inseparable from the slum *qua* sociopolitical phenomenon.

Arendt's appeal to a Kantian "general standpoint" obscures these varying experiences of differently located characters as well as the storyteller's bias in the way she narrates these experiences. Only when we acknowledge this heterogeneity of experiences and this inevitable partiality of the storyteller can we clarify the political implications of different ways of writing a story. Moreover, by making such clarification we see that any standards for historiography will reflect not only epistemological but also political goals.

The strengths as well as the shortcomings of Arendt's analysis come into full view if we apply it to a history that purports to be memory-free. The work of Harvard historian Samuel Elliot Morison provides a fine test case. Morison was strongly committed to objectivity, which he described as the presentation of "a corpus of ascertained fact" the selection of which is "not distorted by queer lenses."[19] In his *History of the American People* he describes a World War II battle as follows:

> Our losses were 226 bombers, 28 fighters, and about 2600 men; but some 600 German planes were shot down. German aircraft production did recuperate, but these February bombing missions denied many hundred aircraft to the enemy when he needed them most.[20]

With Arendt's analysis, we can discern memory-colored lenses subtending this seemingly factual text. For instance, the significance attached to the military data here is not grounded on the data alone. The data is meaningful because Morison organized it (and North Americans read it) in view of a presupposed social memory of World War II—a narrative in which America and Germany are monolithic actors and the plot consists of a series of military battles culminating in America's victory. Her analysis also points us to a more basic discursive framework underlying this memory: a tradition-given lexicon of war wherein "wins," "losses," "enemy," and "victory" have meaning as part of a zero-sum game between nations. The meaning of phrases such as "shot down" or "bombing mission" also derives from this lexicon, as well as remembrance-given images accompanying the lexicon. In this way, an Arendtian analysis elucidates how "memories" make possible a meaningful text. Yet it cannot address the simultaneous obfuscating effects of these memories with, for instance, respect to the racism within the United States military and to the tension between enlisted men and officers.[21] Nor can it address the relation of these obfuscating effects to political and social practices. We thus need to go beyond Arendt in order to address fully the political significance of specific kinds of memories. We also need to exceed Arendt in order to see how her own revaluing of storytelling prepares the way for invoking less orthodox, more "feminist" memories.

Griffin's Radicalization of Storytelling

Susan Griffin's *A Chorus of Stones: The Private Life of War* realizes the radical potential of Arendt's call for storytelling. What Griffin calls the "private" or "feminine" sphere is akin to Arendt's sphere of human meaning. Barring the difference in terminology, Griffin's thesis echoes Arendt's: that political events ultimately consist of deeds and sufferings in human lives; therefore, to understand these events we need a story that helps us to confront these as part of our own heritage and as revealing humanly possible kinds of experiences. Griffin's terms "private" and "feminine," however, mark her advance beyond Arendt. For they indicate that the "subjective" dimension that has been excluded in the name of "objectivity" is not simply human experience in general; rather, it corresponds specifically to experiences associated with femininity, and its exclusion from history is linked to a gendered division between public and private. Thus Griffin argues that histories that dismiss subjective aspects of private life are not merely detached and irrelevant. They are also systematically sexist and elitist. The claim that so-called objective history has privileged male, European, and upper-class perspectives is not new.[22] Griffin's original insight is that a bias towards machoist values and status quo inequalities is *inherent* in an objectivity that is built on the suppression of storytelling.

Griffin illustrates this thesis through artful storytelling. Although her focus is "experience," she does not simply substitute experience for scientific history's data and thereby lapse into only another type of positivism.[23] Instead, she presents her material within narratives depicting her own process of research, including her interactions with witnesses and her personal responses to what she reads and hears. In this manner, she shows her "data" to be context-dependent, individually created, and inherently subjective memories whose telling affects both teller and listener. Moreover, like Arendt, she does not seek to reproduce an objectively given sequence. She actively rearranges the memories and juxtaposes these with her personal reflections so as to intimate lines of similarity and complicity with elements in our own world. *A Chorus* thereby defies every realist convention, foregoing any pretense to represent the past "in itself." Yet, ironically, it is precisely Griffin's engaged listening to personal stories and her creative rewriting of these that offers a rich understanding of historical phenomena—that is, understanding not of a specific event, but of cycles of violence and denial woven through our past and present.

Consider, for instance, the text's account of Yoko, a Japanese woman whose parents were killed by the atom bomb, who lost her siblings soon afterwards, and who was then shuttled back and forth between unwanting relatives. *A Chorus* presents this story in terms of Yoko relating her memories to Griffin. It then shifts to Griffin's recollections of her own broken family. Such a narrative does not pretend to conclusively judge U.S. military actions towards Japan. Yet it does make more vivid one element of those events, namely, suffering related to family loss. It does this not by reducing Yoko's experience to Griffin's, but by allowing a more familiar story (Griffin's remembrances or those evoked in the reader) to serve as a guide to appreciating the lived significance of one aspect of the other's story. The effect is precisely the contribution that Arendt deemed appropriate to storytelling: it enhances our sense of the subtleties and complexities of the event *qua* lived phenomenon, thereby enriching our further reflections and stories.

Griffin also enriches future stories of war because her engagement with specific stories challenges the reductive battle-centered narrative paradigm. For instance, surrounding Yoko's story are stories of a nuclear energy plant engineer who lies about the dangers to workers and the community in order to keep her job; stories of a U.S. soldier who was subjected to nuclear weapons testing and is now refused compensation for his leukemia because the Pentagon denies his participation in the tests; and stories of Rita Hayworth, her father's clandestine raping of her, and the photo of her placed—against her wishes—on the tip of a nuclear warhead. While the particularity of these story fragments mitigates against any single, coherent picture of World War II, the combination nonetheless provokes us to consider the significance of phenomena incommensurate with the logic of zero-sum victories and losses, phenomena such as long-term mental anguish suffered by Japanese survivors, war-related illnesses afflicting GIs and their offspring, and a similar misogynistic machoism underlying both U.S. and German military behavior.

By treating the complexity of life stories, and combining these in such a way as to open up new narrative possibilities, Griffin, like Arendt, reveals seemingly anomalous, shocking events to be nonetheless part of our world. While both authors emphasize the need to understand history's darker moments in order to understand the present, Griffin suggests how this understanding can help us face our own relation to state-violence. For instance, Griffin's account of Hiroshima at once makes foreigners more human and foregrounds the unspoken, disturbing aspects of familiar human relationships. Her narrative of Nazism likewise brings racism close to home; in one section, she interweaves stories of Heinrich Himmlet's obsession of defining himself in opposition to Jews with memories of her own grandfather's antisemitism. Such a narrative does not name causes or origins. But it does help us to discern the kinds of attitudes and practices that sustain cycles of violence and of denial. Further, because Griffin's characters resist categorization into "us" or "them," or into "criminal" or "victim," and because the open-ended form of the narrative leaves space for further reflection, the text invites readers to consider how their own actions may participate in such cycles.

Storytelling as Feminist

Griffin's narrative also links the exclusion of certain elements from history to the derision of these as "feminine." Consider the following account of a soldier compelled to deny his fear:

> At the sight and sound of flying shrapnel, bullets exploding, his flesh shrinks, his head ducks, his whole body cowers, even though he rails at himself, calling himself coward, poltroon, sissy.
>
> Not the idea of death but a wall of flame, not the abstract notion of sacrifice but the bodily knowledge that just under your foot, as you take your next step, there may be a mine. . . .
>
> If you turn in one direction you betray the honor of your gender. You are, as Homer said, unmanned. . . .
>
> But your mind will not admit its complaint. You cannot put what you are feeling into words.[24]

This unusual present-tense fictional construction, which shifts subtly from third- to second-person narration, invites the reader to imagine aspects of combat that are suppressed in national-level generalizations and aggregate data. Further, by thematizing the language available to express these emotional and bodily experiences, Griffin exposes the misogyny operative in their suppression; that is, we see that military lingo censors responses that threaten military discipline by feminizing them: the soldier fears that he will be called "sissy." The military ethos thereby exploits and abets ideologies of women-hatred. Moreover, if the soldier cannot even admit his complaint nor articulate his feelings, then his emotional and bodily experiences of war are not only deemed "unmanly," but are simultaneously excluded from language. Griffin alludes to Elaine Showalter's argument that what we call "shell shock" is a bodily protest against war and "manliness" that resembles female hysteria insofar as a complaint that cannot be articulated finds indirect, somatic expression. Significantly, Showalter also observes that the term shell shock disguises the "feminine" powerlessness, frustration, and deprivation of speech that such soldiers endure.[25]

Griffin's poetic construction does not prove a causal connection between military machoism and biases entrenched in our language. Yet it does reveal a coinciding among that called "feminine," that suppressed by the military, and that without ready signifiers. This has far-reaching consequences for historiography, for it suggests that official data and literal language—the very tools of objective history—tend to mirror military, machoist standards. Arendt criticizes such detached language as inadequate to the subjective essence of political phenomena. Griffin is more specific: historiography that treats as real only public records and seemingly neutral data participates in the silencing of the victims of military violence.[26]

Towards a Feminist Metahistory

Griffin reveals the connection between, on the one hand, Arendt's aim to tell stories that convey the human significance of historical phenomena and, on the other hand, the explicitly political goal of publicizing marginalized views. She demonstrates that what Arendt described as storytelling is crucial if the experiences of politically and economically disempowered persons are to reach a wider audience. First, these persons lack the means to transform their experiences into public images or official documents. Further, these persons tend to bear the negative repercussions of public policies (e.g., long-term physical and mental illnesses from warfare, weapons testing, or storage of toxic wastes)—phenomena that are systematically omitted from the official reports that "objective" histories tend to replicate. Not only do government and corporate-sponsored reports evade the contradictory aspects of official policies, but, as a result, we lack categories of analysis adequate to the aforementioned phenomena. We can remember, discuss, and document such phenomena only after storytellers create, from personal memories, new images, names, and narrative matrices.

Griffin also indicates another respect in which the project of bringing "feminine" experience into history is tied to the revaluation of storytelling. She shows that the costs of war are borne largely in people's emotional, bodily, and interpersonal lives. These areas of life are not only typically associated with women; they are precisely those aspects suppressed in histories when we dichotomize public and private, the representable and the merely particular, and history and stories. Narrating these therefore requires changing what counts as publicizable and as historically important. It also requires the empathetic listening and the skillful rewriting that can bring to language that which has been dismissed as private or unsayable. Similarly, if we are to narrate the actions and struggles of subordinated groups without such narrations being viewed as mere sideshows to the important acts, then we cannot simply present more information to be added to a single "correct" picture. Rather, we must assert with Arendt that the very identification of a meaningful event depends on the making of a story from memories, because to do so is ultimately to problematize taken-for-granted images and narrative matrices, and to see that feminist history can—indeed must—change these basic materials of our language.

Finally, Griffin shows that if the revaluing of storytelling serves "women's history," it also revises and enlarges the meaning of the term. If history does not represent reality in itself but instead creatively reconstructs the stories by which we interpret experience, then "women's experience" is identifiable as such only through our stories. "Woman" is certainly a meaningful category, given that social and political arrangements have generated effects that have been stratified along lines of gender (together and in interrelation with other politically and economically overdetermined differences, such as race and class). Yet, as Griffin's stories demonstrate, identity categories do not define who actors are. Rather, categories such as "woman," "white," or "worker" have significance only as one element in historically specific stories. Their meaning depends on other elements in that story, and also on the chain of stories intimated by Arendt, that is, the stories available to historical actors and to storytellers to make sense of their worlds. Women's history therefore does not represent the empirical reality of "women." But this was never the intent of storytelling. As I have suggested, "storyteller" connotes someone who does not merely report on a fixed content, but who listens to others and then retells their stories in light of the concerns of a specific audience. Thus, the storyteller does not pretend to be a disinterested knower vis á vis a fixed object; she is instead a historically- and politically-located actor who promotes public recognition of certain kinds of experiences and who, in so doing, affects how her subject matter—for example, "women"—is defined. To recognize that "women" is a construction of our stories and that gender is inseparable from other relations of difference is not to forego a feminist historiography—if by *feminist* we understand a project defined not in terms of the identity it represents, but in terms of its inquiry into the devaluation of "woman" and its interest in challenging this devaluation, a project that inevitably intersects with other emancipatory projects.

Griffin demonstrates one possible approach to such a feminist historiography. Her creative rewriting of private lives as they have interfaced with recent wars sensitizes readers to the ways in which our everyday dealings with pain, with personal shortcomings, and with the telling (or not telling) of our stories are interrelated with state-violence. The critical insight this affords affirms that any history that excludes "private" or "feminine" experience tells a distorted story. Conversely, it shows that stories that present themselves *as stories,* using creative and interested approaches to bring into language the "feminine" sphere of emotional, bodily, and interpersonal life, are necessary for understanding not just narrowly-defined "women's issues" but all historical phenomena. Finally, it shows that stories that enhance understanding of political events *qua* lived phenomena are necessarily political, for such understanding challenges detached and machoist narratives of violence and the practices these support.

Certainly, not all stories will speak for women or for the silenced. But a metahistory like that suggested by Arendt and Griffin that registers the storytelling character of all historiography is a crucial feminist project. Such a metahistory affirms that "objective" histories are no less story and no more history than are the innovative and engaged writings that relay phenomena suppressed in public discourse.

Notes

I am grateful to Sara Ebenreck and John Stone-Mediatore for illuminating criticism of numerous versions of this paper.

1. Many such debates are couched in terms of a debate over whether interested, particularized narratives have a place in history proper; see, for instance, Frank Kermode, "Whose History is Bunk?" *New York Times Book Review,* 23 February 1992: pp. 1, 33; remarks by Edith Kurzweil and William Phillips in "The Changing Curriculum: Then and Now," *Partisan Review* 2 (Spring, 1991) pp. 249–81; and National Association of Scholars, "Is the Curriculum Biased?" (Princeton: National Association of Scholars, undated). A recent *Lingua Franca* cover story attests

to the high profile of debates over the role in historiography of creative and personal writing (David Samuels, "The Call of Stories," *Lingua Franca* 5:4 [1995]: pp. 35–41).

2. Kermode, "Whose History is Bunk?", p. 1.

3. See, for example, John Higham, *The Reconstruction of American History* (London: Hutchinson & Co., 1963); Stull Holt, "The Idea of Scientific History in America," *Journal of the History of Ideas* 1:3 (June 1940), pp. 352–62; Peter Novick, *That Noble Dream: The "Objectivity Question" and the American Historical Profession* (Chicago: Cambridge University Press, 1988), pp. 1–41; Trinh Min-ha, "Grandma's Story," in *Women, Native, Other* (Bloomington: Indiana University Press, 1989).

4. Roland Barthes, "From History to Reality," in *The Rustle of Language*," trans. Richard Howard (Berkeley: University of California Press, [1986] 1989); Louis Mink, "Narrative as a Cognitive Instrument, in *The Writing of History*, eds. Robert Canary and Henry Kozicki, (Madison: University of Wisconsin Press, 1978); Hayden White, *The Tropics of Discourse* (Baltimore: John Hopkins, 1978).

5. Walter Benjamin, "The Storyteller," in *Illuminations*, ed. Hannah Arendt and trans. Harry Zohn (New York: Schocken Books, 1968).

6. Hannah Arendt, *The Origins of Totalitarianism* (New York: Harcourt Brace Jovanovich, [1951] 1973), pp. vii–ix, 333, 350–3, 438–56; Arendt, "Understanding and Politics," *Partisan Review* 20 (1953), pp. 377–9, 388–9; and Arendt, "A Reply," *Review of Politics* 15 (January 1953), pp. 76–80. On the relation of Arendt's storytelling approach to her experience of Nazism, see also Lisa Disch, *Hannah Arendt and the Limits of Philosophy* (Ithaca: Cornell University Press, 1994), pp. 14–18 and 112–40.

7. Arendt, *Origins*, pp. 146, 234, and 447.

8. See Lionel Abel, "The Aesthetics of Evil," *Partisan Review* 30 (1963), p. 224; Martin Jay, in "Hannah Arendt: Opposing Views," *Partisan Review* 45 (1978), p. 361; and Eric Voegelin, "The Origins of Totalitarianism," *Review of Politics* 15 (1953), pp. 68–9 and 72.

9. Hannah Arendt, *The Human Condition* (Chicago: University of Chicago Press, 1958), p. 192.

10. Ibid., pt. IV.

11. Hannah Arendt, *Between Past and Future: Eight Exercises in Political Thought* (New York: Penguin, [1954] 1968), pp. 5–7.

12. Ibid., p. 262.

13. Hannah Arendt, *The Life of the Mind* (New York: Harcourt Brace Jovanovich: [1971] 1978), p. 133.

14. Arendt, *The Human Condition*, pp. 50–1. Her more rigid notion of public is woven through this same text, chaps. 5–7, 10.

15. Arendt, *The Human Condition*, pp. 57–8.

16. Kant, *Critique of Judgment*, trans. J. H. Bernard (New York: Macmillan, 1951), pp. 136–7. For Arendt's interpretation, see Hannah Arendt, *Lectures on Kant's Political Philosophy*, ed. Ronald Beiner (Chicago: University of Chicago Press, 1982), pp. 65–74, and Arendt, *Between Past and Future*, pp. 220–1 and 241–2.

17. Kant, cited by Arendt, *Lectures on Kant*, p. 71.

18. Arendt, lecture course at the New School, March 24, 1965, cited by Ronald Beiner in Arendt, *Lectures on Kant*, pp. 107–8.

19. Samuel Elliot Morison, "Faith of a historian," *The American Historical Review* 56:2 (1951), pp. 263–4.

20. Samuel Elliot Morison, *The Oxford History of the American People* (New York: Oxford University Press, 1965), p. 1028.

21. On these phenomena, see Howard Zinn, *A People's History of the United States* (New York: Harper & Row, 1980), pp. 406–10.

22. The staunchest defenders of "objectivity" belie this bias: Morison and Kurzweil identify historical objectivity with, respectively, "spiritual preparation for war" and "compet[ing] effectively"; and Kermode remarkably characterizes those threatening his "correct" history as "anti-homophobes, anti-racists, and anti-whites." (See Samuel Morison, "Faith of a Historian," p. 267; Frank Kermode, "Whose History is Bunk?," p. 33; and Edith Kurzweil in "The Changing Curriculum," p. 254.)

23. Recently, the project of narrating "women's experience" has been criticized for its tendency to reify the categories in which experience is represented and to mystify the connections between personal oppression and broader mechanisms of domination and exploitation. (See Rosemary Hennessy, *Materialist Feminism and the Politics of Discourse* [New York: Routledge, 1993], chaps. 3 and 4; and Joan Wallach Scott, "The Evidence of Experience," *Critical Inquiry* 17 [1991], pp. 773–92.) While I recognize the potential dangers of appeals to experience, I believe that Griffin's work shows how stories of marginalized experience can supersede these dangers.

24. Susan Griffin, *A Chorus of Stones: The Private Life of War* (New York: Doubleday, 1992), p. 239.

25. Elaine Showalter, *The Female Malady: Women, Madness, and English Culture 1830–1980* (New York: Penguin, 1985), pp. 172–5.

26. Contemporary historiography continues to exhibit these contradictory effects of "objectivity"; a case in point is Gerhard Weinberg's acclaimed work, *A World at Arms: A Global History of World War II* (Boston: Cambridge University Press, 1994). Like Morison, Weinberg writes in a detached, seemingly nonjudgmental style. Ironically, this style facilitates his uncritical repetition of received military terms such as "enemy," "defense," and "strike" that presuppose the legitimacy and rationality of war. While Morison reduced battle deaths to aggregate "losses," Weinberg buries the human effects of war in a seemingly neutral catalog of technical and strategic details.

Sara Ebenreck

10   Finding New Roots as a Woman Philosopher

When we began the process of editing this book, Cecile Tougas and I agreed that, as we came near its conclusion, we would each reflect on the significance of this work for our lives as women philosophers. The moment came, and I could discern reluctance within myself, not because there was nothing to say, but because what needed to be said involved speaking directly of my own life as a philosopher, something I have rarely experienced in academic philosophical discourse. Descriptions of the women philosophers in the papers I worked with had evoked resonating echoes within me of the joy and the pain, the promise and the frustration of being both a philosopher and a woman in a profession traditionally dominated by men. Put simply, the work radicalized my thinking, literally taking me into digging about the clearly constrained roots of my own philosophical identity in order to create fertile space for new roots to grow. Following, then, is a portion of that story.

When I finished my graduate course work in philosophy in 1970, I had read (briefly and outside any requirement) only two women philosophers: Susanne Langer and Hannah Arendt. In courses on the history of philosophy and thematic areas from epistemology to theories of human nature, I remember no mention of work by other women philosophers nor discussion of issues related to women's perspectives. I had had no women faculty in my graduate studies, and so no mentoring that involved exploring women's perspectives even in informal ways. The search for philosophical insight was studied as gender-neutral; offensive passages about women in philosophical texts were omitted from discussion, as if a consensus existed that these were only historical matters not relevant to the larger ideas being pursued. In my philosophical studies, clearly, gender issues were not yet out in the open.

Looking back, I recall the atmosphere of my graduate studies as somehow sterile, despite warm contacts among students and with faculty, but I was then far from making a connection between this sense of sterility and gender-based issues. If I could not easily identify with Socrates, Aquinas, Kant, or Marx as archetypal philosophers, as so many of my male colleagues seemed to do, I did not speak of it lest I be perceived as something less than a philosopher in good standing. Lack of such identification did not mean lack of interest in their insights, but simply a curious inability to ever see myself as a philosopher behaving like Socrates or Kant, in class or out of it. I took pride in the ideas I developed both in classes and in my papers, but I didn't tackle the misogynist slurs of thinkers I studied. *I* was thinking, after all, and apparently as well as my male peers, so what did it matter if in centuries long ago Aristotle, Thomas Aquinas, or Rousseau had doubts about women's ability to think as well as men?

Yet the general silence about gender issues, in the midst of programs focused solely on the traditional canon of male philosophers, left those issues simmering just below the level of my conscious attention to them. The absence of work by women philosophers produced its inevitable effect: a tacit assumption on my part that no women had yet accomplished philosophical work significant enough to warrant inclusion in a curriculum that studied important Western theories. Only later, as I experienced the liberating movements of feminist philosophy and the study of women philosophers, did I realize how great a burden this silence and assumption placed upon my own philosophical work.

After finishing my degree, while teaching part time and mothering a son—two activities that left me somewhat outside the intense information flow of graduate school—chance browsing through publications catalogs led me to the work of feminists who were analyzing the gender-bias in the canon of philosophy and developing alternate insights. I began rereading some classic philosophical texts, asking questions that had remained muffled during my graduate studies. As I considered Plato's and Aristotle's ideas on the virtue of courage, for example, I found myself comparing the classic instances of men at war with my grandmother's courage in creating a vegetable-market business from a small, sandy family farm in northwest Michigan in the late nineteenth century, and with my mother's courage in supporting a family of four children while my father was in the South Pacific during World War II. In a paper coauthored with a woman colleague, we looked at courage as exemplified by women in transition to a radically new understanding of personal, social, and professional possibilities for themselves. Instead of continuing to assimilate to an abstract "philosopher's voice," with the stimulus of feminist philosophy I began to link my personal philosophical interests with my life as a woman in community with other women, to develop my voice as a woman philosopher.

In 1987, when an announcement of the first meeting of the Society for the Study of Women Philosophers came to me in the mail, I found a second important community: women deeply committed to the affirmation of the voices of women thinkers from the past as well as the present. Work to recover and link women's insights over long stretches of history seemed to me an absolute necessity. My feminist turn had led me into a constant struggle with texts as I questioned the more or less overt male gaze to discern how and if its insights cohered with my woman's gaze on my inner being and the world about me. A philosophers' society that encouraged study of work in which the textual "I" was always a woman promised to lessen the tensions raised by the need to translate insights across perceived gender boundaries. Although I would quickly discover that the myth of a "woman's voice" with which I could easily identify was exploded simply by the diversity of women's voices and, indeed, would discover that many women do not think of themselves as speaking in a "woman's voice" at all—nonetheless the society provided stimulus and support for these discoveries. In a way that still surprises me, even when I found myself in forcible disagreement with the insights of a particular woman philosopher, I could sense myself in a conversation that began and continued with an empathy that I might call a feeling of sisterhood. I was, clearly, a plant reaching down to grow new roots in a rich soil that I hadn't known even existed.

A second circumstance also motivated my desire to know about earlier women thinkers. In 1987, I was returning to academic teaching after an extended sojourn outside academic life, from work that I had turned to in the midst of my frustration with life as an adjunct instructor in philosophy at two college campuses. In Washington, D.C., my philosophical vision had been both challenged and opened by the rich experience of being part of the community of nonprofit organizations that worked on land-policy issues. As the editor of a quarterly whose centerpiece was based in multidisciplinary forums on such issues, I saw how the voices of major thinkers in the land conservation movement functioned within a context of conversations and events that quickened their thought. Including in the forums a diversity of voices— from artists, poets, and philosophers as well as from economists, scientists, and public policy analysts, from women as well as from men, and from diverse economic and social backgrounds—was essential to opening up the discussions so that new insight emerged. The life-force of this conversational process was striking, and I learned that not hearing a diversity of voices deprives a community of much-needed truth.

When I returned to teaching, I carried with me a determination to work with this sense of philosophy as itself a conversational process, one that would gain illumination by inclusion of the diversity of perspectives. Just as I had found that, in traditional patriarchal Washington, D.C., ensuring the inclusion of women's voices had required deliberately focused attention, so did I rediscover this need within academic philosophy. Not surprisingly, I was teaching courses whose previous syllabi had included few if any women thinkers. My own search for the work of previous as well as contemporary women thinkers became intense, and I knew that I needed community in that process.

It was with these deeply personal and practical desires that I joined the Society for the Study of Women Philosophers and eventually, in company with Cecile Tougas, undertook the work of this book. Every step of the process has been rewarding. Slowly, the names and thoughts of previous women philosophers are becoming part of my life and thought. I have welcomed with joy the rediscovery of Hildegard of Bingen's naming of feminine powers in God and her anticipation of some contemporary ecofeminist philosophy. I have felt pain as I recognized the pattern at work in the need for "recovery" of the black feminist perspective of Anna Julia Cooper, a perspective that deserved recognition both in its time and in the history of American feminist thinking. I've appreciated learning how both Hannah Arendt and Susanne Langer, the only two women philosophers whose work I had read in graduate school, found it necessary to break through conceptual forms to express ideas that arose from their life experiences. As Elisabeth Young-Bruehl has noted about biographers of women, an "air of amazement"[1] has suffused this process, slowly loosening the tight knot of tacit conviction that no significant philosophical work had been accomplished by earlier women. Intellectually, I have not only found material for my courses, but also a profoundly satisfying sense of rootedness precisely as a woman in a philosophical world inhabited by earlier as well as contemporary women.

To belong somewhere—to be rooted—is to love that place; to love a place is to take unceasing delight in the exploration of its features, to recognize the inner truth revealed in them. Working to hear the voices of women philosophers involves such an exploration. In turn, hearing these voices has irrevocably changed both my approach to the history of philosophy and my present conversation within this discipline.

A stark truth has become visible as I have pursued this study: I have learned about many of the ways in which important but culturally nondominant voices can be muted, rejected, or forgotten in a philosophical conversation, and about how much is lost when those voices go unheard. As I read Katie Canon's description of the ethical values taught by generations of black women struggling for survival in America, for example, I hear how important it is to recognize that the ethics of those in power—who include academic faculties and their voices in professional publications and texts—may still fail to address the ethical dilemmas faced by marginalized groups. This suggests to me that learning to listen carefully to voices not considered "important" by a dominant professional culture is absolutely important in the practice of philosophizing. New questions then open up. In addition to the study of the classic philosophical texts and the work of analyzing the logic of arguments within positions, might philosophy become a discipline also marked by the work of listening for truth in voices and places that are all too easily ignored? Philosophizing this way, in a class or in a conversation, becomes more an art than a logical exercise, an art of helping the culturally (or academically) invisible become visible to our minds. If we practiced philosophy this way, would the discipline be embraced more readily by those who perceive themselves on the margins of the worldview created by the dominant thinkers of the West? Would philosophy courses then be sought out more often by students hungry to discover if indeed they too could develop a voice in responding to the deep value conflicts that rend our culture?

Work on this book with the diverse forms in which women's philosophical thinking has presented itself has led to a further radical question about the kinds of "thought forms" that are used when we try to move past those forms created by the male philosophers of the classic Western canon: with what new "thought forms" do we express ourselves?[2] Can the boundaries of philosophy deliberately be loosened, so that the abstract, dispassionate discourse that traditionally seemed to be the voice of philosophy becomes only one of its voices? Might not only the work of women but also the thought of ancient cultures of indigenous peoples around the planet, often expressed in story or myth, be widely recognized as truly belonging within philosophical study? And might this path of discovery return philosophy to its origins as a study designed for all those who seek wisdom?

As these questions and reflections open up for me, I know that study of the work of women philosophers has not only provided practical benefits and a new sense of rootedness for my intellectual life, but has also accomplished what good roots do: convey nourishment and energy to help the life of the mind blossom. Study of the work of women has transformed my vision of what philosophy is and how I want to practice it. The burden of the false assumption—that no women philosophers did significant work—has been laid down. My hope is that no one, especially women philosophy students, might ever need to carry it again. This book, then, is one contribution to that goal.

Notes

1. Elisabeth Young-Bruehl, "The Education of Women as Philosophers," *Signs,* vol. 12, no. 2, (Winter 1987), p. 207.
2. Ibid., p. 214.

III

Philosophical Friendships

Cecile T. Tougas

Introduction to Part III

Mary Ellen Waithe sees Heloise as a model for a true philosophical friend, in the best of senses while under perhaps the worst of circumstances. Heloise was sixteen and already had a great reputation for learning when Abelard, twenty years older than she, became her private tutor. Their later correspondence shows that they fell in love and that he seduced her, forced her to marry him in secret, and later cloistered her. Her authenticated philosophical writings consist in her letters to him and her *Problemata*, also addressed to him. While a most renowned scholar in her own right, she philosophized in relation to a man who was her teacher, lover, seducer, husband, religious director, and abandoner. Most importantly, she lived according to philosophical principles that they had discussed well, particularly Cicero's view of love and Abelard's teaching on moral intention—which Waithe discusses in the framework of, respectively, "the fruit of true love is the love itself" and "the moral value of an act depends upon its intention." Tragically, Heloise came to understand, as her letters strongly suggest, how Abelard had compromised his moral ideals in order to satisfy his sexual passion for her; he did not love her to help her attain her highest good, nor was his intention in marrying her honorable. To that extent, the philosophy he spoke was merely an outward appearance, separated from a lived, felt, bodily experience of love that was at the same time intelligent and altruistic. Heloise, however, was true to her word, in Waithe's estimate. She subordinated herself to Abelard's good, in wifely obedience and humility, while keeping in her letters a subtly critical attitude toward his hypocrisy.

Elisabeth, Princess Palatine, also philosophized in letters to a famous man, through her correspondence with René Descartes. Perhaps the most important outcome of this remarkable collaboration, despite the distance and the differences over which it took place, was, according to Andrea Nye, "their final agreement that ethics and knowledge are inseparable." Nye shows how Elisabeth questioned Descartes's separation of mind and body, insofar as bodily feeling is intelligent and mental substance moves body. Elisabeth found that the interrelation of mind and body—rather than a dualist metaphysics—was the root of all knowledge. For her the trunk of knowledge was ethics proper and the branches were all the sciences. Descartes, on the contrary, had posited on the roots of his dualist metaphysics a value-free science as the tree trunk, with moral science as merely a branch. Her active, public, political life was evidence to her that knowledge is no more value-free than the mind is body-free. Hence, she critically viewed both Descartes's protective isolation and his contrary-to-fact assumption that passion is an illness to be cured, asserting instead that emotions as human responses to events are not only unavoidable but are also sources of moral knowledge. All our knowledge is rooted in a practice of continual moral weighing and bodily suffering. She felt it was only in fantasy that bodily passion and rational thought are unmixed. In reality they are mixed, just as one person's moral action is inseparably related to the state of one's affairs and the family and community in which one lives. The friendship between Elisabeth and Descartes was both emotional and rational, thanks in large part to her intelligent liveliness.

Gloria Anzaldúa, a Chicana feminist theorist, accounts for much vitality in the university classroom of Lisa A. Bergin, who compares and contrasts Anzaldúa's writing with that of René Descartes. Anzaldúa conceives of the human self as a *mestiza* consciousness that is multiple, connected to the material world, in transition, and ambiguous. In developing this concept, Anzaldúa uses a mixture of languages—mostly Tex-Mex, Spanish, and English—in both prose and poetry. She uses dreams, memories, and lived experience in making her argument, writing with anger and passion. She describes aspects of her life history and tells how she began with a pervasive dissatisfaction. Her definition of her self is problematic, yet she comes to value what she most truly is, in part through her reverence for the North American goddess Coatlicue who depicts the contradictory. Anzaldúa writes: "In her figure, all the symbols important to the religion and philosophy of the Aztecs are integrated. Like Medusa, the Gorgon, she is a symbol of the fusion of opposites: the eagle and the serpent, [the male and the female], heaven and the underworld, life and death, mobility and immobility, beauty and horror." With such a model inspiring her conception of what it means to be a self, Anzaldúa makes possible a respectful relation of her thought with a philosophy quite different from hers, as Descartes's is. Students in Bergin's classroom learn how to approach what they find to be unfamiliar, even as they question it critically. Bergin in turn has become more comfortable being authoritative in the classroom. "Part of what helped me . . . [do so] was that I was teaching women as philosophers," Bergin explains. "Giving them authority gave me authority."

Heloise and Abelard, and Elisabeth and Descartes, philosophized through their letters. Each couple lived friendship in ways we might find strange today. In both cases there were wide distances—both physical and spiritual—to be bridged in some manner. Why then did the woman and man in each couple continue to correspond? Why were they interested in each other? Some philosophical affinity, and some need, must have drawn them. Still we may wonder. Why are students attracted by a comparison and contrast of Anzaldúa and Descartes? Connections that occur over apparently impossible distances intrigue us. Despite their unlikeliness, such ties continue to appear nonetheless in a variety of forms. We can speak of philosophical friendship, then, in a variety of ways—perhaps one way for each individual case. (Veda A. Cobb-Stevens spoke of "fifty forms for fifty philosophies," suggesting the unique character of each instance.) When we find congruity of thought and coincidence of interest, then, we may have grounds to assert that some form of philosophical friendship is present. Accordingly, I want to affirm that, in ways she did not recognize consciously, Mary Astell was a philosophical friend to people she did not even know— to Christine de Pizan who lived long before her, to David Hume who wrote half a century after she did, and to nineteenth- and twentieth-century feminists who came much later.

As Jane Duran clearly indicates, Mary Astell was a Christian, an empiricist, and a feminist. But she experienced the solitude of being first—in fact, she has been called "the first English feminist." She argued strongly for women's education on the basis of women's natural equality, for she saw that women's actual social and political domination by men was an unfortunate outward circumstance, not a natural essential inferiority. Yet (like Christine de Pizan, although Duran does not name her) Astell felt a certain inevitability that the actual condition of domination "may need to be bended to," for men are physically stronger than women. Still, she does not call for the abolition of marriage but rather advises women to give up their gullibility and self-deceptions about the married state. Marriage is a trial of a woman's soul. It can allow a woman to develop Christian virtues if she enters into it with the right attitude. In her straightforward observations of the experience of marriage, Astell reveals a great empiricist frame of mind, and Duran shows in particular how Astell is a forerunner of David Hume. Several of Hume's arguments run exactly the same way as Astell's had, though we have no evidence of his awareness of her work. He seems to recapitulate in parts of his *Treatise* much of what she says in *Some Reflections upon Marriage*, as Duran demonstrates in detail. While Hume does not share Astell's interest in marriage as being a "trial of the soul," his argument about inequalities in marriage nonetheless coincides precisely with Astell's. At the same time, Astell presages modern feminists in her strong criticism of male behavior in marriage, her leading assertion of women's natural equality, and her accurate descriptions of both institutionalized inequality and human vices. Thus, she is in several ways, though without her explicit knowing, a philosophical friend to thinkers in other times and places.

Harriet Taylor Mill, on the contrary, lived with and married her greatest philosophical friend and collaborator, John Stuart Mill. But when, after Harriet's death, John first publicly proclaimed her contribution to their work, few philosophers, critics, and historians believed him. Since then most historians of philosophy have brushed aside his statements about her coauthorship as though they were sentimental exaggerations devoid of fact. Jo Ellen Jacobs considers in her essay the nature of collaboration and the possible ways in which cooperative writing can occur. Then, in great detail, she provides us with textual, biographical, historical, and philosophical evidence that Harriet Taylor Mill did indeed write much that did not bear her name. Harriet and John wrote about the relation of political economy and marriage. They found that marriage as a legal obligation that binds one person to another against their inclinations "makes the person of one human being the property of another." Families ruled by a patriarchal despot rather than a "community of interest" or "necessary mental communion" hinder both personal and economic development. Hence, social improvement requires at its root a change in the political institution of marriage. Harriet and John not only wrote about but also lived a family structure based on individual choice, liberty, and equality, for they felt that "in proportion to the development of his individuality, each person becomes more valuable to himself, and is, therefore, capable of being more valuable to others." Their collaboration thus expressed their lifelong commitment to both cooperative production and women's equality as the most important issues of their time.

Veda A. Cobb-Stevens is a philosophical friend to each person speaking through this book, which she first envisioned. Her poems evoke several distinct philosophical attitudes as the bears the weight of each. After Cobb-Stevens's poems, I add a postscript in which I wonder, in light of the varied examples of philosophical friendship provided here, if it is easy today for a woman philosopher to be friends with a man philosopher. I have to admit that it is not easy, and I show some of the difficulty involved.

11   Heloise and Abelard

I. Biography

Heloise's birth is usually dated to 1100 or 1101.[1] [She died in 1164.] Her mother is believed to have been named Hersinde, but following an early education at the Benedictine convent of Argenteuil, Heloise lived with her maternal uncle, a man named Fulbert. Argenteuil had a reputation for education of women equal only to that of Helfta in Germany, home of Gertrude the Great, Mechtild of Hackeborn, Gertrude of Hackeborn, and Mechtild of Magdeburg. Heloise's early reputation for learning was so great that by approximately age sixteen the greatest living philosopher in France, an unordained cleric named Pierre Abelard, agreed to become her private tutor. Abelard soon seduced her. Although Heloise's letters show that she found their sexual liaison physically and emotionally satisfying, they also show that she always considered it to be morally wrong. According to Abelard's fifth letter, it was on moral grounds that Heloise withheld her consent and physically and verbally resisted his advances to the best of her ability.[2] He admits to Heloise that he had sometimes forced her to have intercourse with him. The passage is translated by Etienne Gilson:

> When you objected to it yourself and resisted with all your might, and tried to dissuade me from it, I frequently forced your consent (for after all you were the weaker) by threats and blows.[3]

Pregnant by Abelard soon after becoming his student, Heloise would argue against agreeing to a marriage intended to legitimize the child and save her reputation. She ultimately obeyed Abelard's command to marry him, and always regretted the decision. She had promised Abelard, as had her irate uncle, to keep the marriage a secret, thus preserving Abelard's public position. Nevertheless, Fulbert disclosed the marriage, which resulted in Heloise perjuring herself to deny the relationship. The uncle, to whose home she had returned following the birth of the child Astralabe, retaliated by mistreating her, so Abelard ordered her to return to Argenteuil and take the veil. Furious that the couple conspired to deny the marriage and made the denial seem true by cloistering Heloise, Fulbert had Abelard castrated. The possibility of conjugal marriage now irrevocably foreclosed, Abelard sought final ordination. Years later, Heloise engaged in philosophical and theological correspondence with Abelard. In what follows, I briefly describe the controversy over the authenticity of her *Epistulae* (letters to Abelard and to Peter the Venerable) and her *Problemata* (problems, also addressed to Abelard), her intellectual background, and some philosophical issues she addressed.

II. Heloise the Scholar

There has always been a question of the authenticity of works commonly attributed to Heloise. In part the authenticity question arose because it was widely believed that a woman would not have had an opportunity to acquire the rich intellectual background that the author of works attributed to Heloise obviously had acquired. However unlikely it is that a woman would have received such an education, it is clear that Heloise did, and that she had achieved scholarly distinction prior to meeting Abelard. In part the authenticity question arose out of philologists' usual concern for copyists' interpolations and other textual corruptions. In this section both aspects of the authenticity question are examined in order to establish that Heloise was a scholar in her own right, and not merely a student of a famous philosopher; and that she was the author of those works usually attributed to her, viz., the *Epistulae Heloissae* and the *Problemata Heloissae*.

1. Intellectual Background

It is commonly assumed that because Heloise was Abelard's student, her learning began and ended with Abelard. Since she became pregnant by him not long after he became her tutor, and since he remanded her to the convent at Argenteuil shortly after their child's birth, the assumption that Heloise owed all her learning to Abelard entails that he had less than two years in which to bring her to the level of intellectual development she reached. However, her education at Argenteuil had been a "state of the art" twelfth-century women's education. According to Abelard, Heloise knew Latin, Hebrew,[4] and Greek.[5] She would have been able to study Latin versions of the classical works of Greek and Roman philosophy, theology, history, and literature. She would have learned rhetoric—the art of persuasion through logical argument grammatically and aesthetically composed. Even a cursory glance through Heloise's writings would reveal a list of theorists with whose views she was familiar: Aeschines Socraticus, Ambrose, Aristotle, Augustine—to name some at the beginning of the alphabet.

According to Abelard, Heloise was a renowned scholar before she met him. Peter Dronke, referring to results of his comparison of Heloise's writings to those of Abelard, notes:

This seems to warrant an inference that may cause many scholars surprise or even alarm. It has been tacitly or expressly assumed hitherto that, in their relationship, Heloise, some twenty years younger than Abelard, was in all respects the disciple and he the master—that he imparted knowledge to her while she absorbed it. And yet we know from [Abelard's] *Historia calamitatum* that Heloise, when Abelard first met her, was already "supreme in the abundance of her literary knowledge" . . . and that this had made her "most renowned in the whole kingdom" of France.[6]

If Heloise was the more talented at rhetoric, as Dronke claims (see below) and the more knowledgeable in literature, might she not also have some original philosophical contributions to make to the dialogue with Abelard? To paraphrase a comment Dronke makes:

She who at seventeen was renowned in all France for her literary knowledge was assuredly capable, in her thirties, [when the *Epistulae* and *Problemata* were written] of thinking independently.[7]

According to Dronke,[8] J. T. Muckle suggests that Abelard was guilty of wholesale borrowing of Heloise's arguments without attribution. Muckle points out that the quotations Heloise uses in *Epistula II* in her argument against marriage all appear in Abelard's *Theologia Christiana*, Book II, written prior to the *Historia Calamitatum* but after Heloise was installed at Argenteuil. (Muckle implies that Heloise therefore would not have seen *Theologia* prior to composing the letter.) According to Muckle, it appears that Abelard filled in the details of Heloise's arguments drawn from those of earlier philosophers, as though he had constructed the argument himself.[9] Whether or not Abelard borrowed arguments from Heloise, it is clear that by the time he met her, she was sufficiently well-educated as to be renowned for her scholarly knowledge. But her ability to develop the quality of philosophical and theological writing evidenced in the works attributed to her addresses only one aspect of the authenticity issue. The other issue is whether the same writer is responsible for the entire corpus, and if so, whether Heloise is that writer. I now turn to a brief examination of that issue.

2. *Authenticity of* Epistulae *and* Problemata

Dronke claims[10] that the fact that only one manuscript of the *Problemata* has survived, the fact that it is from Saint-Victor, and the quality of the copy suggest that the *Problemata* come to us in a form that was probably not heavily edited or revised for publication by copyists.

Etienne Gilson argues on different grounds for the authenticity of the Heloise-Abelard correspondence. Gilson refutes Orelli's claims[11] that the correspondence was created posthumously by an admirer of the alleged signatories. Abelard's *Historia Calamitatum* reports a complaint of Heloise that she hadn't seen nor heard from Abelard since their "conversion" to monastic life. If this were true, it would contradict a claim by Heloise, made in the correspondence, thus calling into question the authenticity of the correspondence. (It would not call into question Abelard's *Historia Calamitatum*, authenticated on other grounds.) Gilson[12] informs us that Lalanne questions the authenticity of the *Epistulae* attributed to Heloise, primarily because Lalanne's reading of Heloise's text is based on that of Oddoul, (and following its repetition by Lalanne, the reading was repeated by Greard, Schmeidler, and Charrier).[13] Gilson argues that if these translators realized the common interchangeability of the terms *conversio* and *conversatio* in the critical editions of the text of the Benedictine Rule as explained by Dom C. Butler,[14] they would read *conversio* as synonymous with *conversatio* and would realize that Heloise's letter to Abelard does not contradict facts recorded in Abelard's *Historia Calamitatum,* but confirms those facts. Having shown the controversy over the authenticity of the correspondence to be based on a failure to recognize the synonymity of two words, Gilson considers the authenticity question moot.

Gilson wrote the lectures on which his book is based in 1937. His work is still considered the definitive commentary on the *Epistulae*. Later scholars, using validated methods of linguistic analysis, have been able to buttress Gilson's claims regarding the authenticity of the *Epistulae* and *Problemata* attributed to Heloise. Dronke uses the highly validated Chi-square test, a statistical method that, when used in philological and linguistic analysis, can identify stylistic details of an author's writing that occur due to the author's preference for, e.g., a particular cadence and those cadences that cannot be shown to be any more than fortuitous occurrences. From this analysis, Dronke has drawn two conclusions that will be of interest to philosophers studying Heloise's writings. First, Heloise and Abelard write in styles that are identifiably distinct from those of other twelfth-century writers including Hildebert, John of Salisbury, Bernard Silvestris, Peter the Venerable (who corresponded with Heloise), and Peter of Blois. Furthermore, Heloise writes in a style that is markedly distinct from Abelard's. This means that concerns about the authenticity of her works, specifically, questions whether Abelard or another contemporary writer might have authored or edited her works, can be put to rest. Dronke's second conclusion is that both Heloise and Abelard were strongly influenced in their style of writing by the stylistic treatise *Praecepta dictaminum* of Adalbertus Samaritanus. He says:

> Yet the evidence indicates that both Abelard and Heloise must have known either Adalbertus' *ars* itself or one that was very close to it, and that they were stylistically influenced by such an *ars*, though Heloise followed the teachings more consciously and extensively than Abelard. That is, not only is Heloise's writing a product of high artistic nurture, but we can see how it was schooled by one of the most modern and most unusual stylistic currents of her day.[15]

From this Dronke concludes[16] that the highly expressive style that Heloise mastered liberated her powers of self-expression.

If Dronke is correct in his scientific analysis of Heloise's writing style, then we must conclude that just as Heloise was capable of developing a rhetorical style that was of a very high technical and artistic calibre, and that was unique among writers of her time, she could have been capable of developing the philosophical views that were expressed through her rhetorical style.

On the strength of the foregoing, we can conclude that there are two senses in which the writings attributed to Heloise are authentic. First, she had a background from which she could have been expected to become well-educated; her considerable literary abilities, clearly superior to Abelard's, and her scholarly renown prior to her relationship with Abelard evidence that she had in fact become sufficiently educated to have produced the corpus attributed to her. Second, the corpus of the work is a unique style identifiable as that of the author of the *Problemata* who is known to be Heloise; therefore, the corpus of the work is authentically Heloise's. These two senses in which Heloise's writings are authentic merit examination of her ideas as though they were her own, and not as though they were indisputably derivative of Abelard's. Although she and Abelard had major areas of agreement, it is mistaken, I shall argue, to assume that Heloise was merely writing what she thought Abelard wanted to hear. If we assume that Heloise merely parroted Abelard's philosophy, we overlook some significant philosophical positions that are not at all derivative of Abelard. Indeed, Heloise's views are cunningly critical of Abelard's ability to apply philosophical ideas, which he professed, to his own moral decision making. I now turn to an examination of some of Heloise's philosophical views, specifically, her views on the nature of love, on material vs. moral responsibility, and on marriage. These views are found in her *Epistulae* (letters) to Abelard and her *Problemata* (problems), also addressed to Abelard.

III. Heloise's Philosophy

1. Philosophy of Love

In a long discussion Gilson identifies the philosophical foundations of Heloise's views on love and friendship, and interprets Heloise's actions towards Abelard in terms of that philosophical orientation.[17] It is important to note also that, in Gilson's estimate, Heloise does not simply seek to enunciate and work out a philosophy of love, but lives according to it also. From the *Epistulae* it is clear that Heloise based her views of love on Cicero's philosophy. The central principle both Heloise and Abelard derived from Cicero was that the fruit of true love is the love itself. That is to say, love is disinterested in anything but the giving of love. All the true friend or the true lover wants in return is the experience of giving love to the beloved.[18] According to Gilson, Heloise's attempt to avoid marriage has its basis in Ciceronian principles. Examination of Heloise's letters strongly suggests that Heloise realized that these were principles Abelard taught but did not live by. In her correspondence, and in Abelard's recording of her earlier arguments in his *Historia Calamitatum*, it is clear that Heloise understands, but Abelard does not, how to apply Ciceronian principles to the living of one's own life. For, too late, Heloise recognized that Abelard's character was missing an important component of moral action: the psychological commitment to acting as one believes one ought to act. In Aristotelian terms, the practical syllogism did not result in practical action. Abelard's application of Ciceronian principles of love was purely theoretical, not practical. He did not perceive that the relationship with Heloise was just the kind of situation in which those principles ought to be acted upon. Abelard, a man of theoretical reason, was not a person of practical reason. Heloise was.

Heloise's primary philosophical objection to agreeing to the marriage with Abelard was that to agree to marry him would be inconsistent with loving him disinterestedly, i.e., for himself, rather than for herself. Loving him disinterestedly would require that she love him in a way that was for his highest good, and that consisted in fulfilling the ideal of philosopher-cleric. Heloise wanted to love Abelard in a way that was conducive to his fulfilling what she assumed was his intention to live according to his ideals. To her that meant total and complete separation. Their sexual relationship and its ensuing pregnancy evidenced that formulating a moral intention was insufficiently strong to avoid being overcome by irrational passion. Their sexual relationship represented, in her view, her innocent (because coerced) role in his lapse in living according to his intention. That intention was to live a life fulfilling the duties of the offices of philosopher and cleric. But, Heloise reasons, there is no justification for turning a temporary triumph of passion over reason into a permanent abandonment of the pursuit of those ideals.

What it takes Heloise a long time to understand is that Abelard was all too willing to abandon moral ideals for passionate satisfaction. He is not so willing to practice what he has preached. She may have temporarily allowed passion to triumph over reason, or she may have thought that he allowed passion a temporary victory over a moral ideal, but when he insists on marriage following the birth of their son, it becomes clear to her that he is in danger of making passion's victory permanent. For Abelard, living according to the ideal does not matter quite so much as creating the impression in others (Heloise excluded—why? Does her opinion of his virtue not count?) that his life is lived according to those moral principles. He wishes to marry her secretly, so that he can have access to her sexually—she would be sacramentally required (and passionately inclined) to maintain a sexual relationship with him—while maintaining the outward appearance of living the virtuous life of a celibate. For Heloise, loving Abelard for himself entails loving him for those ideals he has rationally chosen as his own. It does not entail providing him with the opportunity to permanently abandon the ideal of being a celibate philosopher by marrying.

And, while Abelard's *Historia calamitatum* has scrupulously recorded Heloise's arguments about marriage, he does not appear to understand, she complains, that her arguments against marriage are not the same arguments she raises in favor of free love.[19] Heloise views their marriage as something others would take to be evidence that she did not love Abelard in the sense that she did. She loved him for himself, even though he wanted marriage only to guarantee sexual access to her, and did not love her for herself. Heloise's first letter reminded Abelard that because she was known to be the subject of the many popular love poems Abelard had written, others would assume that she would benefit from their marriage. She had refused to marry him because marriage would benefit neither of them. Marriage would thwart Abelard's interests in living up to his ideal of being a celibate philosopher cleric. Marriage would make it appear that she permitted the seduction in order to secure the benefits of marriage:

> From the very moment she became his wife, Heloise would never again be sure that she was not becoming an accomplice to Abelard's moral fall for the purpose of satisfying her personal interest. Such, in sum, was Heloise's drama. . . .[20]

But Abelard was determined to acquire Heloise sexually one way or another. For him the only question was a contextual one: would it be inside a secret marriage or outside marriage altogether? Prior to his castration, he was not considering celibacy at all, although he wanted dearly to preserve the impression of celibacy. He wanted to *appear* to live the moral ideal, not *actually* to live it. Abelard, then, had lost sight of what he really wanted. By refusing marriage, Heloise was acting as a true lover in the Ciceronian sense: she was loving him disinterestedly. She was acting paternalistically in an important sense, too. By refusing marriage, she was helping Abelard to secure his rational wants, his freely chosen moral ends. She was helping him to exemplify his real will, rather than his apparent, passion-directed will.

Heloise wanted to have no part in Abelard's abandonment of his ideal. She may have *caused* that abandonment, caused that passion, but she was not morally responsible for it.[21] She would not agree either to the seduction (Abelard admitted to force and threats), nor to the marriage, for marriage merely legitimized passionate abandonment of the ideal. Heloise had begged Abelard to exclude her participation in solemnizing and legitimizing through marriage his fall from idealism.

Heloise's second letter reports an important concession she made to Abelard's abandonment of the moral ideal. Abelard's persistence in allowing passion to dominate reason, she argued, should still have preserved the option of reinstating reason to its proper role in his decision-making process. If he would allow his passion to cloud his reason and to become interpolated between himself and his ideal, if he would not refrain from having Heloise's physical love, then at least he could have preserved the option of chastity in the future. She had offered to help him preserve that option, she said, by offering herself as his mistress. He continued to press for marriage, a sacrament requiring conjugation. Finally, and to her endless regret, she had relented. Why? The devil had, without her consent, caused her to acquiesce in sinning against Abelard. That sin was the sacrament of marriage.[22] And while Heloise acknowledges that she has sinned, and has committed a crime against Abelard, she maintains that she was not morally responsible for having done so.

When, shortly after their marriage, Abelard took Heloise to live at Argenteuil, she might have been persuaded that after all, he intended to live life of celibacy. She might have hoped that his love for her would become as purely disinterested as hers continued to be for him. Was Heloise hoping that the passion that had led Abelard to coerce their sexual liaison and subsequent marriage had finally been subdued by reasoned morality? Perhaps she was, but hope was soon to be dashed. When

Abelard was castrated by Fulbert's accomplices shortly after Abelard hid Heloise in the convent, his professed love for Heloise ceased.

Later, when Heloise learned about the attack, she felt responsible for the mutilation. After all, had she persisted in her refusal to marry him, Fulbert might not have retaliated:

> The punishment you suffered would have been proper vengeance for men caught in open adultery. But what others deserve for adultery came upon you through a marriage which you believed had made amends for all previous wrong doing; what adulterous women have brought upon their lovers, your own wife brought on you. . . . You alone were punished though we were both to blame.[23]

We can speculate about the conclusions drawn by a woman as intelligent and perceptive as Heloise. Perhaps she came to realize that once castrated, once sexual liaison was impossible, Abelard no longer loved her. The passion that had endured in her was in Abelard merely temporary. And in Abelard, passion had more than temporarily overwhelmed a pure Ciceronian love. Abelard had never had a love for Heloise separate from his passion. Did it ever become clear to Heloise that overcoming passion would not have meant a return to "disinterested, selfless friendship" because none had ever existed for Abelard? Overcoming passion would only have meant the end of their personal relationship. Did Heloise come to realize that Abelard never really loved her, but had only desired her? Did this realization prompt her appeal to him for attention, concern, and respect based on the legal and ecclesiastical relationships they shared? Is that why she demanded her rights as wife and as abbess?

2. Material and Moral Responsibility

In her first letter[24] Heloise joins Abelard's doctrine on moral intention to the Ciceronian doctrine of pure, disinterested love.[25] According to Abelard, the moral value of an act depends upon its intention. Thus, one can act in a way that is morally wrongful, but not be morally responsible, or guilty for the commission of the act if one did not intend a wrongful act to be committed. One can sin merely by forming the intent to sin, whether or not one carries out the intention. This is the position Heloise maintains: that she caused harm to Abelard (in many ways: by arousing his passion, by marrying him, by providing Fulbert with a reason for castrating him). But she is not guilty. She has committed a sin, but she is not responsible; she is innocent:

> In a wicked deed, rectitude of action depends not on the effect of the thing but on the affections of the agent, not on what is done but with what dispositions it is done.[26]

This position on moral responsibility may help us to understand better Heloise's judgment of Abelard's virtue. She is devastated to realize that the very arguments and principles of morality she learned from Abelard and subscribed to did not move him or guide his actions towards her. Worse, she cannot even say that he was, like her, innocent. She somehow separates her action from her intention and survives morally nonresponsible. But can Abelard? It becomes clear to her, in *Epistula II*, that he never had the same good intentions towards her that promoted her behavior towards him. Where she refused marriage out of disinterested friendship, he pursued marriage out of lust. Where she accepted the veil so that he could pursue the ideal chaste life of a philosopher and cleric, he hid her to avoid social sanction. Where she extended the same selfless love both before and after his castration, he lost interest once the possibility of satisfying his physical desires vanished. At every turn, Abelard's actions were consistent with the moral worthlessness of his intention. His actions toward Heloise were motivated only by power, position, and pleasure. Therefore, if we are to carry Heloise's arguments further than she explicitly does, twelve to fifteen years following the events under consideration, at the time she writes to Abelard, Heloise would hold that Abelard was morally blameworthy and not just materially responsible. Heloise, while materially responsible, would remain morally nonblameworthy.

3. Views on Marriage

Gilson notes that Abelard's confession of his violence and brutality towards Heloise tells us much about his moral character, but it tells us much about Heloise, too. Heloise believes that the dignity of a philosopher and a cleric requires continence. Abelard's conclusion was that he therefore should be secretly married to Heloise, ensuring him the outward facade of continence and the private privilege of sexual access to Heloise. In short, he could keep his job without sacrificing an active sex life. Heloise concluded differently, Gilson explains. From the premise that the dignity of a philosopher and cleric required continence, Heloise concluded that they should not marry, and, indeed, should not maintain any personal connection.

> She was not satisfied that Abelard should have the air of greatness, she wanted him to be great. . . . Thence her direct arguments and the decisive conclusions she drew from them. By marriage Abelard was sanctioning forever a lapse that would otherwise be temporary. Unquestionably, once married, their love would become morally and religiously legitimate but judged from . . . the ideal of cleric and philosopher, their life would remain as impure as it was before, save that now it would be irrevocably confirmed in its impurity.[27]

Abelard was a philosopher, Heloise argued, and philosophers belong to the world, not to domestic life. How could a poor philosopher fulfill duties to the world and duties toward family simultaneously? Moreover, marriage would alter his clerical status by foreclosing the option of becoming a priest and hence the possibility of retaining his faculty appointment. In this sense he would be choosing the life of domesticity over that of the intellect and the spirit. In support of her arguments, Heloise cites Paul, Jerome, and Cicero. She pleads to be Abelard's mistress rather than his wife. He refuses. Ultimately, sorrowfully, and, portending disaster, she agrees:

> Of a certainty we shall both be destroyed; and our sorrow match in its intensity the love that has been ours.[28]

Heloise's first letter to Abelard after receiving the *Historia Calamitatum* acknowledges that the arguments against marriage he attributes to her are indeed hers, but that he has omitted some of them. Specifically,[29] he has failed to report that she had preferred love to marriage, freedom to a bond. Even though she now has a position of some respectability, and even power, she has maintained the earlier view. Given another opportunity to make the choice, she would make the same choice. But Heloise's "free love" views are only deceptively feminist: she prefers prostitution, as she calls it, to marriage because marriage would not be for Abelard's good. It would bind him, limit his career and his freedom more than it would her own. Heloise loved him only for himself. In her view, his good was not to be found in the married state. Yet she insists on the prerogatives of marriage once the marriage has taken place. In her first letter she reminds him that after the marriage (to which, in her view, she acquiesced but did not consent) she fulfilled her new duties of obedience to her husband. She returned to Argenteuil and later established the Paraclete at his direction. She had no say in these matters but obeyed his will completely. Part of her duty as wife includes reminding him of his spousal duties towards her. Part of her duty as the abbess under his direction is to help him fulfill his ecclesiastical duties toward the religious community that she established under his order. As his wife she is entitled to love from him, and as the abbess under his priestly direction she is entitled to solicit guidance and direction from him. These are not quite the kinds of demands a prostitute could hope to make. As Elizabeth Hamilton notes:

> That Abelard should neglect to interest himself in the well-being of Heloise; that he who is not only the founder of the Paraclete but her husband should take no steps to help her in the life that she is leading at his order, is in her eyes a grave defect.[30]

It is worthwhile, when considering Heloise's views on marriage, to bear in mind that her views on material vs. moral responsibility are consistent with her assessment of her own moral innocence and Abelard's guilt. We will recall that in the last question of the *Problemata* she asks, referring to marriage, whether it is possible to sin in a matter that has been allowed or even commanded by God. Here her views on marriage are made to fit more squarely within Abelard's own ethic of intention. Since it is the intent and not the act itself that is sinful, Heloise must examine both her intent and Abelard's in partaking in the sacrament of marriage. Both, we know from her letters, were found wanting. She never fully formed the intent and, claiming innocence and weakness of will, notes that the devil tempted her to do that which was wrong. Abelard, on the other hand, suffered no such temptation. His intent was evil: to have sexual access to Heloise while publicly maintaining the appearance of a celibate cleric solely for the purposes of fostering his own career. Abelard was not concerned with the way in which the marriage would impede his concentration as a philosopher and a cleric, but only with the way public knowledge of the marriage would cost his career. For Heloise, the sin of marrying was related to the harm it would do to Abelard's ability to concentrate and write philosophy. As summarized by Radice:

If her arguments are read closely it is clear that she was much less concerned with the possible loss of Abelard's services to the Church than with the betrayal of the ideal which they both admired, that of the philosopher as a man who is set apart and above human ties. . . . She points out the distractions and petty hindrances of domestic life which are inimical to philosophic contemplation, and compares the philosophers with "those who truly deserve the name of monks," that is, the dedicated solitaries such as John the Baptist or the ascetic sects of Jewish history.

Referring to Heloise's first letter, Radice continues:

. . . a lasting relationship should rest on the complete devotion of two persons; this is true disinterested love, based on what she calls "chastity of spirit." To such an ideal union a legal marriage could add nothing, and the presence or absence of an erotic element is, in a sense, irrelevant. The intention towards the ideal relationship is all-important. This is the "ethic of pure intention" in which both Abelard and Heloise believed and to which she often returns.[31]

IV. Summary

Dronke, referring to the *Problemata*, says that

. . . Heloise should be considered not only in relation to Abelard, as has always been customary, but also in relation to other medieval women writers, to see precisely in what ways a womanly awareness comes to be expressed—and to be called in question—in her writings, and how her self-understanding compares with that of other medieval women who have left us written testimonies.[32]

Prudence Allen[33] studies Heloise's views on women. In Allen's view, Heloise represents a curious contrast. One of the best educated and intellectually accomplished women of her time, Heloise clearly expresses a view of women's inferiority to men, even though that view becomes modified over time. Yet we can assess what Heloise says and contrast what she says to what her words reveal about her and about Abelard. Her letters reveal her teacher, her husband, and her religious superior to be a man of enormous gifts and enormous shortcomings. The most brilliant philosopher of his day, Abelard could not live by the very principles he taught to Heloise. As his student, Heloise not only lived by those principles but would have been disillusioned to realize that Abelard did not live by them. The man who fathered her child and became her husband against her better judgement cloistered his wife when marriage no longer served his career needs and ignored her when he could no longer take advantage of her sexually. The priest who was Heloise's religious superior had to be scolded into finally attending to the needs of the nun of the Paraclete.

Heloise's comments about the inferiority of women to men are explicit. But we must remember that those comments came from a philosopher who held Ciceronian views on love and who shared Abelard's "ethic of intent." In light of her philosophical views, and in light of the life that she had led consistent with those views, Heloise's comments ought to be understood as placing a high moral value on humility expressed as so-called "feminine inferiority."

Notes

1. Elizabeth Hamilton, *Heloise* (London: Hodder and Stoughton, 1966), p. 15.

2. Petrus Abelardus in Migne, *Patrologia Latina* 178: 206 CD.

3. Étienne Gilson, *Heloise and Abelard*, L. K. Shook authorized tr. of *Héloïse et Abélard* (Chicago: Henry Regnery Company, 1951), p. 48.

4. See Chronicle of Guillaume Godel (d.? 1173) in *Recueilles des Histoires: Les Obituaires français au moyen age*, Molinier, ed. (Paris, 1880).

5. Petrus Abelardus, *Patrologia Latina* (hereinafter referred to as *PL*) 178: 33.

6. Peter Dronke, *Women Writers of the Middle Ages* (Cambridge: Cambridge University Press, 1984), p. 111.

7. Ibid., p. 149.

8. Ibid.

9. See ibid., p. 111.

10. Peter Dronke, "Heloise's *Problemata and Letters:* Some Questions of Form and Content" in *Petrus Abaelardus, Trierer Theologische Studien*, R. Thomas, ed., Band 38: (1980), p. 53, hereinafter as Dronke, *Problemata*.

11. Gilson, op. cit., p. 145.

12. Ibid., p. 149.

13. Ibid.

14. Ibid., p. 151, Gilson citing D. C. Butler, *Le monachisme bénédictin* (Paris: de Gigord, 1924), pp. 144–5.

15. Dronke, *Problemata*, pp. 56–7.

16. Ibid., p. 57.

17. Gilson, op cit., pp. 47–65.

18. M. Tullius Cicero, *De amicitia*, IX, xiv, xxvii (London and New York: Loeb Classical Library, 1914–1949).

19. Heloise, *Epistula II, Patrologia Latina* 178: 184 ff.

20. Gilson, op. cit., p. 47.

21. Heloise, op. cit.

22. Ibid.

23. *Epistle II* in *The Letters of Abelard and Heloise*, Betty Radice, tr. (Middlesex: Penguin Books, 1974), p. 130.

24. Heloise, op. cit.

25. Abelard, *Scito te ipsum*, in Migne, *Patrologia Latina* 178: 640B.

26. Heloise, op. cit.

27. Gilson, op. cit., pp. 49–50.

28. Elizabeth Hamilton, *Heloise*, p. 42.

29. Ibid., p. 72.

30. Ibid., p. 73.

31. Betty Radice, *The Letters of Abelard and Heloise*, p. 17.

32. Dronke, op. cit., p. 54.

33. Prudence Allen, *The Concept of Woman: The Aristotelian Revolution 750 B.C.—A.D. 1250* (Montreal: Eden Press, 1985), pp. 291–2.

Andrea Nye

12   Elisabeth, Princess Palatine: Letters to René Descartes

Elisabeth, Princess Palatine, Abbess of Herford (1618–1680) was driven with her family from the Palatine by imperial troops and given refuge in Holland by William of Orange. At the age of twenty-four Elisabeth initiated a philosophical correspondence with René Descartes that lasted until Descartes's death in 1650. In her letters Elisabeth questioned Descartes's dualistic metaphysics, his understanding of the soul, his conception of God, and his morality of prudence. Her extant letters have recently been made available in English.[1] In the following pages I examine aspects of her letters in which she questions the modern resolve to put values aside and concentrate on objective knowledge.

Descartes used an organic metaphor for human knowledge. He wrote:

> The whole of philosophy is like a tree. The roots are metaphysics, the trunk is physics, and the branches emerging from the truck are all the other sciences, which may be reduced to three principle ones, namely medicine, mechanics, and morals. By morals I understand the highest and most perfect system which presupposes a complete knowledge of the other sciences and is the ultimate level of wisdom.[2]

So Descartes expressed what he saw as the proper relation between ethics, science, and a dualist metaphysics of mechanical bodies and autonomous minds. For him, metaphysics is foundations. If science is to be immune to interference from politics or theology, it must be grounded in reason free from any form of passionate enthusiasm. Ethics comes only after science has established its grasp on what is best.

In her letters to Descartes Elisabeth reversed his order of priority, putting emotion and value first. She questioned the independence of the mind from the body and went to the root of the claim that rational science is the proper support for ethics—to Descartes's dualist metaphysics. She writes:

> How can the soul of man determine the spirits of the body, so as to produce voluntary actions (given that the soul is only a thinking substance). For it seems that all determination

of movement is made by the pulsion of a moving thing, so that it is pushed by that which moves it, or, by the qualification (quality) and figure (shape) of the surface of that thing. For the first two conditions, touching is necessary, for the third extension. For the one, you exclude entirely the notion that you have of the soul; the other seems to me incompatible with an immaterial thing. This is why I ask you to give a definition of the soul more specific than that in your Metaphysics, that is to say of its substance, as separated from its thinking action. For even if we suppose the two to be inseparable (which anyway is difficult to prove in the womb of the mother and in fainting spells), like the attributes of God, we can, in considering them separately, acquire a more perfect idea of them. (May 1643)[3]

Elisabeth asks Descartes to define the soul or mind more specifically than he has, for she cannot conceive how his definition of soul accounts for the soul's relation to body and matter. If the mind were truly different from the body, it could not move the body. And if mind and body are not separate, then Descartes's rational mental bedrock is quicksand. If different temperaments, different predispositions to feel for others or to feel for oneself, skew how one judges what is best, it is only in fantasy that bodily passion can be kept out of rational thought.

Elisabeth did not hide her disappointment at Descartes's puzzling answer to her questions. Here is a convenient way to think of the separation of mind and body, he told her. When we think of a body moving another body, we tend falsely to imagine that qualities of body, like heaviness, are separate substances that do the moving. False though this is in respect to physical phenomena, such a conception may have been given us as help in understanding the interaction between mind and body. We can imagine the soul to move the body in the same way a fictitious "heaviness" moves a body (May 21, 1643).

Elisabeth's response was characteristically dry:

This idea [of a separate quality of heaviness], given that we are not able to pretend to the perfection and objective reality of God, could be made up out of ignorance of that which truly propels bodies towards the center of the earth. Because no material cause represents itself to the senses, one attributes heaviness to matter's contrary, the immaterial, which, nevertheless, I would never be able to conceive but as a negation of matter and which could have no communication with matter. (July 1, 1643)

Elisabeth doubted the adequacy of Descartes's concept of soul and felt it did not fit the facts of experience. Contrary to fact conceptualizations may cover up ignorance; they may cover up the possibility, as Elisabeth put it, that "there are properties of the soul, unknown to us, which could, perhaps, overturn what your Meditations persuaded me of with such good arguments: the non-extension of the soul" (July 1, 1643).

So Elisabeth recalled Descartes to his own skepticism. "This doubt can be founded on the rule which you yourself laid down there in speaking of the true and the false: that all errors come from forming judgements on that which we do not see clearly enough" (July 1, 1643). The problem, as Elisabeth saw it, is not with faulty arguments nor with the illogical implications of dualism, but rather with the fictionality of

Descartes's metaphysical concept of the separation of mind and body, a concept of separation that he imagined would allow science to proceed without attention to emotion or the impulses of the body.

Other critics besides Elisabeth worried about the moral effects of metaphysical dualism. In response to their objections, Descartes added a "provisional morality" to his *Discourse on Method*. Now he offered a version of that same interim morality to Elisabeth: until science finds out the truth, repress distracting emotions, rationally decide what is best, resolve to do it, don't be bothered by hindsight or remorse. Out of rational control of emotion will come true science and potentially perfect knowledge, and, in consequence, the doing and achieving of what is best. In the meantime, follow established law and social custom.

In the havoc of European politics during the Thirty Years' War, in the struggle to the death between autocratic Catholicism and a democratic-leaning Protestantism, following law and custom was hardly a guarantee of virtue for Elisabeth. Nor did it help when Descartes added a theological guarantee: not only can we trust that God has aligned our rational mathematical ideas with physical reality, he told her, but God also has arranged the world so that the interests of one individual are complementary to those of others. Favors prudently asked are granted; good deeds are to one's own advantage. Consequently it is not necessary to be so exact in evaluating the interests of self and others; it is enough to go with inclination and trust to God who has arranged these things so that human society is "tightly woven." Even if one lives only for one's self, "prudence" requires one to work for others.[4]

In relation to this "theological guarantee," Descartes and Elisabeth debated at some length the question of how the supposed infinite power and goodness of God can be reconciled with free will and evil deeds. Free will is necessary if we are to have moral responsibility, but then free will means that there are events over which God has no control, seemingly limiting God's power. Alternately, if the will of men and women is determined, it seems God is responsible for evil actions. Descartes resorted to some theological hair-splitting to explain. We are free and we are not free, he said. God determines everything, but seen another way we are responsible for our actions. Elisabeth remained unwavering in her refusal to overlook the indeterminacy in human life and its implications. Experienced in the tumult of public and private events, not ready to trust either to unassisted reason or to a divinely prearranged harmony of interests, she argued from experience, not from a script of divinely guaranteed "clear and distinct" ideas:

> The consideration that we are a part of a whole, whose advantage we ought to seek, is really the force behind all generous actions; but I find much difficulty in the conditions that you prescribe. How measure the evils which one gives oneself for the public against the good which would come of it, without them appearing more grand, inasmuch as their idea is more distinct. And what rule would we have for the comparison of things which are not really equally known to us, such as our own merit, against that of those with whom we live? A natural arrogance would make us always tip the balance our own way; a natural modesty would always esteem itself at less than its value. (September 30, 1645)

Reason, Elisabeth pointed out, can easily be induced to be the servant of emotional inclination. In a selfish temperament, reason finds arguments for self-interest; in a sympathetic temperament, it finds reasons for self-sacrifice. Descartes, she charged, was assuming a situation contrary to fact: "To profit from the particular truths of which you speak, it is necessary to know exactly all the passions and all the predispositions the majority of which are insensible" (September 30, 1645). In other words, the perfect knowledge that Descartes's dualist metaphysics is meant to guarantee—as product of a mind separated from the body, untainted by emotions or sensation, attending to its own clear and distinct ideas—is impossible. Therefore, the moral offshoots of a science supported by a fictional separation between mind and body may be equally fictitious, reflecting not perfect goodness but rather moral insensibility.

As Elisabeth's friend and advisor, Descartes applied his ethics of prudence to several catastrophic events in her life, causing misunderstanding and rifts in their friendship. When she is devastated at her brother's casual abjuration of Protestantism, Descartes is cold and distant, lecturing her on the virtues of having friends in all camps. When a courtier boasts of the sexual favors he has received from Elisabeth's mother and sister, and is killed by one of her brothers in a street brawl, Descartes advises Elisabeth, seriously ill and banished to Germany for supporting her brother, to forget the past and smell the flowers. When her uncle, King Charles I of England, is beheaded in London, Descartes reassures Elisabeth that such a dramatic death is preferable to dying in bed because it is painless and contributes to fame.[5] To these, no doubt well-meant, reassurances, Elisabeth often could respond only with silence.

In medical matters Elisabeth regularly spoke out and questioned Descartes's advice. Suffering often from fevers, infections, rashes, and digestion problems, she refused to think of the mind as separate from body and believe that the cause was either purely emotional or purely physical. When Descartes recommended willful suppression and control of emotion, she cited instead physical restraints, environmental factors such as bad air, dampness, and lack of hygiene. A woman's body, she reminded him, is often restricted by tight clothes and forced to be inactive, all of which affects both mental and physical health.

> Know that I have a body imbued with a great part of the weakness of my sex, know that it registers very easily afflictions of the soul and does not have the strength to be quit of them, being of a temperament subject to obstructions and remaining in a climate which contributes to illness. For persons who cannot do much exercise like myself, a long oppression of the heart from sadness is hardly necessary for the spleen to be disrupted and the rest of the body infected with vapors. I think that the slow fever and dry cough which are still there even with the heat of the season and the walks which I take to rally my forces, come from that. (May 24, 1645)

Pathological sadness or melancholy is not the only cause of illness that is without obvious organic cause. For anyone, diet, climate, the quality of the air can lead to illness and depression. There is no way, when one's physical circumstances are poor, Elisabeth insisted, to stop wanting what we cannot get. The very fact of being physical means we desire and cannot stop desiring health and the means of subsistence. Traveling in Germany after the Thirty Years' War, she noted the wretched poverty of the inhabitants and the intellectual backwardness that was the result of war. She noted that there could be no independence of thought in starving deprived bodies—a consideration much less evident to Descartes, waiting out the war in a well-provisioned retreat in the Dutch countryside.

An ethics of prudence might be appropriate for the exceptional life of an isolated scholar, Elisabeth told him, but what is needed for a life that involves public and familial responsibilities is not detachment and prudent dependence on God's will, but judgement.

> If my conscience were as satisfied with the excuses that you give for my ignorance as I am with the remedies for that ignorance, I would be very obliged. And I would be exempt from repentance for having so badly used the time I have for the use of my reason, which for me is longer than that of others of my age. Birth and fortune force me to use my judgement promptly in order to lead a life sufficiently difficult and free of prosperity to prevent me from thinking of myself, just as if I were forced to trust in the rule of a governess. (September 13, 1645)

Elisabeth chides Descartes for his patronizing attitude. Her situation as royalty, she reminds him, does not relieve her from intellectual duty, nor is it an avoidable distraction from the life of the mind. Rather it is a stern teacher that forces her to develop good judgement. In such a life, the point of moral action is not the self-satisfied state of one's own soul, but the state of one's affairs. If they are in disorder, there is no avoiding mental pain, and, in extreme cases, mental and physical dysfunction. In response to Descartes's criticism of Machiavelli for not being true to his own idea of justice, Elisabeth notes: "any opinion [a ruler] might have of himself, even of the justice of his cause, may serve to put to rest his own conscience, but not his affairs, where the laws restrict his authority or when the powerful undermine it and the people speak against it" (October 10, 1646). When one has civic responsibilities, it is not the comfortable state of one's soul that is important but the state of the community in which one lives.

Philosophers like Socrates or Epicurus may die happy and without regrets, Elisabeth argued, but in responsible civic life, repentance is inevitable.

> When Epicurus tells a lie at his death bed, assuring his friends he is well instead of crying out like an ordinary man, he lives the life of a philosopher not of a Prince, Captain, or courtier. He knows that nothing outside prevents him from following his rules and acting like a philosopher.
>
> But with a Prince or a Captain, repentance is inevitable, and one is not able to defend oneself with the knowledge that failure is as natural for a man as being sick. For one does not know if one can be exempted from each particular fault. (August 16, 1645)

Subtly, Elisabeth turns around Descartes's order of priority. Descartes moved up the root of dualist metaphysics to the tree trunk of value-free science, and then to the branches of applied sciences like medicine, psychology, and mechanics. Elisabeth begins from embodied existence, moves to ethics, and only then to sciences that accomplish good. Her metaphysical foothold is not "I think therefore I am" but rather embodied intelligence in time. Because of temporality and the irrationality of much of human behavior, possible future goods and evils are infinite and incalculable. Even past good and evil are not fixed, but always open to reinterpretation in the light of present events. This is why, as she sees it, Descartes's rationalist calm is morally retrograde and the failure to achieve such a calm cannot be blamed on the worldliness and self-absorption of the rich and famous. She writes:

> It isn't always prosperity, nor the flattery which accompanies it, which I believe can decisively keep fortitude of spirit from well-born souls and prevent them from bearing changes of fortune philosophically. I am persuaded that the events which surprise people governing the public, who are without the time to find the most expedient means, carries them (no matter what virtue they have) into actions which afterwards cause the repentance which you say is one of the principle obstacles to happiness. It is true that a habit of valuing goods according to how they contribute to contentment, and measuring that contentment according to the perfections which make pleasure remain, and judging without passion those perfections and pleasures, protects us from many faults. But to evaluate goods, it is necessary to be completely acquainted with them and to be acquainted with all those among which we must choose in an active life would require an infinite science. You say that one must be content when one's conscience witnesses that one has used all possible precautions. But this never happens, because one does not simply find one's history; one always revises things which remain to be considered. (September 13, 1645)

Again Elisabeth questions the counterfactual character of Descartes's priorities. The conception of science as offering a potentially perfect knowledge assumes a fixed eternity of facts about past and future. The world as a rationalist scientist conceives it waits to be discovered, a pre-established order that will be reflected in sets of true propositions either derived from elementary mathematical truths or collated from sets of sensory data. Elisabeth constantly comes back to the fact of the surprises of a life in time, in which decisions must regularly be made before one has complete knowledge. In such a life, complete knowledge is never possible. Imperfect knowledge, painful afterthought, emotional turmoil are an inevitable part of human experience. For this reason, and not excessive emotionality, Elisabeth protests, she is both unable and unwilling to adopt the atemporal attitude that Descartes urged on her so often—she could not watch painful events in her life as if she were at a theater, with rational faculties unruffled by painful emotion.

Such advice might make sense to Descartes, concerned with his own work and with university squabbles surrounding its teaching; for Elisabeth, it was bad advice. Given life in time, given the impossibility of predicting future goods and evils, given the free will of those who seldom act according to reason, rationality for her required the rooted support of morality and experience, especially the experience of continual weighing and reweighing of self-interest against the interests of others—a weighing that cannot be conducted according to any predetermined rational plan or calculation but that depends on continual re-estimation of the value of interests. To omit or ignore that weighing, said Elisabeth, is to blindly allow temperament, self-interested or other-interested, to rule, with reason's line of argument constantly in danger of being undermined by inclination.

What would have made Descartes's perfectible mechanistic science possible is the mind's independence of the body. If the mind were indeed separate from the body, it might achieve immunity from the distractions of temporal existence and focus solely on truth. But, Elisabeth pointed out, given that body and mind are irrevocably linked, thought is always mixed with bodily passion and bodily passion is always mixed with thought. If the rational mind is to move the body, Elisabeth argued, it must do so by "information" and so the body must in some sense be intelligent. Similarly, if intelligent voluntary bodily action is to be possible, the mind must be of weight, of substance. Therefore, temperament and emotion cannot be set aside as irrelevant to rational thought. On the contrary, science requires stable rooting in their proper weighing and correction.

It was at Elisabeth's request and in answer to her questions about clarifying the relation between emotion and reason that Descartes undertook his last work, the treatise *On the Passions*. In it he prescribed a regime that he thought would guarantee the mental independence necessary for rationalist science. As a guide for Elisabeth and other aspiring scholars and scientists, Descartes produced a physics of emotion, identifying the various emotions as controllable and manipulable muscle tensions, flows of blood, body temperatures. In the systematically numbered sections of Descartes's treatise, much of the moral advice he had given Elisabeth reappeared, generalized as a theory of emotion. The "method" of distanced rationality became a state of mind, a mental order that guarantees independence of mind and freedom from pain. Once a man determines what is best and acts on it, he distances himself from painful events, watches events as if in a theater, and, most importantly, cultivates self-generated inner "emotions" of self-satisfaction that override any excessive pain for others. When all else fails, he refrains from acting on emotion and puts himself in pleasant circumstances so that past trouble is forgotten; he gets on with his work. The same advice that Elisabeth had persistently rejected in her letters as practically and morally impossible in a committed and responsible life was now given scientific status as a theory of emotional classification and ordering.

Elisabeth's response to the treatise was supportive but critical. First, she argued, it is impossible to identify various emotions physiologically.

> I do not see how one can know the diverse movements of the blood, which cause the five primitive passions, since they are never alone. For example, love is always accompanied by desire and joy, or desire and sadness, and to the measure that it is strong. . . . How is it then possible to tell the different beating of the pulse, the digestion of meats, and other changes of the body, which serve to reveal the nature of these movements? Also, as you note, none of these passions is the same in all temperaments: mine is such that sadness, such as comes only from the death of a friend, takes away the appetite (that is as long as it is not mixed with any hate).
>
> When you speak of the exterior signs of passion, you say that admiration, joined to joy,

> makes the lungs fill up with many jolts to cause laughing. To which I ask you to add in what way admiration (which, according to your description, seems to operate only on the brain) could open up so promptly the orifices of the heart to create this effect.
>
> The passion that you note as the cause of sighs does not seem to be what you say, since dress and the fullness of the stomach can also cause sighs. (April 25, 1646)

The physiological effects that Descartes cites can be caused by other things than emotion, she argued, by overeating or by tight dress. Furthermore, different people experience emotion in different ways. Because emotions do not come simply but in complexes, it is impossible to sort out what are the effects of one emotion rather than another. As she saw it, there is an even deeper problem with Descartes's theory of the passions than mistaken physiology: to carry out the advice that follows from that theory—to remove oneself from events so that no pain is felt—can lead to moral weakness.

> But I confess that I find the difficulty of separating sense and imagination from things which are continually represented in conversation and letters such that I can't do it without failing in my duty. I understand well that in taking away from an idea of an affair everything that makes me angry (which I believe is only represented by the imagination), I would judge more sanely and would soon find a remedy for my afflictions. But I have never known how to practice this except after passion has played its role. (June 22, 1645)

Hindsight is one thing. After the fact, perhaps, one might separate sense and imagination from tragic events without moral compromise. But the surprises of life in time and dutiful involvement with others inevitably bring painful emotion involving both feeling and the imagining of unhappy events. In this case, to respond coldly and rationally to what is told to one in diplomatic conversation, dispatches, news bulletins, is to fail in one's duty. As Elisabeth had discovered, the rational soul moves the body through intelligent yet bodily "information." Passions of the body have their intelligence and are necessary for knowledge and right action. Sympathy for others in trouble helps one better to know what to do for them; retrospective remorse brings cognizance of faults in oneself and proper remedies for them.

> We are more inclined to make mistakes about our faults than our perfections. And in fleeing repentance for faults we have committed as inimical to felicity, one runs the risk of losing the concern to correct them, especially when some passion has produced them, since we naturally like to be emotionally moved and to follow that movement. There is only inconvenience that comes from the flight that says that recognition of faults could be harmful. (October 28, 1645)

Inherent in the disagreement between Elisabeth and Descartes are differing views of the function and purpose of philosophy. Confronted with Elisabeth's insistence on the inconceivability of the separation of mind and body, Descartes suggests that little time and energy should be spent on metaphysics. One should establish the philosophical bases of knowledge and get on with science (Letter of June 6, 1643). For Descartes, metaphysics or philosophy is rationalization of established commitments, to be established and then left alone. For Elisabeth, concerned with human events, cognizant of the way passion and inclination distort reason, assessing the effect of misguided medical and moral advice, philosophical speculation is continued inquiry into changing conditions. Descartes's metaphysics supports the trunk of an objectivist positivist science and a derivative technological ethics. Elisabeth's nondualist metaphysics of thinking body and material mind nourishes another trunk, a morally sensitive weighing of values and interests from which come flowering branches of science in the service of embodied and temporal human life.

Descartes is not usually thought of as an ethicist. His epistemology more often stands alone as the prototype of modern theories of knowledge. Elisabeth questions some of the possible ethical consequences of that epistemology: a doctor who does not understand the effects of the body on mental disorders, a sociologist who trivializes violent death, a politician with friends in all camps. But perhaps the most important outcome of this remarkable friendship and collaboration between a woman and a man is their final agreement that ethics and knowledge are inseparable. After Descartes, ethics tends to become peripheral to the main concerns of philosophy. Gone are the vast projections of Christian theology that rooted virtue in chains of being. Gone is the Neo-Platonists' insistence on the primary reality of Goodness and Justice. After Descartes, the chief concern of philosophy becomes the nature of physical reality and the methods for knowing that reality. Ethics is either provisional, a posited and agreed upon code of behavior regulating social relations pending the findings of science, or an after-the-fact clean-up job undertaken to answer objections and handle anomalies. Elisabeth and Descartes's collaboration points up some of the dangers in an approach that separates ethics and epistemology. With Elisabeth's questioning, rational isolation no longer seems a superior philosophical stance but rather a failure in emotional attachment that can produce suspect ethics and possibly fictitious science.

Notes

1. Andrea Nye, *The Princess and the Philosopher: Letters of Elisabeth of the Palatine to René Descartes* (Totowa, N.J.: Rowman and Littlefield Publishers, Inc., 1999). See Nye, "Polity and Prudence: the Ethics of Elisabeth Princess Palatine" in *Hypatia's Daughters*, Linda Lopez McAlister, ed. (Bloomington: Indiana University Press, 1996). See also Elizabeth Godfrey, *A Sister of Prince Rupert, Elizabeth Princess Palatine and Abbess of Herford* (New York: J. Lane, 1909).

2. René Descartes, Preface to *Principles of Philosophy* in *The Philosophical Works of Descartes*, edited by E. S. Haldane and G. R. T. Ross (Cambridge: Cambridge University Press, 1979), Vol. I, p. 211. The *Principles* were dedicated to Princess Elisabeth. Descartes cited "the incomparable excellence of [her] intellect," her abilities in both metaphysics and mathematics, and her superior virtue. See his dedication in ibid., pp. 216–8.

3. All letters quoted are from my translations of the French texts in *Oeuvres de Descartes*, C. Adam and P. Tannery, eds. (Paris: Librairie Philosophique, J. Vrin, 1972). Letters from May and June of 1643 can be found in Volume III; from July of 1643 to April of 1647, in Volume IV. The complete texts of all Elisabeth's letters with excerpts from Descartes's replies can be found in Nye, *The Princess and the Philosopher*.

4. See Descartes's long letter of October 6, 1645.

5. See Nye, *The Princess and the Philosopher*, for a detailed account of events in Elisabeth's life during her correspondence with Descartes.

Lisa A. Bergin

---

13   Gloria Anzaldúa's *Borderlands/
La Frontera* and René Descartes's
Discourse on Method:
MOVING BEYOND THE CANON IN DISCUSSION OF PHILOSOPHICAL IDEAS

In this essay I discuss teaching Gloria Anzaldúa (1942–), a Chicana feminist theorist, in philosophy classrooms—specifically, teaching her in conjunction with René Descartes, the French philosopher. Before I begin this discussion, however, I want to trace how I came to be speaking about efforts to expand the canon of Western philosophy.

After I entered the Ph.D. program at the University of Minnesota in 1992, I joined a group of students and faculty members who earlier had formed out of concern over the very low number of women students and students of color in our undergraduate philosophy classrooms.[1] We have been working to change this number by developing course work that is more inclusive than is usually the case with standard philosophy curriculum. At the time I joined, the group had gotten a new introduction to philosophy, Introduction to Philosophy and Cultural Diversity, accepted into the curriculum. I was a graduate teaching assistant for this course in three of its offerings, and in 1997 I taught a version of it myself in the university's night school. This essay is informed by my experiences as an instructor and teaching assistant for this course, as well as my experiences as a participant in the group that developed the course.

Philosophy 1006, Introduction to Philosophy and Cultural Diversity, is structured by groupings of differing philosophical views on three main topics. The quarter begins by exploring conceptions of the human self and takes up René Descartes's unitary consciousness and Gloria Anzaldúa's *mestiza* consciousness. Teaching this pair in conjunction has led to very powerful teaching and learning moments for me.

I begin the classroom discussion of Gloria Anzaldúa and René Descartes with an important method of analysis in which we compare and contrast their works: both authors describe a process by which they move from a problematic conception of the self to a more positive conception. Indeed, there are many similarities between their projects. Yet the conclusions the two theorists come to about the self are quite different. In *Borderlands/La Frontera*, Anzaldúa offers the new *mestiza* consciousness— a conception of the self that is multiple, connected to the material world, in transition, and ambiguous—an alternative to Descartes's conception of the true self as a unitary, pure consciousness. As a class we try to come to some conclusions about the significance of the similarities and differences between the two works. From the vantage of an instructor, I present here some of the important points of connection and disconnection between these two theorists.

In developing the conception of the *mestiza* consciousness—a view of the human self that values complexity, change, contradiction, and ambiguity—Anzaldúa uses a mixture of languages, mostly Tex-Mex, Spanish, and English, as well as both prose and poetry. Rather than using the formal philosophical argumentation of making valid steps from true premises to conclusions, Anzaldúa uses dreams, memories, and lived experience as the important tools for making her argument in *Borderlands/La Frontera*. Moreover, her writing is fused with emotion, as though speaking with a tongue forked in anger and passion. Many would not see her text as a philosophical one. In fact, in teaching the work, I find that the students who have questioned the use of *Borderlands/La Frontera* in a philosophy classroom are the more senior students who have already studied some philosophy.

Yet this is a piece of philosophical importance. One way we can argue for its acceptance is to show some similarities between it and Descartes's *Discourse on Method*. Anzaldúa's work does not merely offer her theory of the *mestiza* consciousness and its social and ethical implications. It is also a work of methodology in which she traces for the reader how she came to her knowledge of the *mestiza* consciousness; it is an intellectual life history. This history begins when Anzaldúa is a young girl growing up in the 1950s in what she terms the "Borderlands" of southern Texas. She describes this area as a region that is neither normatively American nor Mexican, that is inhabited by Chicano peoples who are rejected on both sides of the border—not American enough, not Mexican enough, worthy only of disregard and contempt. From this place she begins a journey that will eventually lead her to the *mestiza* consciousness, a new way of experiencing the world and the self.

At the beginning of her intellectual travel is a pervasive dissatisfaction. Initially, this dissatisfaction is that of a young Chicana girl internalizing the denigrating views of others. This dissatisfaction stems from her conception of her own self as a borderland. She is neither Mexican nor American, yet somehow both. She is a strong-willed girl where girls are to be submissive; she is a woman who desires other women, as only men are "supposed" to. She feels a lack of definition, an uncomfortable mixing of elements that ought not to be combined. Yet this inwardly focused view shifts to examine the standards behind the conceptions others have of her. Through this movement, Anzaldúa begins a skeptical relationship with the human world: she begins to doubt both Mexican and Anglo views that denigrate Chicano people, as well as the numerous cultural views that hold willful women and girls, as well as queer people, as deviant. As a result of this skeptical turn, Anzaldúa "leaves home" in order to find an alternate path to the ones prescribed for most women. In doing so, she comes to reject certain aspects of Chicano culture and embrace others.

In her continued reflective search for self-knowledge, Anzaldúa avails herself of resources that include using a "multi-tongued" language to express her ideas, using early Mesoamerican religions as sustenance and their gods and goddesses as models, and using writing not only as a tool for communication but also as a way of developing ideas and coming to knowledge. With these resources, Anzaldúa completes her epistemic journey to advocate a metaphysics and an epistemology with which her own complicated self, and the selves of others, can be viewed positively: the *mestiza* consciousness.

In his *Discourse on Method*, Descartes also relates to his readers an intellectual history, describing his own journey toward sure knowledge. This journey begins with Descartes's belief that he will attain the heights of current knowledge from his schooling in letters. Yet, finding only confusion and contradiction in the views of esteemed scholars, he becomes skeptical about the possibility of gaining knowledge from instructors or letters and leaves his academic tenure. This leads to his desire to find knowledge himself: "I entirely abandoned the study of letters, and resolved not to seek after any science but what might be found within myself or in the great book of the world."[2] Through his tenure as a traveling world-scholar, Descartes experiences customs that, though different from those in France, are nonetheless practical. Realizing that there are multiple sustainable forms of human life, Descartes becomes skeptical of things taken as given only by custom or example. This philosophical moment leads to his resolve to attempt the acquisition of knowledge as a self-sufficient knower. He will not rely on the works of ancient or contemporary scholars, nor upon common opinion derived from custom. Thus, with only the company of a hot fire, he spends his famous winter in Germany, devising his plan to acquire knowledge.

During this solitude, Descartes devises four rules of method, the first and most crucial of which is that he is to accept only what it is impossible for him to doubt. The remaining three methodological rules concern the mechanics of problem solving and the reflective stance needed to assure complete knowledge. Years later, he applies this method to philosophy: he endeavors to find a secure foundation for knowledge that will lead him to "truth alone." Using the first rule, Descartes finds that he can doubt almost everything he ever took for certain. He finds, however, the *cogito ergo sum* as the only piece of indubitable knowledge, and from this foundation, using the four rules of method, he justifies what can be known of the self, God, and the world.

The theoretical roads that Anzaldúa and Descartes each take contain a few striking similarities. Both journeys begin with self-doubt. For Anzaldúa this is doubt about the worth of her self on many levels, while Descartes's doubt is focused on his worth as a knower. Both individuals question the received knowledge of the day, leading both to leave what is familiar in order to find alternative methodologies and views. Also, both journeys involve isolation, introspection, an intensity of thought, and a critical awareness of the self. These similarities support an argument for placing Gloria Anzaldúa within the field of philosophy. While Descartes is very much at the center of the Western philosophical tradition, Anzaldúa is not. Yet clearly her work is philosophical in nature, and as such there is no reason why it cannot be included within the field. While *Borderlands/La Frontera* does not follow standard philosophical discourse or argumentative style, it is nevertheless a treatise that concentrates upon epistemology, metaphysics, and ethics, in which Anzaldúa examines essential questions of philosophy: What is the nature of the human self? How should humans relate to one another? How do we come to know the things we do? If we can call Descartes a philosopher for being concerned with such questions, we can do the same for Anzaldúa.

As I stated earlier, Descartes and Anzaldúa share a valuing of skepticism about received epistemic and social structures, and both have a methodology of introspection. The views of the self that they arrive at through their journeys of doubt, however, are widely divergent—even opposed. Descartes argues that while he can doubt the existence of his body and the information that it gives to him, he cannot doubt that he exists whenever he takes part in the activity of thinking. Thus for him the essential nature of the human self is the mind. By exploring the differences between the body and the mind, Descartes eventually arrives at a general conception of the self as a unitary consciousness that, he argues, is metaphysically distinct from the body. This metaphysical distinction yields an epistemological valuation in which the mind is the true source of knowledge, while matter—including the body—is dumb, unfeeling, and unknowing.

Anzaldúa in *Borderlands* rejects this metaphysical and epistemological picture. In doing so she is theoretically connected to a history of feminist critiques of political and social consequences of dualist theory. These critiques show ways in which dualist theory has been implemented to support a division between the "privileged" who are imagined as being separate from their bodies (and thus as being proper knowers) and the "underprivileged" who are not imagined as separate from their bodies (for example, women, people of color, the poor, the disabled). One central element in Anzaldúa's rejection of such dualist frameworks is the *mestiza* consciousness, her view of the self.

Remember that originally Anzaldúa's framing of her self is problematic: that she is a willful woman, a lesbian, and a Chicana seem to her to be important elements of the self, and yet she cannot value them positively for the contradictions these elements contain. One possible resolution is to follow Descartes and assert that what she is most truly is unconnected to any physical, cultural, or sexual nature that she embodies. This, however, is not Anzaldúa's resolution. Instead she affirms the centrality of her culture, sexuality, gender, and body to her conception of her self and accordingly forms alternate ways of evaluating the borderland self.

One model Anzaldúa uses to accomplish this re-evaluation comes from the indigenous North American goddess Coatlicue:

> Coatlicue depicts the contradictory. In her figure, all the symbols important to the religion and philosophy of the Aztecs are integrated. Like Medusa, the Gorgon, she is a symbol of the fusion of opposites: the eagle and the serpent, [the male and the female], heaven and the underworld, life and death, mobility and immobility, beauty and horror.[3]

As Coatlicue sustains differing elements within her own being, Anzaldúa discovers ways to integrate her own contradictory positions. This integration is accomplished not through the elimination of tensions in the elements of the self but instead by a valuing of ambiguity, of tension, of a self that is in transition rather than complete, whole, or finished. For Anzaldúa, the *mestiza* consciousness invokes creativity and flexibility, community and coalition, growth and change.

Although Anzaldúa does not argue against Descartes explicitly, she is clearly challenging Descartes's vision: her conception of the *mestiza* consciousness that seeks to meld the dualist mind-body distinction is both metaphysically and epistemologically opposed to Cartesianism. Meanwhile, Descartes would argue that Anzaldúa cannot build a foundation of knowledge as she has; not only does she rely upon dreams, memories, and religious traditions that have not withstood the scrutiny of Cartesian doubt, but also for her the body—an unlikely source of knowledge according to Descartes—is very much central to her epistemological endeavors. Thus Descartes would say that she makes the inessential essential and muddies the epistemological waters of pure consciousness with waves of physicality.

One method of bringing out in the classroom the significance of the theoretical differences between Anzaldúa and Descartes is to discuss the role of language in the two texts. Indeed, students themselves initiate this conversation in response to *Borderlands/La Frontera*. Their reactions to this multilanguage text range from anger at not being able to understand some of the sections of her book, which are not written in English, to excitement at the valuation of Spanish as an academic language. I use these reactions as a teaching tool to ask students such questions as: Why do you think Anzaldúa wrote in the languages she did? In what ways would her book be different if it were all written in one language? Would the meaning of it be the same? I point out that Descartes and Anzaldúa both are deliberate in their choice of language for their texts. Anzaldúa writes in the preface to *Borderlands/La Frontera*: "The switching of 'codes' in this book from English to Castillian Spanish to the North Mexican dialect to Tex-Mex to a sprinkling of Nahuatl to a mixture of all of these, reflects my language, a new language—the language of the Borderlands."[4] Meanwhile, Descartes writes in the sixth section of the *Discourse:*

> And if I write in French, which is the language of my country, rather than in Latin, which is that of my teachers, it is because I hope that those who rely purely on their natural

intelligence will be better judges of my views than those who believe only what they find in the writings of antiquity. And those who combine good sense with studiousness, whom alone I wish for my judges, will not, I am sure, be so partial to Latin that they will refuse to accept my reasons because I explain them in the vulgar tongue.[5]

I point out to students that we are reading Descartes in English translation from the original French, yet I would not supply an English version of Anzaldúa's text even if one existed. I ask them what the philosophical importance of the issue of translation is. The discussion allows students to explore the link between each author's language choice and each one's conception of the human self. The students come to see that according to Anzaldúa's view of the self there are necessary connections between the self, the body, one's cultures, and the languages one speaks. Thus, it is not merely that Anzaldúa's mixed language is a metaphor for her conception of the self; it is also that the self and the language are connected, necessitating her use of the borderland language to express her conception of her self. We would then lose something in translating *Borderlands/La Frontera*. Meanwhile, students also come to see that for Descartes, because the self is a consciousness that is divorced from the material world, language is seen as unconnected to the meaning it conveys. In Descartes's theory of the self, language is not integral to the theory it describes; it is merely a vehicle of communication. Therefore, translating the *Discourse* should not affect its meaning and the only relevance that any specific language has is that it may reach a wider and more open audience than would another language.

I have observed that for most students such a presentation of philosophy as a conversation between differing views functions to engage them with philosophy in ways that I have not experienced in more traditional introductory courses that draw on texts exclusively from the Western tradition. First, students come to understand each position better through the similarities and differences among the views. When put next to each other the consequences for a particular view of the self are brought into focus. Further, examining differing alternatives brings the philosophy alive in a way that it is not when only a single perspective is considered. For example, by learning about Anzaldúa and Descartes together, students begin to see the ways in which philosophy is connected to conversation and debate. This leads students to understand that something is at stake in how one defines oneself, and they become more eager to express and explore their own views. Finally, presenting in the curricula more than one perspective encourages students to combine elements of the differing views we explore and thus develop a view of the self that fits with their own experiences. Becoming more engaged, understanding the material better, adding their own ideas, and developing their own accounts: these are the factors that lead me to conclude that adding diverse voices to standard philosophy curricula creates more intellectually vibrant courses. Of course, we can find different perspectives within standard philosophy curricula, without using voices such as Anzaldúa's. I would argue, however, that voices within Western philosophy currently present a narrower group of perspectives than they would if we were to add other voices. Insofar as philosophy does not take itself to be an examination of how the world looks only to a group of fairly similar people, we should include diverse human perspectives. By doing so we remain consistent with the aims of philosophy.

I want to conclude with a comment on what teaching women authors such as Gloria Anzaldúa has meant to me. This is the first course that I have taught on my own. I was very concerned about my ability to lead the course, not because I thought I wasn't competent to teach it, but because I was afraid that my students wouldn't think I— being a short female graduate student who looks younger than she is—was competent. I was especially concerned because the course attempts to draw into philosophy theorists who are not considered part of the canon. Because my course stretched the definition of the field, I could not easily prove my ability through showing that I was competent in the field as narrowly defined. I expected revolt: "This isn't a philosophy class and you're not a philosopher." But in fact this revolt did not happen. I presented Anzaldúa, Audre Lorde, Malcolm X, and others as philosophers; my students took these authors as developers of philosophical theory alongside Descartes, Locke, and Plato, and they accepted me as an instructor of philosophy. I think their acceptance had to do in part with my becoming comfortable taking authority in the classroom, where being seen as an authority is something that women know we cannot always expect. Part of what helped me establish authority as a philosophy teacher was that I was teaching women as philosophers. Giving them authority gave me authority. And continuing to do so lessens the degree to which I feel like an interloper in this field and so helps me to call philosophy home.

Notes

1. The members of this group during the time I have been at the University of Minnesota are Katy Gray Brown, Melissa Burchard, Professor Douglas Lewis, Anne Phibbs, Pauline Sargent, Professor Naomi Scheman, Ronald Sundstrom, Amanda Vizedom, and myself. Each of these colleagues has contributed enormously to my thinking about teaching philosophy.

2. René Descartes, *Discourse on Method,* Laurence J. LaFleur, tran. (New York: Macmillan, 1956), pp. 12–13.

3. Gloria Anzaldúa, *Borderlands/La Frontera: The New Mestiza* (San Francisco, Calif.: Aunt Lute, 1987), p. 47.

4. Ibid., preface (unnumbered).

5. Descartes, *Discourse on Method,* p. 56.

Jane Duran

---

14 Mary Astell: A Pre-Humean Christian Empiricist and Feminist

The renascence of interest in works by women of the seventeenth century has meant a renewed interest in the work of Mary Astell (1666–1731), especially in her works *A Serious Proposal to the Ladies* and *Some Reflections upon Marriage*.[1] These works are, in some ways, forerunners of the line of feminist thought running directly through the later nineteenth and early twentieth centuries, but in other ways not so. Thus Astell's thought presents us with a difficult case, for, unlike feminists of the nineteenth and twentieth centuries, Astell is reluctant to attack the institution of marriage itself, and she seems to think it a concomitant to the institution that women can exercise their virtues of patience and forbearance within the framework of it. I was drawn to Astell precisely because of her paradoxicality, and I will argue that her attempts at the resolution of the problem of marriage are revelatory for many of us. But one of the remarkable aspects of Astell's work is its relationship to later work by David Hume. *A Serious Proposal* appeared in 1694 and *Some Reflections* in 1700. So her works precede Hume's by almost half a century, and yet the careful style of empirical analysis employed by Astell, and the conclusions to which she comes, are remarkably Humean.

Astell's longer works have been provided with an admirable commentary by the British theorist Bridget Hill, so I will frequently turn to Hill's remarks in order to provide clarification for some of Astell's more difficult positions. Hill titles her edition of Astell's work *The First English Feminist,* and one need not strain to see why.[2] That Astell is indeed a feminist—that is, that she asserts the natural equality of women as persons—is obvious from the first few paragraphs of *Some Reflections*. What makes Astell's work more difficult, however, is that her feminism is tempered by what she apparently regarded as simple common sense, and also by a desire to pay respect to the Christian tradition. Indeed, what makes Astell's thought so unusual is that she attempts not only to defend some of the elements of that tradition that are intrinsically tied to marriage, but that she also attempts to employ Scripture in her feminist argument for the equality of women. As Hill notes of Astell, "If we are to understand her, we have to accept the ambiguities and contradictions of her writing."[3] This is perhaps an understatement, but the complexity of her thought provides us with a challenge, and she makes the intriguing argument that women are perhaps best able to make use of their particular virtues in bad or "shipwrack['d]" marriages.[4]

I

At the opening of *Reflections,* Astell makes it clear that she has severed the apparent inferiority of women from anything occurring naturally to the female sex. In other words, if women appear to be inferior to males in most respects, it is only because social conditions both demand and promulgate that apparent inferiority. As she notes, "That the Custom of the World has put Women, generally speaking, into a State of Subjection, is not deny'd; but the Right can no more be proved from the Fact, than the predominancy of Vice can justifie it."[5] Thus, women have not been allowed to participate in society in such a way that their talents can be made use of; men prohibit the education of women, and then wonder why women appear to be uneducated. The fact that the Apostle Paul and others, in their composition of the epistles forming the New Testament, mention the need for female submission says more about the social conditions of Paul's time than it does about females having been created as the inferiors of males.

Astell writes:

> The Apostle indeed adds, that *the Man is the Glory of God, and the Woman the Glory of the Man,* Etc. But what does he infer from hence? he says not a word of Inequality, or natural Inferiority. . . .

And:

> But what says the Holy Scripture? It speaks of Women as in a State of Subjection, and so it does of the *Jews* and the *Christians,* when under the dominion of the *Chaldeans* and *Romans,* requiring of the one as well as of the other a quiet submission to them under whose Power they liv'd. But will any one say that these had a *Natural Superiority* and Right to Dominion?[6]

Here Astell powerfully makes the case that the seeming lesser qualities of women are only seeming, and the result of accident. The submission of women is required not because of natural inferiority, but because of actual subjugation; those who would argue that women ought to maintain their place are arguing *ad baculum,* as it were, because they are able forcibly to make the argument since they are physically the stronger. What Astell will go on to say about this "quiet submission" is part and parcel of the paradoxical tension of her position, but it derives from her respect for a Christian concept of marriage.

Bridget Hill notes that among motives for the composition of this particular part of the argument, one stands paramount: the appearance the preceding year of a sermon on the topic of female submission in marriage by one John Sprint of Dorset.[7] Sprint had attempted a logically powerful articulation of the classic line that Eve's sin demeaned all women, and that the duty of women within the confines of a Christian marriage was to try to please their husbands so as not to " . . . wickedly pervert the end of [their] Creation."[8] We might expect any "feminist" responses to straightforwardly attack such a line, but the response of women at the time was quite complex, and with good reason, since established belief did not provide a great deal of room for movement. Hill tells us that this sermon had prompted several replies, also published—one by Lady Elizabeth Chudleigh, and the other published anonymously, but titled "The Female Advocate."[9] That Mary Astell's work was intended by her as a longer and more reasoned response to Sprint seems perfectly plausible and, according to Hill, is more than likely the case; its length and the complexity of Astell's thinking may account, at least partially, for our difficulty with it.

What makes Astell's work so remarkable is that her adherence to the doctrine of the natural equality of women is intermingled, at length, with a concurrent assertion that actual domination may need to be bended to. On the one hand Astell claims the natural equality of women, yet on the other hand she remarks upon the actual *de facto* neglect of this equality. The upshot of the intermingling, as it were, of these two lines of argument is that Astell sees marriage as a place for the trial of a woman's soul, a trial that might allow a woman to enlarge upon the Christian virtues. Astell has no doubt that many women, possessed of fine souls and desiring "their ambition heavenward," as Hill has it, will be able not only to survive marriage, but also to grow from it, in a fashion in accordance with Christ's commands. She resists, however, the temptation to call for an abolition of marriage as it then stood, or even, indeed, for much less frequent marriage. Of her own marriage we know comparatively little, but given the marriages of friends and acquaintances of hers, such as the Duke and Duchess of Mazarine, we can see why Astell might be tempted to view marriage as a trial. The view that Astell develops is a sort of early Christian feminism—Christian not only because it does not deny the authority of the Church and Scripture but also because it asks for a certain sort of moral submission, and feminist because it asserts the natural equality of women. But in taking a stance that is heterodox for her time and in delineating the social conditions forcing the apparent inferiority of women, Astell demonstrated a great deal of prescience, and her views make her a seventeenth-century champion of women's rights.

II

In one of the passages cited above, Astell remarks that "The Apostle . . . says not a word of Inequality, or natural Inferiority."[10] As I have indicated, Mary Astell struggles to reconcile this assertion with the actual physical circumstances for women, particularly married women, of her time; however, in making this assertion Astell has interpreted the effect of social institutions upon female life in a manner that demonstrates a great deal of foresight, at least insofar as the eighteenth- and nineteenth-century theorists were concerned. I am most concerned here with trying to show some ways in which Astell might be thought to be a forerunner of Hume; in particular, in "Of Chastity and Modesty" (Book III of the *Treatise*) Hume develops a similar line of argument to account for the lack of parallelism in restrictions on the sexual conduct of the two sexes. While we have no knowledge of any awareness on Hume's part of Astell's work, the parallelism of what they have written is intriguing and requires investigation.

I will examine Hume's line here in some detail, as I want to provide the groundwork for a contrast with Astell. In general, Hume's concern is to try to develop an account of why it is that females are more answerable for their chastity than are males. Like Astell, he starts with the premise that the asymmetry in the relationship is not due to nature; this, of course, is the same point that Astell had made in the earlier quotation where she compared the subjection of women to that of the "Jews and Christians" under the Chaldeans and Romans, respectively. Hume states that it is "obvious" that there is a lack of "foundation in nature for all that exterior modesty [pertaining to females]."[11] He also notes that the length of human childhood forces males to participate, at least to some extent, in the rearing of offspring, but

> . . . in order to induce the men to impose on themselves this restraint, and undergo chearfully all the fatigues and expences, . . . they must believe, that the children are their own. . . .[12]

Now the difficulty is that men believe it is only female fidelity that must be carefully nurtured, as it were, in order to make this assurance, but the simple threat of public punishment for women's infidelity is not enough. When we remind ourselves of the publicly obvious involvement of the mother with the child, through pregnancy, lactation, and so forth, and the not-so-obvious involvement of the father with the child—even from the biological standpoint—we can see that the father needs some reassurance of his paternity, which he can obtain only from the promise of female fidelity. So something more is needed, and that is

> . . . the punishment of bad fame or reputation; a punishment which has a mighty influence on the human mind, and at the same time is inflicted by the world upon surmises, and conjectures, and proofs, that wou'd never be receiv'd in any court of judicature. In order, therefore, to impose a due restraint on the female sex, we must attach a peculiar degree of fame to their infidelity, above what rises merely from its injustice, and must bestow proportionable praises upon their chastity.[13]

The difficulty is, of course, that no such punishment is meted out to the philandering male. Hume goes on to remark upon the evident unfairness of this situation, but what he says—although somewhat more closely analyzed from an empirical point of view—merely recapitulates a great deal of what Astell says in *Some Reflections*. For, as she notes, women have few choices, and are not allowed the same freedoms in their marital state that would accrue to a man: "For when a Wife's Temper does not please, if she makes her Husband uneasie, he can find entertainments abroad . . . [but] tho' he makes it ever so uneasie to her she must be content and make her best on't," and as she later says, he will "make her his [slave] all the rest of his life."[14] Hume notes interestingly with regard to the options available to men:

> Thus batchelors, however debauch'd, cannot chuse but be shock'd with any instance of lewdness or impudence in women. And tho' all these maxims have a plain reference to generation, yet women past child-bearing have no more privilege in this respect, than those who are in the flower of their youth and beauty.[15]

Both Hume and Astell note that there are few options for women; both note that the opprobrium attached to the alleged or purported misconduct of women is unduly severe in comparison to any scandal attaching to the heedless conduct of males. Where Hume and Astell part company, however, is in their interest in the institution of marriage itself. Having no religious point of view, Hume has no interest in this institution except as social phenomenon, while Astell, on the other hand, wishes to make the argument that women can take advantage of their imprisonment, so to speak, to improve their morals and strengthen their capacity to exercise charity. It is here that Astell's Christian analysis collides with her feminism and leads to an interesting set of assertions about the options available to a woman confined in a shipwrecked marriage.

III

Astell's trenchant empiricism—her interest in experience as given through the senses —with regard to the institution of marriage has several interesting consequences: she not only sees marriage as possibly elevating in its moral effect on women, but she is also able to highlight in an empirically descriptive way the actual follies and foibles of women when it comes to the beliefs they bring to marriage. She does not spare women on this account, and her factual reports on the topic of female credulity, although not so severe as her chastisements of males, nevertheless go a fair way toward bringing equality to an analysis of gullibility and self-deception when it comes to the institution of marriage.

Again to some extent presaging Hume, she is able to provide an experientially correct portrait of mistaken beliefs:

> But do the Women never chuse amiss? Are the Men only in fault? that is not pretended; for he who will be just, must be forc'd to acknowledge, that neither Sex are always in the right. . . . She must be a Fool with a witness, who can believe that a Man, Proud and Vain as he is, will lay his boasted Authority, the Dignity and Prerogative of his Sex, one Moment at her Feet, but in prospect of taking it up again to more advantage; he may call himself her Slave a few days, but it is only in order to make her his all the rest of his life.[16]

In other words, the male sex has no monopoly on gullibility and self-deception when it comes to marriage; in fact, to be just to the analysis here, it is not so much that males engage in self-deception as that they attempt to deceive others. It is women, chiefly, who are gullible and who engage in self-deception—for they deceive themselves in wanting to believe that they may benefit from marriage, other than in the way of gaining strength in their pursuit of altruism. Women frequently believe in false promises that men will be their "slaves" when a close, unbiased examination of the situation reveals that it is usually the females who play serving person. Here Astell provides us with an early and astutely empirical commentary on the contemporary notion of self-deception, and does so in a way that may cause us, as women, to examine ourselves more closely.

Ultimately, Astell sees marriage as a device for the betterment of the souls of both males and females, but her experience of the world leaves her with little hope that males will, as a general rule, be able to appreciate the opportunities of the situation. She notes that a bad marriage—which she takes to be the common lot of women of her class and station in life and which, as I have noted, she had much opportunity to observe—allows the woman to gain genuine knowledge and so overcome gullibility and self-deception:

> She now distinguishes between Truth and Appearances, between solid and apparent Good; has found out the instability of all earthly Things, and won't any more be deceiv'd by relying on them. . . .[17]

Part of the knowledge that the woman will gain revolves around making a greater distinction between the temporal and the eternal, as the New Testament asks us to do; that which looks most promising, in earthly terms, is also false. But she also claims that men could use the situation of marriage to improve their morality, if only they could be persuaded to take a more humane view and admit the equality of women as persons—and if only they would listen to women: "There is not a surer Sign of a noble Mind, a Mind very far advanc'd towards perfection . . . but as he is more Wise and Good. . . . A Man therefore for his own sake, and to give evidence that he has a Right to those Prerogatives that he assumes, shou'd treat Women with a little more humanity and Regard than is usually paid them."[18] Nevertheless, the institution of marriage demands that women submit, however unjustly, to its legal and physical force—or, as Astell says, "She then who Marrys ought to lay it down for an indisputable Maxim, that her Husband must govern absolutely and intirely, and that she has nothing else to do but to Please and Obey."[19] The best insurance against the abuse of this force in either sense is a good education, particularly, as Astell claims, in "the Ways . . . of the Age."[20] In other words, our experience of life teaches us both what to expect from marriage and how to benefit from it, but Christianity demands that we be concerned about our immortal souls in relation to our lives here on earth. Unfortunately, very little in Astell's seventeenth-century experience, or in our twentieth-century experience, encourages us to think that a "Man . . . [who] for his own sake" might benefit from treating women better, actually will.

Astell closes by noting the advantages that an education and good temper can impose on a situation that, she implies, we are committed to for the foreseeable future:

To wind up this matter, if a Woman were duly Principled and Taught to know the World, especially the true Sentiments that Men have of her, and the Traps they lay for her under so many gilded Compliments, and such a seemingly great Respect, that disgrace wou'd be prevented which is brought upon too many Families, Women would marry more discreetly, and demean themselves better in a Married State than some People say they do.[21]

Astell neither hopes nor believes that marriage itself will change—what she aims at is convincing the marriageable young (and their elders) that behavior within marriage must change. Men must treat their wives more humanely, and women must go into marriage more aware of and better prepared for the various temptations and miseries that marriage has to offer.

IV

I have been arguing that the philosophy of Mary Astell presents us with a sort of pre-Humean Christian empiricist view of marriage. The tension here arises from the fact that Astell's view is clearly Christian in its reliance on the notion of Christian virtues such as charity and forgiveness, and overtly empirical in its descriptive analysis of the actual facts of married life. Her view salvages marriage as an institution at the same time that it severely chastises male behavior within the framework of that institution, because male behavior falls far short of Christian ideals. Perhaps more so than the labels "empiricist" or "feminist," the label that is most apt for Astell is "Christian," in the sense of the Christian church, for her attempt to recommend for women that they acknowledge the authority of men in the state of marriage and that they utilize some of the injustices attendant to the situation as grounds for the exercise of the virtues is a remarkably Church-centered view.

As I indicated at the outset of the paper, Hill claims that "If we are to understand [Astell], we have to accept the ambiguities and contradictions of her writing." What we find in Astell's work, I assert, is not so much ambiguity but apparent contradiction. Because of the power of Astell's assertions about Christian virtues and internal growth, we cannot fail to take her admonitions seriously; however, we are troubled by her apparent commitment to an institution that is overtly abusive of women. Since Astell's empirical criticism of the conditions that create unhappy marriages (like that of the Duchess of Mazarine) is so strong, we are led to believe that she will prescribe some other course of action (other than marrying) for the thoughtful, intelligent young woman. Yet there really was no other course of worldly action available to the young woman of the period who was not minded to enter a convent—and this Astell knew full well. Astell gives the young woman the option of internal change, education, and Christian growth. Astell's view of natural equality, institutionalized inequality, and the distribution of virtues and vices among humans—male and female—makes her a careful and keen empirical observer of the mores of her day. That Astell distinguishes between "dominion" due to "Power" on one hand and "Natural Superiority" on the other makes her a philosopher, one who argues carefully and makes clear and relevant distinctions. It also makes her, I conclude, a feminist—one who understands that insofar as sex and gender are concerned, there is no natural superiority.

Notes

1. All citations of Mary Astell's work are from *The First English Feminist: The Writings of Mary Astell*, Bridget Hill, ed. (Aldershot, UK: Gower Publishing Co., l986).
2. Ibid.
3. Ibid., p. 36.
4. This phrase refers to the unhappy marriage of the Duke and Duchess of Mazarine and is cited by Hill in her introductory commentary on p. 31.
5. Astell in Hill, op. cit., p. 72.
6. Ibid., pp. 72, 75.
7. Ibid., p. 36.
8. Ibid.
9. Ibid.
10. Ibid., p. 72.
11. David Hume, *A Treatise of Human Nature*, L. A. Selby-Bigge, ed. (Oxford: Oxford University Press, l978), p. 570. All references to Hume are from this edition.
12. Ibid.
13. Ibid., p. 571.
14. Astell, *Some Reflections*, p. 103, pp. 99–100.
15. Hume, *A Treatise*, p. 573.
16. Astell, *Some Reflections*, pp. 99–100.
17. Ibid., p. 96.
18. Ibid., p. 112.
19. Ibid. Many feminists have found these remarks troubling indeed. Astell is, of course, writing in the tradition of the Church. Nevertheless, as we have noted, she is an empiricist in her strong commitment to observation of the evidence.
20. Ibid., p. 118.
21. Ibid., p. 127.

Jo Ellen Jacobs

15   Harriet Taylor Mill's Collaboration with John Stuart Mill

It is billed as one of the great love stories of all times: Harriet Taylor (1807–1858) and John Stuart Mill remained devoted to one another for twenty years in an intimate friendship that involved joint travel, common dining, and expression of admiration and affection. It was an unexpected union. Harriet Hardy followed the usual path for nineteenth-century women when she married John Taylor at the age of eighteen and promptly had two sons, but she veered from the typical path when she fell in love with John Stuart Mill during her third pregnancy. Harriet remained married to John Taylor but lived apart from him for the two decades of her companionship with John Mill. After Taylor died, Harriet and John Stuart Mill married. Their love story is charming, but their philosophical collaboration is even more interesting because it raises questions about the way we write, the way we conceive of authorship, and the way we do philosophy.

Harriet Taylor Mill wrote a long article for the Society for the Diffusion of Useful Knowledge; the essay *The Enfranchisement of Women;* and several book reviews, poems, and articles for the *Monthly Repository.* She also collaborated with John Stuart Mill on a series of newspaper articles, a pamphlet primarily on domestic violence, the essay *On Liberty,* and a chapter in *Principles of Political Economy.* The nature of the collaboration between Harriet and John has been contested by historians of philosophy who question the coauthoring of various writings traditionally assigned to John. In exploring the nature of their work together, I will examine biographical texts, historical conditions, and philosophical evidence.

Joint thinking and writing is a mysterious waltz of questions, suggestions, and eliminations. Those who conspire to write together may contribute by critique, inspiration, or attempts to express what the other is saying. Often this is done in a quiet, unrecorded living space that leaves no trace in history other than the work written and the testimony of those involved. Those looking for manuscripts written in the handwriting of two instead of one may be looking in the wrong place.

Denying a collaboration that constitutes coauthoring, the historian of philosophy Jonathan Loesberg writes in *Fictions of Consciousness:* "Mill never claimed that Harriet had any part in the actual composition of the works, implicitly admitting the contrary when he writes that when two minds form their ideas in unison, 'it is of little consequence in respect to the question of originality, which of them holds the pen.' "[1] Clearly Loesberg equates composition with being a scribe, thus believing that John is denying coauthorship when he denies that Harriet wrote the words on the page. But this view of authorship is one Mill adamantly denies in the very passage Loesberg quotes, for John goes on to say (and is quoted in full by Loesberg as saying) that " 'the one who contributes least to the composition may contribute most to the thought.' "[2] Here John clearly states his view that, in authoring, contributing to ideas is as important as writing the ideas on paper. Yet Loesberg speaks for many contemporary historians of philosophy when he says: "The evidence shows her participation to be only of the most tangential kind, hardly amounting to anything that might be reasonably called joint authorship. . . . Her contributions were probably only in the direction of minor stylistic emendation."[3] Loesberg admits that his assumptions of what constitutes joint authorship do not reflect John's, but in doing so Loesberg blindly dismisses the view of the person who participated in the collaboration, John Stuart Mill himself.

After using collaborative writing assignments in my own classroom, and having written an article myself in collaboration with another scholar, I realized that after editing and reediting, writing and rewriting each other's words, it becomes impossible to determine who contributed what idea or even who contributed more. Beatrice and Sidney Webb, who lived a few generations after Harriet Taylor Mill and John Stuart Mill, worked and wrote together during much of their lives. Before marrying Sidney, Beatrice wrote: "We are both of us second-rate minds, but we are curiously combined. I am the investigator and he the executant; between us we have a wide and varied experience of men and affairs. We have also an unearned salary. These are unique circumstances. A considerable work should result if we use our combined talents with deliberate and persistent purpose."[4] The partnership marriage that they referred to as "the firm of Webb" was a true intellectual union. Their biographer, Mary Agnes Hamilton, says of them: "Almost impossible, nowadays, to think of Sidney and Beatrice Webb except as a couple. It is not only that they have written, together, books in which no one can detach what belongs to one from what belongs to the other. They talk, if you meet them, in the dual, almost always. . . . When they say 'we,' the listener knows, no matter who uses it, that the number is right; the thinking is, somehow—he does not know quite how—a joint process."[5] Hamilton describes their working habits:

> In any work jointly done, there is an element of mystery; and perhaps the question "How exactly do you divide it?" is one that cannot be answered: least of all when between joint workers there is a complete sympathy. But, on a normal morning, after their secretary had left them, they would, together, read the notes of interviews and visits, and the precis of documents, already made; made either by one of themselves or by the secretary. They read, and discussed them. At a certain stage, her eyes would light up. She would spring

to her feet and pace up and down, waving her cigarette. "That implies. . . ." She would then start off, on a chain of argument, he swiftly writing the while, using his matchless power of finding appropriate and exacting words for what she was sketching out in broad and vivid outline. Any idea or general view thus struck out by either was subjected to an intensive mutual testing. Then, after thoroughly thrashing it out together, they took it to be tried on others.[6]

Beatrice and Sidney worked as a team and their work was attributed to them both. It would be absurd to claim that the work was Sidney's alone because the text was in his handwriting or because he probably selected most of the final words for their thoughts. Beatrice's broad vision, her initiation of a line of argument, and her general view were the clay that Sidney refined into written text. The broad swipe requires articulation, just as the hand must write some word. That these two parts of writing might find their home not in one, but in two souls, seems obvious to those who have experienced it, yet impossible to those who have not.

Another kind of collaboration may occur in the writing of documents in business, movies, and television. On "Fresh Air," an interview show on National Public Radio, Tom Fontana, the producer and writer of the television show "Homicide," accepts praise for an episode he confidently asserts "he wrote" and describes his method for producing scripts.[7] Tom comes up with an idea for an episode. He then describes this idea to a freelance television writer who then produces the script. After "looking" at the drafts, Tom suggests revisions that the freelance writer carries out. He then takes the last draft from the freelance writer and "polishes it up." He also has to send it to the censors for changes, and he admits that he sometimes changes the script at the suggestion of the actors. Yet the credits list him as sole writer of the script. He has no hesitation claiming authorship of a work in which the bulk of the writing was someone else's.

In these cases of collaborative writing, the second is today far more common than the first, yet only in the first is there joyful acknowledgment that the final text is coauthored. The script of the television show was written collaboratively by the producer, the freelance writer, the censor, and perhaps the actors, but unlike the collaboration of Beatrice and Sidney, no one other than the producer is given credit. While the enjoyment that collaboration can bring to the participants is enthusiastically depicted by the Webbs' biographer, the collaboration of Fontana and others is acknowledged only in his telling of the process, as he alone takes credit or receives awards for the final product.

Like Beatrice and Sidney, Harriet and John were equally honest in confessing their joint acts of writing, but they have not been so lucky in finding biographers who believe them. If we look at the evidence for their collaboration and what they say it meant to them, we may gain insight into the way many texts may have been produced. We may also find a way of thinking philosophically that serves as an alternative to the "lonely genius in the garret" way.

Without substantial evidence to the contrary, it seems reasonable to believe that work is collaborative if the participants say it is so. While we might understand why Fontana would want to claim single authorship when the process is actually cooperative, it is hard to imagine why someone like John Stuart Mill would want to claim collaboration existed when it did not. Critics and biographers have answered that John was "besotted," "bewitched," or "charmed" by Harriet. Often they have seen John as a naive goof so innocent of women that he is overwhelmed by the first one to cross his path. Alexander Bain, for example, writes that John was subject to an *"extraordinary hallucination* as to the personal qualities of his wife."[8] Yet such biographers offer no evidence that John was bullied into claiming he and Harriet collaborated when they did not. Instead those biographers are imposing their own definition and evaluation of collaboration on Harriet and John's.

There is much biographical and textual evidence for collaborative writing and coauthorship in the intimate letters of Harriet and John, as well as in Harriet's letters to John Taylor and Eliza Flower. Unfortunately, Harriet destroyed most of her letters just prior to her death; hence, we have more evidence of their collaboration in John's voice than in Harriet's. It is clear, however, that John asks for advice and thanks Harriet for editing, writing, and discussing, as well as for contributing ideas.[9]

Since the two were together when *Principles of Political Economy* was written, we do not have letters about its initial writing; however, some of their working habits shine through in the letters about its revision. John writes: "This is probably only the progress we have been always making, & by thinking sufficiently I should probably come to think the same—as is almost always the case, I believe *always* when we think long enough. But here the being unable to discuss verbally stands sadly in the way, & I am now almost convinced that as you said at first, we cannot settle this 2d edit. by letter" (February 19, 1849). Like Sidney Webb without Beatrice, John Stuart Mill clearly feels fettered by their inability to talk about the revisions. "I despatched yesterday to the dear one an attempt at a revision of the objectionable passages" (February 21, 1849). Harriet suggests revisions that John often accepts. "I feel that I never should long continue of an opinion different from yours on a subject which you have fully considered. I am going on revising the book: not altering much, but . . . I have added two or three pages of new explanation & illustration which I think make the case much clearer" (February 21, 1849).

Concerning the type and format, John Stuart Mill writes: "You know what difficulty *we* had before" (emphasis added). Harriet helps make the practical and aesthetic decisions about the appearance of the book as well as the content. John says: "The bargain with Parker is a good one & that it is so is entirely your doing—all the difference between it & the last being wholly your work, as well as all the best of the book itself so that you have a redoubled title to your joint ownership of it" (March 17?, 1849). Concerning a point of contention between them on an idea, John writes: "But we shall have all these questions out together & they will all require to be entered into to a certain depth, at least in the new book which I am so glad you look forward to as I do with so much interest" (March 21, 1849). The text does not always reflect Harriet's suggestions, as he says, for example: "I think I agree in all your remarks & have adopted them almost all—but I do not see the possibility of bringing in the first two pages [from the preceding chapter]—I see no place which they would fit" (March 14, 1854). Some revisions can be done simply by John, but meatier matters require the contribution of both. "One page I keep for consideration when I can shew it to you. It is about the qualities of English workpeople, & of the english [*sic*] generally. It is not at all as I would write it now, but I do not in reality know how to write it" (February 19, 1857). These letters were to her, not to the public; they are genuine evidence for a thoroughgoing collaboration and do not support the statements of biographers like Loesberg. To Harriet and John, composition consisted in dialogue, in lively debates that preceded and intermingled with the writing of words on a page. To ignore such interplay or to claim that it is not philosophical and worthy of the title of coauthorship is to subscribe to a view of philosophizing that Harriet and John rejected.

Harriet is quite open about her intellectual involvement with John when she writes to her first husband, John Taylor. For twenty years John Taylor received reports about Harriet's work on manuscripts with John Mill and sometimes was asked by her to send some of her manuscripts along to her.[10] The openness of their letters displays an amazing amount of good sense in what must have been an awkward situation, as John financially supported Harriet while she traveled, dined, and worked with John Mill yet remained married to John Taylor. About the initial work on *Principles of Political Economy,* Harriet writes to John Taylor: "I do certainly look more like a ghost [than] a living person, but I dare say I shall soon recover some better looks when we get to Brighton. I think I shall not be able to go before the end of next week being just now much occupied with the book" (late 1847).[11] "I am so taken up with the Book which is near the last & has constantly something to be seen to about binding &c that I could not leave town before the beginning of April if even then" (March 1848).[12] "The book on The Principles of Political Economy which has been the work of all this winter is now nearly ready and will be published in ten days" (March 31, 1848).[13] Even as early as 1840 she directs her husband to send manuscripts that she left in London because "I am very busy writing for the printers & want to get some scraps out of that."[14] The depth of her involvement in writing with John Mill is quite clear in these letters to John Taylor.

The only acknowledged period of "bad humor" on John Taylor's part occurs in reference to an attempt by John Mill to include a dedication to Harriet at the beginning of *The Principles of Political Economy.* John Taylor wrote that the "dedication will revive recollections now forgotten & will create observations and talk that cannot but be extremely unpleasant to me" (April 3, 1848).[15] In another letter Harriet suggests an alternative practical reason for not fighting to have her name listed as coauthor or even have the book dedicated to her except in copies given to friends: "My reason being that opinions carry more weight with the authority of his name alone" (May 12, 1848).[16] Harriet was not unaware of the differences in how a text might be received if the title page read "by John Stuart Mill" as opposed to "by John Stuart Mill and Harriet Taylor." To keep peace with John Taylor and to assure that the work would receive a fair hearing, Harriet refused to allow John to proceed with the dedication of the book on which she had worked so hard and to which she had contributed a chapter.

She did not fail to recognize her own contribution in private, however. Harriet sent a copy of the book to the daughter of William Fox, the Unitarian minister who may have introduced Harriet to John Mill. William Fox himself apparently replied with praise for the book, for Harriet wrote in response to him: "I am glad you like the book. It is, I think, full of good things—but I did not suppose you were interested in the subjects which most interest me in it, and I sent it to Miss Fox because when I knew her in her early youth she appeared to interest herself strongly in the cause to which *for many years of my life & exertions I have been devoted, justice for women*" (May 10, 1848).[17] This private letter communicates her commitment to women's causes and suggests a philosophical reason for her collaborative method of writing. I believe that Harriet may have seen collaborative writing as a revolutionary act, as a way of creating philosophical texts that rejected the "single author" pattern which had become the publicly acceptable way of writing philosophy.

Letters also reveal that at this time John was experimenting with collaboration with others besides Harriet, but he never achieved collaboration so well with anyone else besides her. In 1831, he describes a joint project with George Graham, a friend of his, but this work was never completed. Still, John's careful description of their division of work and the assumption of collaborative writing are important bits of evidence about how he and Harriet might have collaborated.[18] In his handwritten bibliography, John also notes other forms of collaboration in his writing.[19] He notes in the *Autobiography* two further instances: first, Alexander Bain's improvement of John's *System of Logic* and a "great number of additional examples and illustrations from science; many of which, as well as some detached remarks of his own in confirmation of my logical views, I inserted nearly in [Bain's] own words."[20] Second, John attests to contributions to the *Subjection of Women* made by Helen, Harriet's daughter, whom he sees as his own daughter as well: "As ultimately published it was enriched with some important ideas of my daughter's, and passages of her writing."[21] These are all the words of a man careful to give credit where it was due, not a henpecked husband or "besotted" lover only trying to appease a pretentious lover or wife, as he is so often portrayed. He both takes credit and gives it when authorship is joint.

Harriet too may have been in the habit of collaborating, but unfortunately with men less scrupulous than John was about acknowledging the mutuality of their work. F. A. Hayek says of some feminist articles by William J. Fox and William B. Adams included in *The Monthly Repository:* "Their arguments often so closely resemble some of Mrs. Taylor's manuscript drafts of the period that one wonders whether it was merely that she imbibed her ideas from them or whether her somewhat unpolished drafts did not perhaps serve as the basis for the articles of the more skilled writers."[22] It certainly would not be the first time well-known writers used the work of lesser-known writers as a hidden source.

In John's *Autobiography,* he claims at the start that his motive for writing is "a desire to make acknowledgement of the debts which my intellectual and moral development owes to other persons; some of them of recognized eminence, others less known than they deserve to be, and the one to whom most of all is due, one whom the world had no opportunity of knowing."[23] Here and elsewhere there is no doubt he is referring to Harriet. He says repeatedly that Harriet collaborated in much of his work, from *The Principle of Political Economy* until *On Liberty*. Listen to these passages:

> It was at the period of my mental progress which I have now reached that I formed the friendship which has been the honour and chief blessing of my existence, as well as *the source of a great part of all that I have attempted to do,* or hope to effect hereafter, for human improvement.... I have often received praise, which in my own right I only partially deserve, for the greater practicality which is supposed to be found in my writings, compared with those of most thinkers who have been equally addicted to large generalizations. *The writings in which this quality has been observed, were not the work of one mind, but of the fusion of two,* one of them as preeminently practical in its judgments and perceptions of things present, as it was high and bold in its anticipations for a remote futurity.[24]

Thus John does not thank Harriet Taylor Mill vaguely for moral support or merely for her inspiration. He specifically thanks her for her contribution to the ideas and the writing published in his name alone but actually the result of "the fusion of two" minds working together.

He describes her contributions to individual texts such as *Principles of Political Economy*. "Up to this time I have spoken of my writings and opinions in the first person singular because the writings, though (after we became intimate) mostly revised by her, and freed by her judgment from much that was faulty, as well as enriched by her suggestions, were not, like the subsequent ones, largely and in their most important features the direct product of her own mind."[25] He distinguishes the revisions and expansions of earlier collaborations from the direct contribution of her ideas in texts from the *Principles of Political Economy* to *On Liberty*. He honestly uses the plural "we" and "us" and "our" in referring to the *Principles of Political Economy*: "We were now much less democrats than I had been, because so long as education continues to be so wretchedly imperfect, we dreaded the ignorance and especially the selfishness and brutality of the mass: but our ideal of ultimate improvement went far beyond Democracy, and would class us decidedly under the general designation of Socialists."[26]

Harriet's contribution is most evident in *On Liberty*, according to John. He writes:

> The *Liberty* was more directly and literally our joint production than anything else which bears my name, for there was not a sentence of it that was not several times gone through by us together, turned over in many ways, and carefully weeded of any faults, either in thought or expression, that we detected in it. It is in consequence of this that . . . it far surpasses, as a mere specimen of composition, anything which has proceeded from me either before or since. With regard to the thoughts, it is difficult to identify any particular part or element as being more hers than all the rest. The whole mode of thinking, of which the book was the expression, was emphatically hers.[27]

After Harriet's death, in his dedication of *On Liberty* to her, John recognizes her importance even further:

> To the beloved and deplored memory of her who was the inspirer, and in part the author, of all that is best in my writings. . . . Like all that I have written for many years, it belongs as much to her as to me; but the work as it stands has had, in a very insufficient degree, the inestimable advantage of her revision; some of the most important portions having been reserved for a more careful re-examination, which they are now never destined to receive. . . .[28]

This dedication was John's first public proclamation of her contribution to their work. But, like many of his statements about his collaboration, it was brushed aside by historians of philosophy as if it were only sentimental oozing, devoid of fact.

There is furthermore historical and empirical evidence for the collaboration of Harriet and John, for Harriet actually did pen some of their joint efforts. Some of their newspaper articles were in Harriet's handwriting and were only signed by John before submission.[29] John lived by his handwriting, as he had the clear handwriting of a scribe, whereas Harriet did not. While John consequently wrote most of their joint projects, Harriet's handwriting of the articles constitutes minor evidence of their collaboration. In discussions of their collaboration in which "penning" is equated with "authoring," the fact that much of what they composed together is written in his handwriting is taken as evidence that he was the primary or only author. So I now point out that at least some of their joint work is in Harriet's hand.

A more interesting historical point concerns anonymous writing and the common use of pseudonyms during this period. George Eliot, George Sand, and Currer Bell were the pen names of just a few of the women who chose to write some of their works under the cover of an alias. These women writers knew that a more objective reading of their works was possible if the sex of the writer was either thought to be male or was at least ambiguous. Magazine articles were typically anonymous or written with obvious *noms de plume*. John wrote anonymously in the Edinburgh Review[30] and used the name "Antiquus" in his *Monthly Repository* articles,[31] using the initials "A" and "S" in his *London Review* articles.[32] Most of John's magazine articles are unsigned or signed by a pseudonym. MacMinn notes the following: "Mill used at least twenty pen names, particularly between 1822 and 1858."[33] He stopped using pseudonyms in the year Harriet died. It is plausible to conclude that John had been using them to conceal Harriet's contributions but no longer needed them after her death. Thus the anonymity in magazine writing and newspaper columns during the nineteenth century allowed women such as Harriet to write without detection. The benefit was that they could be published and their voices could be heard, but the cost was that their voices were not gendered and the history of their contributions was obscured. Although Harriet and John probably took advantage of Victorian publishing practice to conceal their individual and collaborative authorship, John nevertheless revealed it in the handwritten bibliography that he created for his own use and left for future scholars.

There is, in conclusion, some philosophical evidence for John and Harriet's collaboration. Early in their relationship (1832–1833), Harriet recognized that the institution of the family and marriage could be a central roadblock to the development of a progressive society. As a patriarchal institution, marriage, "a legal obligation which binds any person to live with, or be dependant on, another, against their inclination—which makes the person of one human being the property of another,"[34] could prevent the development of half of the human species, thus confounding the development of all of humankind. Harriet saw the reduction of marriage to such an institution along with the spread of capitalism as a threat to all. In the chapter she contributed to *The Principles of Political Economy,* she wrote that "something better should be aimed at as the goal of industrial improvement, than to disperse mankind over the earth in single families, each ruled internally, as families now are, by a patriarchal despot, and having scarcely any community of interest, or necessary mental communion, with other human beings."[35] The connection between the patriarchal structure of the family and the capitalist economic system is not lost on Harriet. Alteration of the institution of marriage and family life was, as feminists in the 1960s would again point out, critical to changing society from the ground up. By living outside a traditional marriage for twenty years and working collaboratively, Harriet and John experimented with a new family structure based on liberty and equality.

In *On Liberty* they finally generalize a nugget of thought written in an early unpublished essay by Harriet: "Every human being has a right to all *personal* freedom which does not interfere with the happiness of some other."[36] Only if women had the right to marry or not as they saw fit, and only if they could get an education that would allow them economic independence, would things in society change for the better. In *On Liberty* the call is to extend to every individual of whatever gender or class the liberty to think, express, and live her or his ideas as far as possible as long as her or his acts did not harm another. The only way to gain the truth is by the vigorous debate of opponents who believe very different points of view, since none of us is infallible.[37] Harriet and John would make critical thinking and discussion, instead of the memorization of classics, the heart of education. "There is always hope when people are forced to listen to both sides" of a debate.[38] The discussion and tension at the center of their collaboration, as shown in the letters quoted above, is living proof of what can result when there is freedom to disagree.

In *On Liberty* they announce that it will do little good to be able to think our own thoughts if we are not allowed to act on them. So Harriet and John advocate "experiments in living." Unless we choose how to live our own lives, we will remain stunted. It is easier and to some extent safer for a person to follow the paths set out by custom, but "what will be his comparative worth as a human being? It really is of importance, not only what men do, but also what manner of men they are that do it."[39] What is the worth of a woman who has no choice in how to live? What is the worth of a worker who has no choice in how to work? Choice is critical to developing our human potential, and liberty is required for choice. This liberty is not an egotistical self-development but rather it adds to the development of us all. "In proportion to the development of his individuality, each person becomes more valuable to himself, and is, therefore, capable of being more valuable to others."[40] No legal alteration can finally advance society to its next great leap forward. Now we need the freedom to develop strength as individuals, the liberty to choose how to live, and the independence to try new family and marriage structures that will revolutionize how children are raised and educated. This bold expansive project of Harriet and John's begins with the development of men and women who can alter the way power is shared in families and then spread the results of these experiments to institutions of education and the economy. Sharing in the writing of their ideas was their way of expanding liberty for themselves, "their" daughter, and all who would listen to their plea that they worked *together.*

The collaborative aspect of their writing is consistent with the socialism and feminism that they tried to live. They did not believe that philosophy, particularly in its political and ethical stands, was meant only for the classroom or the debate club. Rather, they both believed that the two most important issues of the age were "emancipation of women and cooperative production."[41] Writing collaboratively about women's issues was a perfect carrying out and living of their commitment to both of these issues, for they felt that no one person owns a text. The point of their writing, both in what they said and in their collaborative manner of saying it, was to demonstrate the equality of men and women. Harriet and John may have worked as they did as an act of revolution against the practice of philosophy as an individual pursuit, against the silencing of women, and against the capitalist defining of "intellectual property." Their work can serve as an example of cooperative production in the service of women's equality. It can also suggest a model of philosophizing different from the one in which a wise teacher infects a student with the truth: it implies that philosophy is "plural work," to use Michèle Le Doeuff's phrase.[42] Harriet and John's greatest contribution to philosophy may not be so much in what they said but more in their method of producing philosophical texts.

Thus it is evident that Harriet Taylor Mill and John Stuart Mill worked together extensively and regularly beginning at least with *The Principles of Political Economy* and continuing through *On Liberty.* Authorship is a fluid concept that has changed over time and is best defined by the participants involved in the work. Collaboration is the work of thinking, providing examples, expanding kernels of thought, revising, drafting, deciding about fonts and headings and publishing details—most of the elements of what most call writing—all as done together. Given the amount of supporting evidence for John's assertion of coauthorship, especially in light of a thoughtful examination of how collaborative writing can occur as I have indicated above, there is good evidence to accept his judgment. Furthermore, the appropriate criterion for coauthorship should be the one he and Harriet accepted and applied to their work together, and that criterion must be seen in light of the practice of anonymous and pseudonymous writing during this historical period. Harriet and John used a fluidity of authorship to express their philosophical partnership in which talking, exploring ideas, expounding on the other's ideas, initiating a train of thought, suggesting an example, and demanding clarification all played a part. Their practice of coauthorship welded their means of writing to their end of living a life that recognized socialism and the equality of women as the most important issues of their time.

Notes

1. Jonathan Loesberg, *Fictions of Consciousness: Mill, Newman, and the Reading of Victorian Prose* (New Brunswick: Rutgers University Press, 1986), p. 48.

2. Ibid.

3. Ibid., pp. 48–9.

4. Mary Agnes Hamilton, *Sidney and Beatrice Webb: A Study in Contemporary Biography* (London: Sampson Low, Marston & Co. Ltd., n.d. [1932?]), p. 67.

5. Ibid., p. 1.

6. Ibid., p. 75.

7. "Fresh Air," National Public Radio, March 9, 1993.

8. Alexander Bain, *John Stuart Mill: A Criticism with Personal Recollections* (London: Longmans, Green & Company, 1882), p. 171, emphasis added.

9. Appendix G of Volume 3 of the *Collected Works of John Stuart Mill: Principles of Political Economy* (hereafter *CW*) contains all of John's letters to Harriet about the revisions of that work. It is a good source for understanding their working habits on at least the revisions for this work. Letters cited can be found in that appendix, according to dates.

10. Some of the evidence offered about Harriet's letters is also contained in my article, "'The Lot of Gifted Ladies is Hard': A Study of Harriet Taylor Mill Criticism," in *Hypatia* 9:3 (1994), pp. 154–5.

11. Harriet Taylor Mill, *The Complete Works of Harriet Taylor Mill*, Jo Ellen Jacobs and Paula H. Payne, eds. (Bloomington: Indiana University Press, 1998), p. 471. Hereinafter this collection will be referred to as Jacobs.

12. Jacobs, pp. 473–4.

13. Jacobs, p. 472.

14. Jacobs, p. 451.

15. Jacobs, p. 472.

16. Jacobs, p. 392.

17. Jacobs, p. 390, emphasis added.

18. See *CW* XII, p. 43.

19. Ney MacMinn, J. R. Hainds, and James McNab McCrimmon, eds., *Bibliography of the Published Writings of John Start Mill* (Evanston, Ill.: Northwestern University Press, 1945).

20. *CW* I, p. 255.

21. *CW* I, p. 265.

22. F. A. Hayek, *John Stuart Mill and Harriet Taylor: Their Friendship and Subsequent Marriage* (Chicago: University of Chicago Press, 1951), pp. 28–9.

23. *CW* I, p. 5.

24. *CW* I, pp. 193, 198–9, emphasis added.

25. *CW* I, early draft, p. 234.

26. Ibid.

27. *CW* I, p. 259.

28. *CW* XVIII, p. 216.

29. Ann Robson in *CW* XXII, p. xci, ftn. 142.

30. See *CW* I, p. 292.

31. See *CW* I, pp. 328, 368.

32. See *CW* I, pp. 396, 432.

33. MacMinn, Hainds, and McNab McCrimmon, *Bibliography of the Published Writings of John Start Mill*, p. ix.

34. Jacobs, p. 19.

35. *CW* III, p. 768.

36. Jacobs, p. 19.

37. John Stuart Mill, *On Liberty* (New York: Penguin Books, 1982), chap. 2.

38. Ibid., p. 115.

39. Ibid., p. 123.

40. Ibid., p. 127.

41. Letter to Parke Godwin in *CW* XVII, p. 1535 (January 1, 1869).

42. Michèle Le Doeuff, "Women and Philosophy" in *French Feminist Thought*, Toril Moi, ed. (Oxford: Basil Blackwell, 1987), p. 208. For an extended discussion of the connection between Le Doeuff's ideas of philosophy and Harriet and John's work, see my article " 'The Lot of Gifted Ladies is Hard': A Study of Harriet Taylor Mill Criticism" in *Hypatia* 9:3 (1994), pp. 154, 158–9.

Veda A. Cobb-Stevens

---

16 Poems from *Fifty Forms for Fifty Philosophies*

Veda A. Cobb-Stevens is a philosophical friend to each person involved with this book, for she is the one who first envisioned the book for us. She founded the Society for the Study of Women Philosophers and invited us to speak before one another. She challenged us to discover philosophical insight in unconventional forms, such as novels, poems, and letters. Ironically, she herself held back the publication of her own poetry under her name while she was alive. She died before she was able to put such impassioned expression into the world as her own. We editors find it fitting now to present some of her poems here, as sketches of several philosophical attitudes. She knew forms and shapes of philosophy in both spiritual and tactile ways, and she loved them. I remember her being a passionate servant to them. In the following selection she bears the weight of each, one at a time. She is clearing the field of philosophy and dividing it in a new way. As she writes in her poem "The Mason" (which will be given in full below):

> I gave my hands acquaintance with the shapes
> that I found. I would chose no others.
>
> I lift each stone for my sisters and brothers.

Your Gestures

You do not have to explain your gestures to me:
they are music, they hold me in a stillness
the way melody does as it moves through time.

I move through time, but in the loving surround
of your gestures, I seem to rest and am
content. No, you do not have to explain.

There are some things which find expression
naturally, the way moods are manifest
through the sway of trees: how they brood,
their tender sadness, or in a high wind,
their unmatched exhilaration. You need not

explain. As your hand reaches out,
the world is composed, memories make order
and my life takes on the elements of peace.

Lines on Paper

I wanted to draw Anselm secluded in his room
with an angel or two hovering nearby, unseen.
He was quite clear in my mind, the *credo ut intellegam*
knitting his brows, his heart wild with a placid fervor.

How many times had he tried to find that one proof,
he who already believed, who in a sense did not need
further demonstration, possessed as he was of God's pulse
to regulate his days?

Credo ut intellegam.
This phrase continues to sound underneath the logic,
credo into crescendo as the conclusion is drawn.

My only God, how could one put such lines on paper?

Is it possible, with a mere pen, to render symphonics?
Visual forms, aching with absence, hunger for a higher life.

And Beethoven knew: at a certain point even the sounds go deaf.

The Architect

I follow the arduous circuit of my thoughts
until I reach an exemplar, a perfect form
that can constitute a template which I can use
over and over, repeating the original figure
in many dimensions, constructing innumerable patterns
from combinations of this single excellent shape.

One mode of variation is to be attained
through the materials: the rough-hewn feel
of granite (even highly polished), the lichen-like
weathering of unpainted steel with the rich rusts
forming in brown, orange-gold, burnt siena
and umber, covering the structure in italic crusts,
baroque annotations on the underlying simplicity
of cast. These arrangements I make to last.

The Sceptic

I believe in nothing, affirm everything
at once, lavish the world's ridges
with randomness.

        All in all
I may discern thoroughly faint cycles,
imprints in the chaos, shadowy evidence
of eternities of repetition, of roses left
to must and dark, only to green again,
their stems and leaves become slow exaggerations
into some spring air.

          But I believe in nothing.

I see everything fail and turn twice again
into rot. I see the same thing always:
how nothing matters, how lives come to death,
how history flows back from desire to ash
and vexatious waste is the mind's only balm.

The Physicist

Searching through reality's inventory, I am overcome
by palindromes, opposites becoming each other
in a kaleidoscopic jugglery.

When I make inquiry
into particle or wave, I sense the intercalations
of interim forms of energy, in whose mutual interferences
are found worlds working out: hot interiors become extrusions,
surface crusts folded in, forming hinterlands in recession
ready made for some new age adventurer.

No immoderation
in these magnitudes. Force and counterforce, the intention
of a dance—could we but discern its connotations.

At times, I feel in the shifting junctures a certain
warning, amounting almost to an interdiction: leave us
alone. It is we who are observing you, quickened observer,
as you peer into your formula, on you we make regardless impress.

The Mason

Slaves built those walls, my mother would say,
pointing to the long low structures stretching out
through field after field, each stone fitted
to the other, no mortar. Those strong walls
were raised under duress, made monuments
to nameless hundreds who hauled rocks down
in carts or wagons, at times in bare hands.

Things have changed. I chose my job,
and went to school for it, well, in a way.

I learned my trade from those already skilled,
walking the rich fields by day and by night.
I gave my hands acquaintance with the shapes
that I found. I would choose no others.

I lift each stone for my sisters and brothers.

The Mathematician

I have spent ignorant hours, lamenting concepts
that I have lost, sensing the world somewhere
outside perception's reach. I have let it go,
the world, in the hope of something new,
an idea never glimpsed before or some stance
to assume in the face of those too familiar.

What if, what if . . . The effort exhausts me,
squeezing blood from my brain, nothing
to soak up now but the pallor, which circles
all around.

Have I been wrong, perhaps,
all these long years to concentrate so
on presumptive objects no one has ever seen,
not even I, making accurate calculations
of quantities far transcending my own mind?

The Solipsist

Were I not alone, I might turn my hand
to accomplishment, thus hoping to extend
certain lucky finds into something more
durable. I would make amends with all
whom I have offended, become reconciled
to brevity and to the vacuities of want.
I would take up all my tasks with the certain
easeful demeanor of blessedness. Were I not
alone, I could seek into the mysteries,
putting down the urgent question marks
into all hours. As it is, my interrogations
reach no one. My voice resounds in emptiness.

But, oh, it does resound.

A comfort, perhaps?

Echoes return in circles from lack to nothingness.

Realists

It is a daily sacrifice, the unblinking consent
to the world's presentations, taken as plain truth.

We are not glad of such clinical perceptions.

It is how we were born: we are capable of no
make believe, are as suspicious of imagination
as a doctor is of microbes. Conventional solaces,
salvific hopes, comfortable moments of blindness
are not ours, though we are often nostalgic
for dreams we have never had.

                Others occasionally
approach us, gesticulating, in front of our composure,
and we note carefully the various purples and reds
on their livid faces.

            We avert our eyes from nothing,
not from human flesh nor from our inherent inability
to join hands.

          Our own sadness is carefully noted down.

God is Love as an Emerald is Green

I am a stranger here and yet a friend.
I am acquainted with everything, own nothing,
love whatever I am privileged to see. Love.

Yes. The good and the bad. All together
making one life. I am a part of this world
and yet not of it. My destiny is here
in bones, in blood, and in future ash.

My end is elsewhere. I do not know where.

I simply trust the conjugations: subject,
verb, object, all linked together, or perhaps
fused into one, so there is no distinction
between one pole and another, nor between
the poles and what holds them, tenderly, together.

Somewhere, that clear green light glows and waits.

Eve's Ribs: Paradise Regained

The sanctified relief of daybreak where the sky is grey-white:
    a single bird has begun restorations of all that night had
    revoked.

On the bare table are relics, unsparing residua that prompt
        renewed commitments, recollections of old rebellions,
        now reconciled, made into foundations for the future.

These bones can never be worn down into mere symbols.
Their material character is known as the hand passes over
        them,
            their curvature constant, composing space from its wrested
            tangents.

Sister, mother: I can feel your urges still there in the marrow,
        that essence of desire, transmuted into a fine powder.
This morning, looking into the world's mirror, I brush it lightly
        over my face to give my cheeks color. It makes me ready
        to enter life with just the right restrictions, to seek
        accomplishment
            as one with you and with that other, bone with bone:
            father, brother.

In the Midst of It

What would it mean to be a survivor?
No one survives. The concept is inconceivable.
But destruction is not more intelligible,
not a whit. So where does that leave us?

Where we've always been: in the midst of it—
life, death waiting, certain spontaneous smiles
when eyes have met in implicit understanding,
spring snowmelts, the water rushing quickly
like excited breath, the daffodils again,
the red tulips and, later, their withered stems.

We continue into the density of it, happy
for the most part, mysteriously so, knowing
all along that it shall end, not knowing
why it must or what, afterwards, awaits us.

Cecile T. Tougas

17 Philosophical Friendship, 1996: A Postscript

In closing this section and pondering the examples of philosophical friendship that it provides, I ask myself, is it easy nowadays for a woman philosopher to be friends with a man philosopher? Reflecting on two of my own attempts at philosophical friendship (the ones I describe in my essay, "Why I Have Worked on This Book for Several Years," at the end of this book), I have to answer that I do not find it easy to be myself and at the same time to expect that a man philosopher will be glad to take me seriously as both a woman and a philosopher.

A Japanese philosopher who had sent me an essay of his that I found to be terribly upsetting was offended when I told him kindly yet frankly of my feelings about his essay. He wrote me a bitter postcard that I will refer to later (at the end of the book). I then sent him a five-page letter to clarify and substantiate what I had meant, expecting he would still respect me as I continued to respect him. Several weeks later, however, he phoned me while he was in North America—to say goodbye. He did not wish to hear me or to continue the friendship when I disagreed with him.

An American colleague whom I had known and worked with for several years had also sent me an essay. In it he had written that the actual reality of community is located in "polyvalent semiotic networks." But in this essay on community no one was present—not even himself. His writing was eerily distant from his living experience and his actual situation. It also ignored the very difficulties we have in being friends. I responded to him honestly, gently, and truly; I had never criticized his work before. In my letter I suggested that he bring personal presence into his metaphysical talk on human community. But he misunderstood my suggestion and in writing back only defended his work.

This philosopher trivialized my critical pleading that he be himself in his philosophizing. At the same time, in his letter he failed to address me as a philosopher equal to him, as a metaphysician in whose company he was as he was writing. In effect, he was not himself before professional philosophers, and insofar as I knew him personally, I was not a philosopher to him. Accordingly, he did not think that philosophizing could occur in personal letter-writing—despite the fact that I had just sent him a copy of my introduction to this very section on philosophical friendship. He did not mention that Heloise and Elisabeth had philosophized intently in their letters. He did not take them seriously into account nor esteem their writing as genuine philosophy, despite all I had written about them. He believed that only his impersonal style of writing was the proper way to speak in the company of metaphysicians. The only alternative he mentioned was a style used to address teenagers.

He thus left me wondering what I might do to help this man to be my philosophical friend. I sighed, summoned my courage, and decided to write him again, honestly, clearly, and passionately. I reread his essay and his letters, took notes, and marked what pained me most. I took out my fountain pen and my finest plain paper, and I wrote:

Dear _____ ,

I have been rereading your address to the _____ Society and want to talk about it with you through this letter. In doing this I will show that philosophizing can occur well in letter-writing because it is occurring now in this one. Act proves potency.

My style is not one used to address teenagers. You will see that it is rather a style expressing respect and rigor. Yet it is also personal, for it is from me to you, in response to what you have sent me.

If it were not possible to philosophize in a personal letter, then several women philosophers (who are studied in our women's book) would be excluded from philosophical recognition, just as they were excluded from public intellectual life. But many of us are finding genuine philosophy in letters of these women.

Accepting that philosophical discussion can and does occur in a letter involves accepting a new mode of expression that is different from old ones. This mode, as I see it, is both personal and abstract, both rooted in present living experience and working in strict logical distinctions.

What I and women philosophers I know through this book give is not "a better abstraction" or "a more correct metaphysical system," but rather erotic relation, a feeling sense that demands that abstract concepts be connected to the fullness of the experience founding them. We women know that we must always feel what we say as we are saying it. We must be undergoing and watching what our words mean. As we make distinctions, we cannot pretend we are making ourselves separate. As Victor Hugo writes in *Les Misérables*: "*Il faut que l'idéal soit respirable, potable et mangeable à l'esprit humain*" (ed. Yves Gohin; Gallimard, 1995; p. 665 of the first volume) "The ideal must be breathable, drinkable, and eatable by the human spirit." The ideal must be intimate, closely felt, and mixed with the ordinary necessities of life.

Systematic metaphysics depends on small, individual actions. The continuity it is supposed to provide—bridging natural and human environments, as you say in your essay—is already there from the beginning. The "semiotic richness" and growth of learning in felt intelligence that philosophy is said to enhance depends on a continuum of feeling and enduring that is not expressed in words. As Husserl remarks (I cannot remember where), so much of the meaning we intend never comes to fulfillment in perception or intuitive givenness. Our experience is temporal and finds itself inadequate and incomplete at any given moment. Still less of the meaning we intend comes to expression in words and symbols. Even bodily expressions fail to "say it all." I know this is so—it is evident to me this moment as I write to you. I am intent on so much that has import, and it is such a great abundance that I cannot find words adequate to tell it. So I suggest, I say something on a small scale, I understate, I speak imperfectly. In this, however, I know that "the semiotic networks" that you speak of depend on the inexpressible that we live, feel, breathe, drink, and eat every day. The ideal transcends semiotics and largely is beyond words. The attitude Hugo suggests towards it, then, is prayer and reverie. The preverbal is felt and it is our ground. We live it in small, individual ways each day. Our feeling together, before we have abstractions, is the original continuity that founds what we do, interpret, and say. Metaphysics cannot create what is already there, but rather should recognize it and give it credit.

The absence of an awareness of pain grieved me when I first read your paper. I imagined members of the _____ Society in suits, listening. They don't want to hear about pain; they are all dressed up nicely and have titles, degrees, professional positions. But as you and I—who have suffered divorces, painful love affairs, and horrible working conditions at _____ —as we know well, human community occurs "more often in the breach than in the observance" (as Shakespeare writes somewhere). When you speak about community in an abstract way as semiotic structure, as a "context of signs" providing the conditions for "healthy growth or sick decay" (p. 11), you're not showing you remember how bad it hurt when we tried to make a community when we married the people we married and when we worked the jobs we worked. Community is so wretchedly difficult to live. Yet we are inseparably with people. Oh, all the failures, the hurt caused to others, besides what we personally suffered! No wonder the Society people don't want to hear about the truth: we fail in human community. Can our systems of thought make amends? No, we need to seek forgiveness and a new way of life.

Not having your personal presence in your paper disturbs me greatly, especially since your address received applause. But the truth is not in what receives applause so much as it is in what suffers. Today I was reminded of what life was like when my first marriage failed. Our two-year-old son used to wake up in the night, crying and gnashing his teeth. The pain was terrible and he knew it without words, without "semiotic networks"—he knew it in his sleep. No words were sufficient in this breach of continuity to make things better. Our whole feeling as parents and our wills needed to change. We should have been open to prayer and reverie. They alone could have made communication possible: *feelings* of sorrow and grief.

Near the end of your essay you challenge Rorty's call to us to "read the novels of writers like Dickens and Kundera" so we can "revive for ourselves the sense of pain and loss experienced by others" (p. 15). For you say it is not enough just to read novels; we must also make "concrete positive prescription" for establishing community. Rorty's vision "lacks a systematic metaphysical and semiotic ground," you say on page 16.

But the ground already exists; we need to recognize the feelings that unite us immediately. As Victor Hugo writes, we are *metaphysically one* already—we all belong to God. It is forgiveness—it is love—that saves us, not a metaphysical system. What changes the whole life of the person is neither a prescription nor a systematic metaphysics, but rather—crying.

If reading a novel helps us revive the pain and loss we have experienced inadequately—

that we have denied and hardened ourselves against—then it may build community better than systematic metaphysics ever can. If Dickens or Hugo helps us bear our pain, then they are helping us to have empathy, to recognize our lack of community despite our ultimate ground of connection.

You wrote on page 9: "the more independent the individual, the greater the potential contribution to the community." But if I am extremely independent, why should I contribute anything to the community? Rather, I give because I have something, I need to give it, and I need to receive in return. We depend on each other and at most are relatively interdependent. We are vulnerable and even miserable. Awareness of this fosters community in a most fundamental way. Semiotics is an abstraction from the reality of the grief of life. Why don't you show who you are in your philosophical writing? It is humiliating to do so, but it is truthful and provides a sense of what grounds semiotics. Novels and letters have much philosophy to teach us—*rigorous* philosophy.

Your friend,
Cecile

IV

Love, Feeling, and Community

Cecile T. Tougas

Introduction to Part IV

When Christine de Pizan gazed into the mirror of Lady Reason, as Tracy Adams tells us, she saw herself and all women in a way that men of her time did not. She found that women were the intellectual equals and often the moral superiors of men. While women's social and political domination by men, according to the fourteenth-century hierarchy of female subordination, indeed prevented women from exercising power in public life, Christine knew that the dominating philosophical view did not reflect women's true being.

Christine's writings provide many examples of famous women and criticize men's failures in governing society. Yet she did not propose a new system of relations between men and women, because she felt that open defiance to the intolerable situation of her time would lead only to injury. She acknowledged through her own experience that even widows enjoying some degree of authority and freedom could never rise publicly above their status as supplements to men. At best women could become mediators or *moyennerresses,* making peace when men could not cease fighting, thus benefitting social life immeasurably. All this Adams tells us in an absorbing way, but then reflects sadly: "Her writings on women thus arrive at a dead end: she lays out the problem, refutes the adversary's claims, but can go no further. There is no real solution mediating woman and public life."

Then Adams brings to our attention what hardly anyone seems to know about the last part of Christine's life: Joan of Arc transforms Christine's vision. The young Joan and her miraculous accomplishments move the elderly Christine so much that she comes out of retirement to compose the *Ditié de Jehanne d'Arc.* Christine is moved to express how the frail Joan is *moyennerresse par excellence:* she mediates between God and humankind, saves France, and brings peace. Only a divine power can bring such victory against great odds. Joan communicates directly with God, who bestows on her a great sign of favor. Joan functions publicly not only on a level with men, but also on a level that transcends that of men—"above all the heroes past"—for she is guided in her heart by God. Thus, all women are honored through Joan. Woman is sovereign insofar as it is Joan—not Charles VII—who deserves the crown because of her personal closeness to God. The power of divine love, appearing through a woman, is stronger than the power of violent political force—this she sings.

John J. Conley describes several small societies in which the concept of woman was sovereign: the salons of seventeenth-century France. Directed by women, these salons enhanced feminine intellectual life despite its exclusion from university and academy. They fostered the examination of ethical questions, particularly about love, the mind, and war. Prominent among them was the Jansenist salon of Madeleine de Souvré, the Marquise de Sablé. She moderated political oppositions and was a genuine mediator in Christine de Pizan's sense. But even more significant is her contribution to moral theory "through a genre that she virtually invented": the *maxime*, a concisely ironic observation of manners, tinted with dissidence and aiming to unmask vices. Mme de Sablé's *maximes* avoid the extreme of bitter skepticism, for they moderate a stark view of human failings with a sense of authentic virtue through love.

The production of *maximes* was a collaborative enterprise in Mme de Sablé's salon. Both la Rochefoucauld and Pascal participated in this group effort and received public acclaim for their compositions, while Mme de Sablé's *Maximes,* collected and published posthumously in 1678, were reprinted in full only in the last few years. She was recognized only as a helper of famous men, not for her own achievement in moral theory. Conley helps to right this wrong now by bringing several of her most interesting *maximes* to light through his translation, for instance: "It is sometimes useful to pretend that one is mistaken" (*Maxime* 4); "It is quite a common fault never to be happy with one's fortune and never unhappy with one's soul" (*Maxime* 67); and "Love has a character so particular that one can neither hide where it is nor pretend where it is not" (*Maxime* 80).

Other *maximes* criticize the theater as a diversion, dangerous insofar as it promotes illusions about love. Conley says epigrammatically: "For Mme de Sablé, the deleterious effect of theater lies primarily in its power to imprison us in an imaginary society, in which sacrifice and pleasure take root in manufactured emotions rather than in the struggle for virtue." She knew that what frees us is not the imaginary but rather the real society of reciprocal friendship and community, in which love without pretense inspires us to live more virtuously. Through her writing, her salon, and her new genre of moral reflection, she enabled devout friendship to grow, as the genuine basis of moral life.

In the eighteenth century the salons continued to sustain a dissident intellectual life for both Enlightenment *philosophes* and women. But by the end of that century, the *philosophes* drove out *l'amour*, love, as the central topic of salon conversation. Enlightenment rationalists felt threatened by woman's social importance and her superiority in the love relationship. They denigrated what Ann Willeford calls "a woman-centered philosophy," one that derives its model of human excellence from a seventeenth- and eighteenth-century concept of woman "as the essence of civilization and refinement." They preferred their contemporary concept of man, their established philosophical tradition, their formally recognized education, and their ability to propagate their views publicly. While a woman-centered philosophy integrated some supposedly masculine traits, a man-centered one treated anything different from itself as an inferiority to be excluded, reduced, or overpowered.

Salon women left us a remarkable perspective on human nature in general—in their personal essays, letters, and philosophically rich novels that have gone unnoticed until recently. Their basic view of human being, as Willeford indicates, is that each person is an individual with an essence to be developed. Each has innate qualities to be transformed and perfected; the inner reality is most important. Feeling best determines our behavior and indicates what is valuable. Imagination, taste, and sensitivity as modes of feeling not only give us genuine knowledge but also guide our actions well. Society is best organized by attention to the authority of inward life, the heart.

Man-centered *philosophes*, however, identified themselves with universal laws of reason and the external public authority that was supposed to promulgate them. They believed that society ought to be ordered to function smoothly by force. To them progress did not mean development of one's inner qualities (for all are born as "blank slates") but rather improvement in outer material conditions. In their view, reason—not feeling—gives us genuine knowledge and moral guidance. The *philosophes* believed that they embodied reason and so naturally, as the social group in power, that they should be obeyed. They ignored the authority of the heart—Joan of Arc's courage, Christine de Pizan's passion, Mme de Sablé's friendship. "Enlightened" reasoners refused to integrate what was opposite to their preferences and wanted for themselves the power that salon women had. Willeford approaches the end of her essay somberly: " . . . with the [French] revolution, women lost almost all traces of their former power and influence."

Still, the woman-centered perspective on human being and the importance it places on an inner life of feeling were not annihilated. Karin Brown finds them now through the work of Sophie de Grouchy, Marquise de Condorcet, who translated Adam Smith's *Theory of Moral Sentiments* into French. Mme de Condorcet had written eight long letters on sympathy to her brother-in-law, a physician and philosopher, and she appended them to her translations of Smith. Brown discovered an original 1798 copy of this rare book at the Fales Library, New York University. Unable to photocopy such an old book, she photographed each page as it was gently held open by Maxime La Fantasie. Then Brown enlarged and studied every page. Here she presents a careful summary of Mme de Condorcet's analysis of sympathy.

Unlike Adam Smith, Mme de Condorcet traces sympathy to its original causes in our first sensations of pleasure and pain. On the basis of particular concrete experiences early in life, we quickly form a general and abstract impression of pain that can be recalled and felt again strongly. So when we perceive another person suffering, we can feel pain directly insofar as we can remember our general abstract impression of it. Such pain has a moral presence, for it produces a moral reaction: sympathy. Reciprocally, moral suffering involves a bodily reaction; sympathy is both emotional and physical. Mme de Condorcet is original in distinguishing how we have a "general abstract idea" in our feeling, not just in our thinking. She remains rooted in actual bodily experience, even as she provides a more complex understanding of sympathy than Smith does, inasmuch as he does not trace sympathy to its origins, believes we have no strong and immediate experience of what another person feels, and thinks we have to imagine another's situation (and how we would feel in it) before we can sympathize.

Mme de Condorcet traces our moral constitution to sympathy and our primary familial relation. As infants we feel pleasure at the hands of our caretakers on whom we depend, and so we reciprocate with care. "Specific dependency begins in the crib; it is our first tie to another human being," she writes. It yields a disposition of sympathy "that develops and expands to other people throughout one's life," as Brown reports, and so is the ground of our moral capacity. We are responsible for cultivating a sense of our human interdependence, "the sentiment for humanity." Through such feeling a moral conscience is born. Through reflective reason it is developed. Reason and sentiment are thus as interdependent as human beings are, and Brown concludes by indicating how Mme de Condorcet bridges the gap between the rationalists and the sentimentalists of her time.

Approximating a salon, at least for our time, the Society for the Study of Women Philosophers meets annually in hotel conference rooms during the American Philosophical Association meeting. At a typical session in December 1994, Society members turned their attention to an examination of love, empathy, and practical ethics. The last presentation was devoted to Dame Iris Murdoch's philosophical view of love and its illustration in her novel, *The Bell.* Patricia J. O'Connor explained how, according to Murdoch, love is central to living a virtuous life. Love involves attention to the other as a truly different person and so requires a purifying of imagination—"the clear eye, the just *and* compassionate gaze." Moral interaction with others depends on such disciplined loving attention. The beauty of both Murdoch's philosophy and her fiction lies in their complementary ways of showing what love and a good human life are. Theoretical insight informs the novel, while the story demonstrates realistically, concretely, and particularly what moral theory means. When a character begins to develop the discipline of attention and comes to recognize the distinct features that others have, the reader also gets practice in paying attention and purifying imagination, as preparation for moral interaction. The novel, O'Connor writes,

> shows us in detail how difficult and valuable it is to attend to the reality of other people, not by theoretical assertion but by suggestive eloquence—by creating a large imaginative space that both serves the needs of the characters and engages the attention and the unconscious mind of the reader.

Reading fiction can thus help us to be moral. But morality is no fiction. Murdoch takes pains to make careful distinctions in these matters, as O'Connor explains at length. We can now glimpse how Murdoch's appreciation of the novel has fundamentally the same roots as Mme de Sablé's criticism of the theater, for both women are concerned about dangerous diversions that promote illusions regarding love. They would agree wholeheartedly that a major enemy of excellence in both morality and art is fantasy or false perception that is based on egocentricity. Unexamined, uncritical fantasy imprisons us, keeps us from attending to others, and prevents moral interaction. Empathic attention, however, extends both our intellects and our hearts, without becoming either a rapt fascination or a merely factual impartiality. Purified imagination makes possible a "non-violent apprehension of difference," and so it is essential not only to ethical living but also to novel writing and theatrical presentation.

Empathic attention is important in this book. I hope for it from the reader, and in a personal essay at the end of this last section, I tell why I paid much attention to this book for several years.

18 Christine de Pizan and Jehanne d'Arc: Above All the Heroes Past

While Anglo-American feminism developed on the basis of the notion of individual freedom, this notion by itself neither leads inevitably to women's rights, nor is it the only basis from which a society might move towards equality between the sexes. Feminism conceivably might develop on another basis than the notion of individual freedom, as Christine de Pizan's (1364–1430) last work, the *Ditié de Jehanne d'Arc* illustrates.[1] This poem rearranges the hierarchy of the sexes in a way that derives nothing from the notion of individual freedom. In her panegyric to the Maid of Orleans, Christine suggests that God has sent a sign to a chaotic world ravaged by the Hundred Years' War: that a new age is about to begin, an age in which a woman will be the savior of the French people.

The *Ditié de Jehanne d'Arc*, however, treats a future broader than the immediate concerns of battle-ravaged France, frightening as they were. Christine's poem takes on a prophetic dimension when she proclaims that Joan of Arc will deliver France from the Saracens, restoring the Holy Land. The Joan portrayed by Christine is more than a battle strategist. Long before composing the *Ditié*, Christine had described several victorious feminine warriors, and although she cited these women to disprove misogynist claims of female weakness, she did not use their stories as she did Joan's to proclaim the advent of a new era in which a woman would occupy a central position. Joan of Arc represents a new figure of womanhood for Christine, one whose coming is providentially ordered. Joan is thus a sign from God that salvation history is about to enter a new phase, this time with a woman delivering humankind.

For Christine, male domination reflected a divine hierarchy, and such a hierarchy could be changed only with the divine approval of which Joan was the sign. Before writing about Joan, Christine had developed a philosophy of women's rights, but this body of work, while serious in its own right, achieves its fullest potential in the *Ditié*. As if awaiting final confirmation, Christine pushes her claims about women to their conclusion in the last work of her life. Her writings on women assume a bolder aspect read retrospectively, in light of the *Ditié*. We will turn first to the earlier works on women to consider them from this perspective.

Christine de Pizan's restoration of feminine history constitutes one of the most familiar aspects of her *oeuvre*.[2] Several works seem to prefigure her "rewriting" of women's history: among these are *Le Livre du Duc des vrais amants*, ca. 1403, where she clarifies the meaning of courtly love, and her criticisms of Jean de Meun's *Roman de la Rose*, 1401–1403—criticisms that came to play a central role in the famous "Querelle de la Rose." Christine's works expose some of the fallacies of the prevalent male perception of woman and presage her systematic rewriting of women's history in *Le Livre de la cité des dames* of 1405, a work in which she comprehensively rebuts the misogynist tradition.[3]

Having reclaimed women's history, Christine withdraws to the ubiquitous medieval hierarchy that required feminine subordination, for she advocates wifely obedience in *Le Livre des trois vertus*, a sort of practical book of everyday advice to accompany its more theoretical predecessor, *Le Livre de la cité des dames*.[4] Christine is now viewed as a herald of feminism, progressive in her analysis of women's problems but conservative in her proposed solutions. She envisions a subsidiary social role for women: at best they can use their influence to sway men's decisions, or they may replace men when necessary, as widows replace their husbands. While she does not demand a new system of relations between men and women, she nonetheless suggests women's roles that subvert male dominance. One such role is that of mediator. An examination of this role in the companion books will illustrate Christine's way, in *Le Livre des trois vertus*, of working out for everyday life what she suggests theoretically through her exempla in *Le Livre de la cité des dames*.

The role of mediator was in fact an important one during Christine's lifetime, as she stresses in her writing. But for all its historical validity, the role becomes subversive under Christine's pen when she suggests that while men hold all positions of political power in fifteenth-century French society, they are incapable of conducting their affairs intelligently among themselves and therefore need women to mediate for them. In *Le Livre de la cité des dames* (hereafter *Cité*) she first makes a criticism of the male-centered history of her day, then she replaces that history with a version recounted from a feminine perspective. Female mediators play a role both in the masculine history Christine criticizes and the feminine one she writes.

What is this "history" Christine criticizes in *Cité*? Traditionally, "history" has carried a dual meaning, referring both to the actual occurrence of an event and to its recording. In *Cité* Christine demonstrates that history in both of its senses has been the purview of men and that they have mishandled both. The unrolling of public events has been controlled by men. They legislate, declare wars, control the government—and they have not always done an admirable job. Furthermore, they have distorted the recording of history in misogynist writings; Christine echoes the Wife of Bath's indignant "Who painted the lion?" but unlike the Wife of Bath, she responds to the question in detail. The entire *Cité*, in fact, becomes a response as Christine shows how a very different record appears when women instead of men "paint the lion" or tell the story.

Women, Christine proffers, are better suited by nature to run the world, being innately more peaceable. Furthermore, women are not sufficiently strong to be dangerous, even if they wanted to be; their lack of strength guarantees their abiding gentleness in comparison to men, whose physical strength has allowed them to wreak atrocities upon the world. God and Nature, she writes, have done women a good turn in making them less powerful of body, for at least they will never be guilty of the "horribles cruautés, les murdres et les grans et griefs extorcions" that have been and continue to be perpetrated in the world.[5] The world would be a pleasanter place with women in charge. But even though women are powerless in that they wield no direct force, feminine intervention keeps men in some semblance of order, and for this reason Christine insists, in *Le Livre des trois vertus* (hereafter *Trois vertus*), upon the importance of the feminine role of mediator. Without the feminine ability to mediate between warring men, the world would be in an even sorrier state than the one it is in. In *Trois vertus,* Christine provides everyday advice on how to be a good woman and emphasizes the importance of the feminine role of mediator between a woman's husband and his antagonists:

> O de quans grans biens ont maintes fois esté cause au monde roynes et princepces en mettant paix entre anemis, entre princes et barrons et entre peuples rebelles et leurs seigneurs, les escriptures en sont toutes pleines! Si n'est en terre plus grant bien que de princepce et haulte dame et sage. Eureux est le pais et la contree qui telle l'a.

> Queens and princesses have greatly benefitted the world by bringing about peace between enemies, between princes and their barons, or between rebellious subjects and their lords. The Scriptures are full of examples. The world has no greater benevolence than a good and wise princess. Fortunate is the land which has one.[6]

In her *Epistre a la Royne* of the same year, Christine reiterates her notion that women are essential to harmonious government by calling on Queen Isabeau to negotiate peace.[7] She writes that it behooves a princess to act as mediator (*moyennerresse*) in negotiating peace treaties and reminds her "Très excellent et . . . très redoubtée Dame" of the infinite reasons why the Queen should be moved to work for peace, reasons the Queen's good sense grasps very well: "infinies raisons vous pourroient estre reccordees des causes qui vous doivent mouvoir a pité et a traictié de paix, les quelles vostre bon scens n'ignore mie."[8]

If, however, in Christine's eyes men have done a very bad job of making history, and even though women could do as well if not better, the realities of fifteenth-century society prevent her from suggesting more than an auxiliary role for women in government. She is by no means a proponent of dramatic change but instead casts herself as a restorer of truth. In *Cité* she requests only that her readers grasp the fundamental intellectual dishonesty of misogyny, and she insists that God has decreed that women be treated well. She proposes that the truth be allowed to reveal itself, and one of her first purposes is to demonstrate her own credibility as its conveyer. In order to speak truthfully about women, she must establish a new stance as subject from which she can examine women, including herself, without the distorting influence of misogyny.

Dame Raison, Lady Reason, helps her establish this stance. Holding up her mirror, Lady Reason orders Christine the narrator to gaze into it, explaining, "Si saiches de vray qu'il n'est quelconques personne qui s'i mire, quel que la criature soit, qui clerement ne se congnoisse" ("I would thus have you know truly that no one can look into this mirror, no matter what kind of creature, without achieving clear self-knowledge").[9] In the mirror, Christine, the narrator and subject about to write the history of women, sees who she is. The role of subject informed by *Raison, Droitture,* and *Justice* (Reason, Rectitude, and Justice) Christine assumes throughout the rest of the book gives her a position that surpasses the traditional male point of view that was limited to ancient authorities found in books. Christine as historian of woman occupies a unique position, untouched by the misogynist preconceptions to which men fall prey. Through the reflection held by Lady Reason, she can see the object she describes.[10]

From this vantage point, Christine admits that men are lying and selfish when they project all their worst traits onto women. Yet she advocates remaining within the bounds of traditional female behavior. For her, the foremost examples of virtuous women—those with a "sens naturel en fait de policie et gouvernement"—are nearly all widows.[11] Christine, left a widow at the age of twenty-five with three children, was well aware of both the disadvantages and advantages of widowhood. She relates with great feeling the disadvantages in the autobiographical sections of *L'Advison Christine* of 1405. On the positive side, however, widows during the Middle Ages were sometimes regarded as substitutes for their deceased partners and therefore could theoretically exercise authority far exceeding that allotted to dependent women. Thus, Christine's use of widows as political actors is not particularly controversial. Like the mediator, the role of widow is not an independent one—it is based on substituting a woman for a man—and yet it allows a certain amount of power and provides an arena for demonstrating feminine competence. After her opening example of virtuous women, Christine describes a series of widows who replaced their husbands as rulers.

Christine thus seems to be positioned within the bounds of tradition. Her attention to widows is irreproachable and even inevitable for gathering contemporary examples of virtuous women, for materially powerful women in Christine's world were most often widows—married women were subject to their husbands, unmarried women to their fathers or brothers. Widows were free from the dominance of guardians and therefore enjoyed greater freedom in the public sphere than did their married sisters, for even if wives could sometimes appear in the public sphere, they were not accorded power there. It is true, as Martha Howell explains, that women of the late Middle Ages "made and sold textiles, clothing, beer, bread, pottery, and other goods used both locally and abroad," and that they ran

taverns and inns; they belonged to guilds and confraternities; they brokered deals between visiting merchants and local manufacturers; they borrowed and lent money; they took oaths; they led religious movements; they ran charities; they joined popular political demonstration; they sued and were sued; they learned and taught reading, writing and arithmetic; they delivered babies for pay; and they dispensed medicine and medical advice.[12]

It is also true, however, that they were not involved in the decision-making process of the public sphere. Howell continues: "In northern European cities, a line separating a world exclusive to men from the world that men and women shared was drawn around a small but very significant kind of public activity—the formal, direct exercise of public authority."[13] As Christine shows in *Cité* and *Trois vertus*, however, widows could sometimes play an active public role because they were not really considered women but rather substitute men, and as such enjoyed male privileges.

What initially sounds like a traditional formulation of the possibilities for female action soon reveals a subversive undertone. Lady Reason's discussion of widows suggests a view of men somewhat less than flattering. Certainly she begins innocently enough:

> t'en ramenterray aucunes de ton temps, affin que tu myeulx congnoisses ma verité, qui sont demourees vesves, dont le bel gouvernement qu'elles ont eu, et ont, en tous leurs affaires après la mort de leurs maris donne magnifeste experience que femme qui a entendement est convenable en toutes choses.

> I will remind you of some women of your own time who remained widows and whose skill governing—both past and present—in all their affairs following the deaths of their husbands provides the obvious demonstration that a woman with a mind is fit for all tasks.[14]

Midway through her catalogue of exempla, Lady Reason summarizes, providing a favorable assessment: "D'autres dames de France unes et autres, qui bien et bel en leur vesveté gouvernent elles et leur juridiccions, assez te pourroye dire" ("I could tell you much about other ladies of France who, as widows, governed themselves and their jurisdictions with fairness and justice").[15] Lady Reason's conclusion, however, overcomes the conventionality of her initial approach. What a pity it is that women are allowed public exercise of power only under extraordinary circumstances, she says, for the world would be better off if men realized the unavoidable truth these widows represent.

> Que t'en diroye? Je te asseure que foyson de grandes, moyennes et petites pareillement se puet dire, lesquelles, qui prendre y veult garde, on puet veoir qu'en leur vesveté ont soustenu, et soustiennent, en aussi bon estat leur seigneuries que faisoyent leurs maris a leur vivans, et qui autant sont amees de leur subgiez; et mieulx de telles y a, car n'est pointe de doubte, n'en desplaise aux hommes, [que] quoyqu'il soit des nices femmes, qu'il en est maintes qui ont meilleur entendement et plus vive consideracion et judicative que n'ont tout plain d'ommes, est il? et desquelles, se leurs maris les creussent ou eussent pareil scenes, grant bien et prouffit seroit pour eulx.

What should I tell you? I assure you that the same can be said of a great many women, whether from the upper, middle, or lower class, who, as anyone who wishes to pay attention can clearly see, have maintained and maintain their dominions in as good condition as did their husbands during their lifetime and who are as well-loved by their subjects. There are better examples, too, for there can be no doubt—no offense to men, certainly—that although there are ignorant women, there are many women who have better minds and a more active sense of prudence and judgment than most men—isn't it so?—and if their husbands would believe them or would have equal sense, it would be a great boon and profit for them.[16]

In *Trois vertus*, her follow-up to *Cité*, Christine develops her perspective on widows to its logical conclusion. She divides her instructions into three sections (respectively, for princesses, for ladies and maidens who live at court, and for the masses), and she describes for each group the advantages of being widowed.

For princesses no longer enjoying the first bloom of youth, Christine emphasizes the possibility of increased influence in the political arena. Women are particularly good negotiators; the widowed princess has the opportunity to achieve her potential in this domain.

Mais s'il avient cas que la princepce demeure vesve a tout son aisné filz encore joenne et meindre d'aage, et que par aventure guerre et contens sourde entre les barons pour cause du gouvernement, la convient il qu'elle employe sa prudence et son savoir pour les mettre et tenir en paix, car nulle guerre d'estranges anemis ni lui pourroit estre tant perilleuse comme ceste. Et pour ce, la dame qui sera toute sage, sera si bonne moyenne entre eulx par son prudent maintien et savoir—pensant le mal qui pourroit venir de leurs debas, veu son enfant encores joenne—que bien les saura apaisier. Et pour ce faire querra les plus convenables manieres qu'elle porra, les traictera par doulceur et par bel, et vouldra que tout soit fait par bon et loyal conseil.

If the princess is widowed while her oldest son is still young and a *minor*, and if war and civil troubles arise among the barons concerning the government, then necessarily she will employ her prudence and her wisdom to reconcile the antagonistic factions and maintain peace among them. No war waged against her by foreigners could be as dangerous as civil war. Therefore, the wise lady will be such a good mediator by her prudent conduct and her knowledge that she will succeed in appeasing all her factions. Her constant thought must be to avoid all the troubles resulting from quarrels consequent upon the youth of her child. The troublemakers she must handle with gentleness and courtesy. Good and loyal counsel will guide her every act.[17]

Author herself of two treatises on arms and war, *Le Livre du corps de policies* and *Le Livre des faits d'armes et de chevalrie*, Christine concludes: "Et n'est pas doubte que estre extimé ne pourroit le bien que telle princepce peut faire en royaume ou contree" ("The benefit such a princess hereby would give to her realm is immeasurable").[18]

For Christine husbands are a burden to be assumed only when absolutely necessary. She suggests that older princesses avoid remarriage if at all possible. To the younger princesses she mentions remarriage as something they may need to do at the behest of their friends and advisors—never as a voluntary choice. To the widows of the non-nobility, Christine specifically warns against remarriage. Only out of dire necessity should a widow of this group place herself under the dominion of a man.

> Et pour ce que en l'estat de veuvté a tant de durtéz pour les femmes, si que nous disons, et il est vray, pourroit sembler a aucunes gens que doncques seroit leur meilleur que toutes se remariassent. Si pourroit a ceste question estre respondu que s'il estoit ainsi qu'en la vie de mariage eust tout repos et paix, vrayement seroit sens a femme de s'i rebouter, mais parce que on voit tout le contraire, le doit moult ressoigner toute femme, quoy que aux joennes soit chose comme de nécessité, ou tres convenable; mais a celles qi ja ont passé joenne aage, et qui assez ont du leur, ne povreté ne les y contraint, c'est toute folie.

> Because widowhood truly provides so many hardships for women, some people might think it best for all widows to remarry. This argument can be answered by saying that if it were true that the married state consisted entirely of peace and repose, this indeed would be so. That one almost always sees the contrary in marriage should be a warning to all widows. However, it might be necessary or desirable for the young ones to remarry. But for all those who have passed their youth and who are sufficiently comfortable financially so that poverty does not oblige, remarriage is complete folly.[19]

Thus first in *Cité*, then more directly in *Trois vertus*, Christine slips away from male dominance as she explores the possibilities of a well-established social phenomenon: the relatively wide range of independence that was allowed to widows. While *Cité* culminates with an account of martyrs—women who could only retain their integrity and identity through death—it opens with politically powerful and independent women. If Christine idealizes the patient Griselda pattern of goodness, she begins her story with exempla of skilled governors. For Christine, good women are devout and willing to accept the hardships God sends them. But she is practical, too, and understands the advantages of being able to lead a public life.

Within the limits of the medieval hierarchical ordering of society, then, Christine systematically cordons off a space in which women can function independently, and she shows through exempla how different women have developed their own histories in a world ruled by men. In *Trois vertus* she urges women who are free of husbands to remain so, but she acknowledges the reality that many women are subject to their husbands and advises them on how best to bear this burden. She suggests they conceive of themselves as Christian martyrs. As the allegory of *Cité* gives way to the everyday life of *Trois vertus*, Christine continues to urge women to rise above their husbands psychologically. The City of Ladies exists within the individual woman. Through the inspiration of its exempla, the wise woman will see beyond her husband's misbehavior. Christine writes:

> . . . le sens et la prudence de la sage femme, qui que elle soit, quant elle scet tout ce supporter et dissimuler saigement sans faire semblant que elle s'en aperçoive et que elle n'en scet riens, voire, s'il est ainsi que elle n'y peust mettre remede; car elle se pensera comme saige: se tu lui diroyes rudement, tu n'y gaigneroyes riens, et s'il t'en menoit male vie, ty poindroies contre l'aguillon; il t'esloingeroit par aventure, et tant plus les gens s'en

moqueraient, et croistroit la honte et le diffame, et t'en pourroit encore estre de pis. Il faut
que tu muires et vives ave lui, quel qu'il soit.

. . . the wise woman's good judgement and prudence are manifest when she knows how
to bear all this, dissembling, without appearing to be aware of his perfidies or showing
that she observes anything unusual. Even if every suspicion is true, there is nothing she
can do about it. She may well reflect to herself: "If I speak to him harshly, I will gain
nothing. If he mistreats me, I am headed into a storm. Perhaps he might send me away.
Then people would mock me all the more, thus adding shame and disrepute to the whole
despicable affair. Even worse might overtake me. Alas, I am obliged to live and die with
him, whatever he may be."[20]

Cursed with a cruel husband, a woman can emulate the martyrs. Still, Christine never
suggests that a woman suffer in silence; she never condones simple submission.
Rather, she recommends that the mistreated wife gently urge her brutish husband
to reform.

Christine ends *Cité* with an admonition about men's general unreliability and
exhorts women to act well nonetheless:

Et, briefment, toutes femmes, soyent grandes, moyennes, ou petites, vueillés estre sur
toute riens avisees et cautes en deffense contre les annemis de voz honneurs et de vostre
chasteté. Voyez, mes dames, comment ses hommes vous accusent de tant de vices de toutes
pars. Faittes les tous menteurs par monstrer vostre vertu et prouvé mençongeurs ceulx
qui vous blasment par bien faire.

In brief, all women—whether noble, bourgeois, or lower-class—be well-informed in all
things and cautious in defending your honor and chastity against your enemies! My ladies,
see how these men accuse you of so many vices in everything. Make liars of them all by
showing forth your virtue, and prove their attacks false by acting well. Repel the deceptive
flatterers who, using different charms, seek with various tricks to steal that which you must
consummately guard, that is, your honor.[21]

By symbolically establishing a city for ladies and by directly addressing the reader,
Christine affirms that women not dependent upon men for their sustenance are better
off without them. She grants that many exceptions exist—her own lamented husband
among them—but a substantial proportion of men are selfish bullies to women who,
in turn, need all the more to be intelligent, pious, and loyal. In her vision, women
are the intellectual equals and moral superiors of men. Christine's counsel that wives
obey their husbands is based on the realistic assessment of the position of wives in
her society and represents a practical response to an intolerable situation rather than
an advocating of male dominance.

Severely circumscribed by her society, Christine finds ways around it rather than
rebels against it directly, for rebellion could only end badly; open defiance would lead
to shame and physical injury. The City of Ladies represents a private, interior space of
reflection and exempla; it is not the society within which Christine lived. In the latter,
as she well knew, while mediators and widows enjoyed relative influence and power,

they could never rise publicly above the status of being supplements to men. Her writings on women thus arrive at a dead end: she lays out the problem, refutes the adversary's claims, but can go no further. There is no real solution mediating woman and public life.

Yet, after nearly a lifetime of remaining within the confines of traditional ways, Christine in her last writing manifests a transformation. When she composes the *Ditié de Jehanne d'Arc* she no longer views the female role as secondary, for the mediator between God and humankind—the savior of France—is now a young woman. Woman's value as substitute man, a notion represented in Christine's widow exempla, is far exceeded by Joan of Arc whose femininity becomes not only tolerable but desirable in the *Ditié.* God has bestowed a great sign of favor upon a frail woman, and Christine proclaims the meaning of this sign to the world.

Christine's acceptance of the inevitability of male domination, then, is joyfully transformed in her final work near the end of her life. Written in 1429, weeks after the consecration of Charles VII at Rheims, the *Ditié* is a triumphant assertion of a renewal of French history and, more importantly, universal history. While critics have noted that this work represents the culmination and affirmation of Christine's career as a writer, I would like to suggest that for Christine, Joan signifies more than a powerful and worthy woman: Christine sees Joan's appearance as the coming of a new savior and draws authority from this appearance to understand salvation history in a fuller way. Mary, chosen to be mother of God and agreeing to be, functions as mediator between man and God. Through Joan, God continues to invest woman with great significance. Through a woman as mediator par excellence, Christ came to earth to save man; through the Maid of Orleans, God creates a parallel mediation. This new, divinely ordained role authorizes women to fulfill the feminine capabilities Christine had stressed in *Cité* and *Trois vertus* yet, at the same time, to function publicly on a level with men, or in the specific case of Joan, on a level beyond even the bravest of men. Joan is "desur tous les preux passez," above all the heros of the past.[22] Centuries of male domination fall away as woman occupies a central role.

Dropping the historical discursive style of writing that she used in *Cité*, Christine takes up the metrical *dit*, a form used in the mid-thirteenth century to express personal emotion. Christine returns to the *dit* as song and identifies with Carmentis, prophet and poet.[23] Aroused from her retirement in a convent near Poissy, Christine takes up her pen one last time to record the miracle God has sent to the French in the form of Joan and, in so doing, she creates an appropriate epitaph to her own life's work. All of Christine's most optimistic hopes for the role of women are now fulfilled—indeed, surpassed—in the figure of the country girl, the *simple bergère,* who appears and saves France during one of its many dark hours. A new age has begun in this year of 1429, Christine declares; the sun has begun to shine again, bringing good times anew:

> L'an mil CCCCXXIX
> Reprint à luire li soleil.
> Il ramene le bon temps neuf . . .[24]

The ostensible occasion for rejoicing is the accession of Charles VII to the throne of France, but as Christine quickly reveals, he has taken his proper place in history only through the mediation of *La Pucelle d'Orléans,* the maiden of Orleans, Joan of Arc. Although Charles is the King of France, he owes his crown to Joan. Addressing Charles VII in her *Ditié,* Christine reminds him to whom he owes his renown: through the grace of God, the Maid has lifted him up, subduing his enemies beneath his banner. This is a new and wondrous thing.

> Mais, Dieu grace, or voiz ton renon
> Hault eslevé par la Pucelle,
> Qui a soubmiz soubz ton penon
> Tes ennemis (chose est nouvelle!)[25]

Joan's miraculous victories are the result of her communication with God and her mediation of God to the soldiers, Christine proclaims. The restoration of peace in France after a hundred years of war has been achieved in spite of Joan's physical weakness, and Joan has accomplished what no man, however strong, could. Selected and guided by God, Joan is valorous of heart, or *cuer.* Stronger than Hector or Achilles, she has restored the throne of France to its king, and under the direct guidance of God, she is in the process of putting the English army to rout. No hero who has ever existed has been the peer in prowess of the Maid who is chasing the enemy from France.

> Car tous les preux au long aler
> Qui ont esté, ne s'appareille
> Leur prouesse à ceste qui veille
> A bouter hors noz ennemis.[26]

Christine exhorts the French to realize that Joan is an extraordinary manifestation of the will of God. Through maternal imagery she stresses the fact of Joan's femininity: Joan nurses France at her breast with peace and sweet nourishment. This loving mother also "subdues the rebellious people." Joan

> donne à France la mamelle
> De paix et doulce norriture,
> Et ruer jus la gent rebelle.[27]

Joan is no substitute man, nor is she a man in a woman's body, but is more fully a valorous woman, a mother defending her child.

The miracle does not stop simply with Joan. As the *Ditié* recounts a specific historical event, Christine attributes a wide significance to Joan's triumphs: all women are honored through her—"Hee! quel honneur au femenin Sexe!"—for God loves Joan: "Que Dieu l'ayme il appert."[28] All the brute force of men—and physical strength is the only masculine advantage Christine ever noted—could not achieve what Joan has been given to achieve. For all their public power, men without a mediator have no contact with the divine. No show of physical strength would have sufficed, not the strength of one hundred or even one thousand men: "Jamais force ne fu si grant, / Soient ou à cens ou à miles."[29]

Thus the role of mediator, important in *Trois vertus*, takes on a sacred dimension and perfects the process of feminine valorization Christine began earlier in her writing. In *Cité* Christine referred to women's tears, traditionally a sign of female weakness, as evidence of God's blessing: "Car je tiens que à cause des larmes de leur devocion soyent sauvee plusiers d'elles et d'autres pour qui elle prient" ("for I believe that many women, as well as others for whom they pray, are saved by the tears of their devotion").[30] In the *Ditié* woman's weakness is shown to be a receptivity to the special grace of God that is stronger than man. Human might is inferior to the power of love. The role of mediator, previously limited to negotiations among men, now receives a sacred meaning.

Joan's mission supersedes the war in which she has just intervened. She will deliver France from its enemies. Christine no longer has the stance of deference that she adopted in *Cité* and *Trois vertus;* now she asserts that Joan deserves to wear the crown of France, not the man she has helped to procure it.

> Ceste doit porter la couronne,
> Car ses faiz ja monstrent assez
> Que plus prouesse Dieu lui donne
> Qu'à tous ceulz de qui l'on raisonne.[31]

Charles had been incapable of claiming his rightful position until Joan came to his aid. Did she not lead him by the hand all the way to his consecration, Christine asks: "N'a el le roy mené au sacre, / Que tousjours tenoit par la main?"[32]

In emphasizing Joan's status as *pucelle,* or maiden, Christine links Joan both to Eve who lost her innocence and to Mary the Virgin Mother who gained far more than Eve ever had: a physical joining with divinity.

> . . . je di que trop plus hault degré a acquis par Marie qu'il ne perdi par Eve, quant humanité est conjointe a deité, ce qu'il ne seront mie se le meffait de Eve ne fust avenu. Se se doit louer homme et femme de celle mesprison par laquelle tel honneur luy est ensuyie. Car de tant qu nature humaine tresbucha plus bas par creature, a elle esté relevee plus hault par createur.

> . . . I tell you that he [man] gained more through Mary than he lost through Eve when humanity was conjoined to the godhead, which would never have taken place if Eve's misdeed had not occurred. Thus man and woman should be glad for this sin, through which such an honor has come about. For as low as human nature fell through this creature woman, was human nature lifted higher by this same creature.[33]

Women, instead of being relegated to secondary roles as they had been in the old era, will be the leaders in the new, showing the way to salvation through their closeness to God.

In her earlier work, Christine demonstrates that women are equal to men by showing how competently they fulfill their positions when they are allowed to replace men. She does not, however, suggest that society change to the extent of granting women a role equal to that of men's in the public sphere. But in the *Ditié* God specifically chooses a young girl to save France. Perhaps this sign of favor bestowed upon the feminine sex was not sufficient to cause the Church to revise its position regarding women, but for Christine the evidence was compelling. Her movement from a conception of history as writeable from a woman's stance but imperturbably male-dominated to a conception of history as animated by a *pucelle* is a radical one. The view in the *Ditié* of the great value of woman is latent in the earlier works, but Christine required authorization from God to complete the trajectory upon which she had tentatively embarked. The *Ditié* transcends male/female hierarchy and raises a claim for the great importance of women as mediators of the love of God.

Modern readings of Christine as a fundamentally conservative writer fail to take into account the full spectrum of her ideas and furthermore fail to consider that the evolution of ideas is full of regression and forward movement, chance digression and inconsistencies. In noting simply that Christine failed to promote wifely rebellion, we miss the significance of her *oeuvre*. She required confirmation from God before she dared bring her own notion of feminine worth to its conclusion, but once she received what she believed to be that sign, she acted promptly and with complete confidence.

Notes

1. Christine de Pizan, *Ditié de Jehanne d'Arc*, Angus J. Kennedy and Kenneth Varty, eds. (Oxford: Society for the Study of Medieval Language and Literature, 1977).

2. See Patricia Phillippy, "Establishing Authority: Boccaccio's *De Claris Mulieribus* and Christine de Pizan's *Le Livre de la Cité des Dames*," *Romanic Review* 77 (1986): 168. See also Susan Schibanoff, "Taking the Gold Out of Egypt: The Art of Reading as a Woman," *Gender and Reading: Essays on Readers, Texts, and Contexts*, Elizabeth A. Flynn, ed. (Baltimore: Johns Hopkins University Press, 1986); Valerie Wayne, "Zenobia in Medieval and Renaissance Literature," *Ambiguous Realities: Women in the Middle Ages and Renaissance* (Detroit: Wayne State University Press, 1987).

3. I will cite from Maureen Cheney Curnow, *Le Livre de la Cité des Dames of Christine de Pisan: A Critical Edition*, Vanderbilt University Ph.D. dissertation (Ann Arbor, Michigan: Xerox University Microfilms, 1975). I will also cite translations from Earl Jeffrey Richard, *The Book of the City of Ladies* (New York: Persea Books, Inc., 1982). In these notes I will refer to Curnow's edition as *Cité* and to Richard's translation as *City*.

4. Christine de Pizan, *Le Livre des trois vertus*, Charity Cannon Willard and Eric Hicks, eds. (Paris: Champion, 1989). Translations cited are from *A Medieval Woman's Mirror of Honor: The Treasury of the City of Ladies*, Charity Cannon Willard, tr. and ed., with Madeleine Peiner Cosman, introduction (New York: Persea Books, Inc., 1989 and Tenafly, N.J.: Bard Hall Press, 1989). In these notes I will refer to the French edition of Willard and Hicks as *Trois vertus* and to the English translation of Willard as *Mirror*.

5. *Cité*, p. 675.

6. *Trois vertus*, pp. 35–6; *Mirror*, pp. 86–7.

7. Christine de Pizan, *The Epistle of Human Life* with *An Epistle to the Queen of France* and *Lament of the Evils of the Civil War*, Josette A. Wisman, tr. and ed. (New York and London: Garland Publishing Co., 1984). The edition and the translation are on facing pages.

8. Ibid., pp. 76, 80.

9. *Cité*, p. 627; *City*, p. 9.

10. See Laura Kathryn McRae, "Interpretation and the Acts of Reading and Writing in Christine de Pisan's *Livre de la Cité des Dames*," *Romanic Review* 82 (1991): 412–33.

11. *Cité*, p. 666.

12. Martha C. Howell, "Citizenship and Gender: Women's Political Status in Northern Medieval Cities" in *Women and Power in the Middle Ages* (Athens: University of Georgia Press, 1988), p. 37.

13. Ibid.

14. *Cité*, p. 666; *City*, p. 32.

15. *Cité*, p. 671; *City*, p. 35.

16. *Cité*, p. 672; *City*, p. 35.

17. *Trois vertus*, pp. 84–5; *Mirror*, pp. 120–1.

18. *Trois vertus*, p. 86; *Mirror*, p. 121.

19. *Trois vertus*, p. 193; *Mirror*, pp. 200–1.

20. *Trois vertus*, p. 55; *Mirror*, p. 99.

21. *Cité*, pp. 1034–5; *City*, p. 256.

22. *Ditié de Jehanne d'Arc*, XLIV.

23. See Jacqueline Cerquiglini-Toulet, *La Couleur de la mélancholie: La fréquentation des livres au XIVe siècle 1300–1415* (Paris: Hatier, 1993), pp. 118, 121.

24. *Ditié de Jehanne d'Arc*, III.

25. *Ditié de Jehanne d'Arc*, XIII.

26. *Ditié de Jehanne d'Arc*, XXVI.

27. *Ditié de Jehanne d'Arc*, XXXIV.

28. *Ditié de Jehanne d'Arc*, XXXIV.

29. *Ditié de Jehanne d'Arc*, XXXVI.

30. *Cité*, p. 659; *City*, p. 28.

31. *Ditié de Jehanne d'Arc*, XLIV.

32. *Ditié de Jehanne d'Arc*, XLVIII.

33. *Cité*, p. 653; *City*, p. 24.

John J. Conley

19   Madame de Sablé's Moral Philosophy: A Jansenist Salon

Excluded from the university and the academy, the intellectual life of women in seventeenth-century France flourished in the salon.[1] This institution of the late Renaissance, usually conducted by an aristocratic woman in her Parisian *hôtel*, provided more than polite conversation and amorous adventure. It offered a forum for the mutual creation and criticism of literature, especially poetry, and for artistic performance, especially musical. In the rigid social hierarchy of baroque France, the salon broke the barriers between men and women, cleric and lay, and, on occasion, between aristocracy and bourgeoisie. The salon also provided genteel cover for dissidence against the political and religious orthodoxies of the Bourbons. Hôtel de Nevers sang in a Jansenist key. Hôtel de Rambouillet declaimed in the antiroyalist verse of the Fronde.

Philosophical questions occupied a secondary place in the salons of mid-seventeenth-century France. Even the most progressive convent schools, those conducted by the Ursulines and the Cistercians of Port-Royal, omitted philosophical instruction from the curriculum.[2] Nonetheless, the philosophical works of Descartes quickly created what Wendy Gibson describes as a veritable "army of *cartésiennes*" among such *salonnières* as the Duchesse de Maine and the Baronne de Staal.[3] Descartes himself avowed his interest in attracting women readers by composing the *Discours de la Méthode* in French rather than in Latin.[4] Descartes's dualistic anthropology provided ammunition for *salonnières* who defended the equality of the sexes along the lines of Marie de Gournay's *L'Egalité des Hommes et des Femmes*.[5]

In one area of philosophy, the baroque salon demonstrated unusual interest: moral theory. This predilection for ethical reflection is not surprising, given the emphasis placed upon instruction in religion, morals, and etiquette by the prestigious convent schools of the period.[6] Perhaps the most remarkable of the salons committed to moral theory was that headed by Madeleine de Souvré, the Marquise de Sablé (1599–1678).[7] She conducted a salon at Port-Royal inspired by Jansenism. Her salon engineered a new genre of moral reflection, the *maxime*, an epigrammatic exercise in moral psychology. In this genre, Mme de Sablé distinguished herself as both patron and practitioner.[8] La Rochefoucauld's *Maximes* and Pascal's *Pensées* are distinguished representatives of her salon's production. In her own *Maximes* (1678) and treatises, Mme de Sablé proposed a more moderate account of virtue than theirs.

Widowed in 1640, Mme de Sablé played a central role in the political and religious controversies of the period. During the 1640s, as an habituée of the salon of the Hôtel de Rambouillet, Mme de Sablé became an intimate of the partisans of the Fronde, the aristocratic coalition opposed to the growing absolutism of monarchial power.[9] Through correspondence and personal intervention, she played a conciliatory role between the factions in the civil conflict. After her religious conversion in 1652, conducted under the influence of the Jansenist leader Arnauld, Mme de Sablé became a partisan of the Jansenist movement, the quasi-Calvinist sect within French Catholicism.[10] Typically, she attempted to moderate the growing opposition between the Jansenists and their critics. During the "crisis of the signature" (1661), Mme de Sablé repeatedly intervened to soften the resistance of the Jansenist nuns of Port-Royal and to reduce the sanctions employed against them by civil and ecclesiastical authorities.

In 1657, Pope Innocent had issued *Cum Occasione*, which condemned five heretical propositions that he claimed were found in the works of Jansenius (1585—1638), the inspiration of the Jansenist movement. Jansenist leaders agreed that the propositions were heretical, but they disagreed that Jansenius had ever endorsed them. In 1661, Louis XIV demanded that Jansenists sign a statement adhering to the controversial bull. A moderate faction, lead by Arnauld, supported the "signature" under reservations. A militant faction, led by Pascal, supported total resistance. Mme de Sablé repeatedly urged the nuns of Port-Royal to accept the moderate solution.

Throughout her life, Mme de Sablé participated in the salon culture of Paris. She successively became a member of the salons of Mme de Rambouillet,[11] of Mlle de Scudéry,[12] and of Mlle d'Orléans.[13] She organized two salons of her own: at the fashionable Place Royal (1648–1655) and on the grounds of the Jansenist convent of Port-Royal (1655–1661, when the nuns suffered ecclesiastical sanctions, and after 1669, when religious peace had returned to the convent).

Two salons in particular shaped the meetings that Mme de Sablé conducted in her maturity at Port-Royal. In the late 1640s and the early 1650s, Mme de Sablé frequented the famous "Saturdays" of Mlle de Scudéry.[14] This salon focused exclusively upon literary matters. The habitués demonstrated special interest in light poetry, such as the satiric epigram. This literary taste clearly influenced the genesis of the *maxime* as the favored literary product of Mme de Sablé's later salon. Like most salons, Mlle de Scudéry's "Saturdays" mixed social classes (clerics like Bossuet, laity like the Prince de Condé) and genders (male dramatists like Corneille, female dramatists like Mme de Villedieu).[15] Mlle de Scudéry's salon exhibited the academic rigor that the more intellectual salons were borrowing from the scientific academies of the period. Mlle de Scudéry's salon stipulated a formal agenda for each session and produced a regular set of minutes, acts, and historical notices.[16] Conrart,[17] a prominent member of the *Académie française*, served as the salon archivist.

Later in the 1650s, Mme de Sablé participated in the salon of the Palais du Luxembourg, presided over by Mlle d'Orléans. Habitués of the salon included aristocratic authors who were to become close friends of Mme de Sablé: Mme de Sévigné,[18] Mme de Lafayette,[19] and La Rochefoucauld.[20] In 1657, Mlle d'Orléans invented a new type of literary genre: the "portrait."[21] The portrait consists in a witty description of the physical, emotive, and, especially, moral composition of a particular person. Mlle d'Orléans etched the portrait of Mme de Sablé under the pseudonym of the Princess of Parthenie.[22] The portrait evokes one of Mme de Sablé's lifelong vices: her hypochondria. The "portrait" soon transcended the salon at Luxembourg and became a literary vogue throughout France. Jean Segrais,[23] the secretary of the salon, began the successful publication of compilations of the salon's portraits in 1659. The emphasis upon moral psychology, especially the subtle vices of the righteous, was to direct the focus of the *maximes* later produced in Mme de Sablé's Jansenist salon.

In 1655, Mme de Sablé built her lodging on the grounds of the Jansenist convent of Port-Royal. Distinguished women of her salon included Mme de Sévigné, Mme de Lafayette, the Abbess of Fontevrault, and the Abbess of Caen. Prominent men came largely from the Jansenist movement: the theologian Arnauld,[24] the moralist Nicole,[25] the jurist Domat,[26] Abbé Jacques Esprit[27] of the *Académie,* and Blaise Pascal.[28] La Rochefoucauld, although reserved toward the Jansenist movement, elaborated a radical critique of virtue consistent with Jansenist anthropology.

Mme de Sablé's salon pursued a wide range of philosophical interests. Salon members debated the theses of Descartes through discussions of *Pensées sur les Opinions de M. Descartes,* composed by Clausure.[29] Marquis de Sourdis read a paper on physics: "Why Water Rises in a Small Tube."[30] Mme de Brégy[31] delivered communications on the life of Socrates and new translations of Epicurus. The predominant issues of the salon, however, were ethical questions, especially those regarding the nature of love. The salon's records repeatedly note "Questions on Love," "Thoughts on the Mind," and "Thoughts on War."[32] This preoccupation with moral issues, explored through epigrammatic analysis, provided the conditions for the emergence of the salon's distinctive literary genre: the *maxime.*

The *maxime* began as a type of literary salon game. Habitués of the salon would develop a sentence based on the observation of manners. This sentence would usually take an ironic turn. Through successive criticism, offered in salon conversation and through epistolary exchange, salon members would polish the moral observation. The ideal was epigrammatic concision. The *maxime*'s barbed judgments routinely incorporated the Jansenist suspicion of virtue that marked Mme de Sablé's circle. Originally a collaborative enterprise, the production of *maximes* soon revealed a salon genius: La Rochefoucauld, whose *Maximes* (published in successive editions from 1665 to 1678) became the standard of achievement in the genre.[33] Mme de Sablé's intimate involvement in the genesis of La Rochefoucauld's *maximes* has never been disputed. In massive correspondence, Mme de Sablé criticized and proposed alternative phrasing for hundreds of *maximes* that La Rochefoucauld had submitted for comment. In extreme cases, this process of editorial correction would submit the same *maxime* to over thirty *retouches.*[34]

La Rochefoucauld never hid his debt to Mme de Sablé: "You know that sentences are only sentences after you have approved them. I send to you what I took from you in part."[35] As Victor Cousin argues, the influence of Mme de Sablé is just as patent in the work of Blaise Pascal, another habitué of the Port-Royal salon.[36] The epigrammatic style, the moral psychology, and the Jansenist anthropology of the *Pensées* betray clear roots in the *maxime* genre that dominated the literary creation of Mme de Sablé's salon.

Unfortunately, Mme de Sablé's reputation as the patroness of La Rochefoucauld has obscured her own contribution to moral theory through a genre that she virtually invented. After her death, Abbé d'Ailly[37] published Mme de Sablé's own *maximes* under the title *Maximes de Mme la Marquise de Sablé. Pensées Diverses de M.L.D.* (Paris: 1678, in-12).[38] These *maximes* reveal Mme de Sablé's skill in using this tool of moral psychology developed in her own salon. They also manifest her distinctive moral outlook, a synthesis of social criticism and defense of virtue that differs sensibly from the bitter irony of La Rochefoucauld.

Certain of Mme de Sablé's *maximes* provide pragmatic counsels for success. *Maxime* 4 states that "It is sometimes useful to pretend that one is mistaken."[39] Mme de Sablé underlines the importance of style in achieving one's goals. *Maxime* 25: "There is a certain empire in the manner of speaking and acting, which imposes and which wins, in advance, consideration and respect. . . ."[40] Given the laboratory of the salon, Mme de Sablé pays particular attention to the proper conduct of speech. *Maxime* 36 praises the concise phrase: "Speaking too much is such a great fault, that in the area of conversation and business, if the good is the short, it is doubly good, because we win by brevity what we often lose by verbal excess."[41] Mme de Sablé notes the link between power and knowledge, especially the knowledge of others gained through intimate dialogue. *Maxime* 37: "Practically always, we make ourselves master of those we know well, because the one who is perfectly known is in a way subordinated to the one who knows him."[42] *Maxime* 35 traces the strategy of this psychological empowerment: "Knowing how to discover the interior of another and hide one's own is a great mark of a superior mind."[43] Significantly, the more pragmatic *maximes* do not present success in terms of economic wealth or political power. Rather, reflecting the culture of the salon, they conceive success as psychological knowledge achieved through a careful discipline of interpersonal dialogue.

Several of Mme de Sablé's *maximes* possess a more psychological cast, inasmuch as they present variations on Socratic ignorance. *Maxime* 38 argues: "The study of and search for truth often serve only to make us see, by experience, the ignorance which is naturally ours."[44] Mme de Sablé, however, adds her distinctive contours to the philosopher's confession of ignorance. More emotive, Sablean ignorance connotes madness. *Maxime* 8: "The greatest wisdom of man is to know his folly."[45] Mme de Sablé moralizes the quest for authentic knowledge: "It is quite vain and useless to make an examination of everything which happens in the world, if that does not serve to correct oneself."[46] Conversely, moral vice often appears as the outward sign of the incapacity to grasp one's mental and moral infirmity. *Maxime* 7: "Mediocre minds, poorly formed minds, especially the semi-savants, are most subject to opinionated stubbornness."[47] While playing on the Socratic paradox of the ignorance of the wise and the vain knowledge of the fool, these *maximes* evoke the Jansenist portrait of depraved human nature, in which one's confusion constitutes a privileged moment in the personal itinerary of moral and religious conversion.

The majority of Mme de Sablé's *maximes* constitute a critique of aristocratic society. The critique focuses on the vices typical of this milieu. Like la Rochefoucauld and Pascal, Mme de Sablé unmasks the self-interest, especially the pride, that disguises itself as virtue or necessity among the nobility.

Several *maximes* dissect the vanity that animates the salon's commerce: polite conversation. Instead of dialogue, such discourse normally consists of speeches strictly reducible to the speaker's partial interests. *Maxime* 29: "Everyone is so busy with her passions and her interests that she always wants to talk about them without ever entering into the passion and interests of those to whom she speaks, although they have the same need to be heard and helped."[48] In a minute study of the psychology of conversation, Mme de Sablé describes the chasm between the social conventions of politeness and the empire of the will in defending oneself. *Maxime* 31: "One of the things which make it difficult to find pleasant people, who seem reasonable in conversation, is that practically none of them do not think more about what they want to say than responding exactly to what one says to them. The most tolerant are happy to show an attentive expression, but at the same time, one sees, in their eyes and in their spirit, a removal and a precipitation to return to what they want to say. . . ."[49] In this *maxime,* Mme de Sablé not only satirizes the desperate search for personal triumph that dominates the conversation of the salon, but she also underscores the obstinacy of the human will in excluding the presence and interests of others, even in the anodyne exchange of everyday information.

Several *maximes* attack more directly the corruption of social power. Mme de Sablé contests the material wealth and the moral poverty of her peers. *Maxime* 67: "It is quite a common fault never to be happy with one's fortune and never unhappy with one's soul."[50] The link between economic fortune and emotive happiness reveals that virtue no longer motivates the leading members of society. *Maxime* 32 notes that "Good fortune almost always makes some change in the procedure, the tone, and the manner of conversation and action. It is a great weakness to want to adorn ourselves with that which is not ours: if we esteemed virtue more than any other thing, then neither any favor nor any promotion would ever change the heart or the face of people."[51] For Mme de Sablé, the definition of self-worth in terms of material fortune is only one sign of a society closed to the pursuit of virtue. Upon clearer scrutiny, even apparently altruistic actions manifest themselves as strategies of personal empowerment. *Maxime* 74: "Virtue is not always where one sees actions which appear virtuous; sometimes one only recognizes a favor in order to establish one's reputation or to be even more firmly ungrateful toward favors one does not wish to recognize."[52] The courtly rules of politeness themselves become weighted markers in the game of political aggrandizement.

Mme de Sablé's severest critique of French society is presented by her most famous *maxime,* number 81, entitled "On Comedy." This extended paragraph provides a categorical condemnation of theatrical performances. "All the great diversions are dangerous for the Christian life, but among all those which the world has invented, there is none greater to fear than the comedy."[53] This criticism of the theater is hardly novel for a member of the Jansenist circle. The sympathizers of Port-Royal, led by the moralist Nicole,[54] had repeatedly condemned attendance at the theater as incompatible with Christian righteousness. Both Catholic and Calvinist canons of the period banned Christian burial for members of the theatrical profession.[55] Mme de Sablé's criticism of the theater as a dangerous "diversion" echoes the larger Jansenist critique, perfected by Pascal,[56] of a society that suppresses religious questions under a curtain of jaded entertainments.

Strikingly, however, Mme de Sablé does not employ the traditional Christian arguments against the theater. The churches had habitually condemned the theater because of the sexual license of comic pieces and the debauchery, even prostitution, for which many theaters had become notorious. Mme de Sablé, on the contrary, criticizes the comedy because it creates an illusion of authentic love and, through mimetic participation, manipulates the emotions of the public. For Mme de Sablé, the danger is not obscenity or license. These can be rejected easily by the educated spectator. The danger lies in theatrical presentations of moral and reasonable love, illusions that subtly alter and destroy the authentic affections of the self. "It [comedy] is a representation so natural and delicate of the passions, which animates them and makes them arise in our heart, and especially that of love, when one provides a fairly chaste and honest love, because, the more it seems innocent to innocent souls, the more are those souls susceptible to comedy's influence."[57] Exposure to such models of romantic love prods the spectators to engineer such artificial relationships in their everyday lives. "So, one goes away from the comedy with the heart so full of all the sweets of love and the mind so persuaded of its innocence that one is completely prepared to receive the same pleasures and the same sacrifices that one has seen so well depicted in the comedy."[58] For Mme de Sablé, the deleterious effect of theater lies primarily in its power to imprison us in an imaginary society, in which sacrifice and pleasure take root in manufactured emotions rather than in the struggle for virtue. Theater promotes a false sense of "innocence" that precludes the realistic assessment of one's need for moral and religious conversion.

Several *maximes* develop their social critique by examining the gap between appearance and reality, a gap nurtured by the rules of social esteem. *Maxime* 19 diagnoses the contradiction: "We are more worried to appear as we should be than to be in effect what we should be."[59] This desire to appear virtuous, rather than to be virtuous, fosters a distinctive web of social deception. *Maxime* 20: "If we had as much care to be what we should be as we have to deceive others in disguising what we are, we would be able to show ourselves just as we are, without having the trouble of disguising ourselves."[60] Mme de Sablé detects a particularly virulent strain of appearance-reality conflict in the way in which her contemporaries execute their high offices of social trust. *Maxime* 23: "We often have a greater desire to pass for conscientious than to execute conscientiously our office, and often we prefer to be able to say to our friends that we have done well for them rather than having, in fact, done well."[61] For Mme de Sablé, the virtues and offices of the aristocrat often are nothing more than a slothful quest for social applause, artfully concealed under the polish of self-advertisement.

Despite the severe social criticism presented in the preceding *maximes,* Mme de Sablé's moral reflections are distinguished by a refusal to adopt the thoroughgoing cynicism of other authors in her salon. Her correspondence with La Rochefoucauld frequently contains criticism of La Rochefoucauld's extreme dismissal of all "virtues" as masks of interest. Several *maximes* develop a positive moral theory that attempts to defend the veracity of certain virtues and even, paradoxically, the social value of certain vices.

Mme de Sablé insists that, despite its perversions, virtue still constitutes the soul of authentic aristocracy. *Maxime* 72: "Those who are stupid enough to esteem themselves only by their nobility despise, in some way, that which makes them noble, since it is only the virtue of their ancestors which has made the nobility of their blood."[62] Mme de Sablé explicitly condemns the tendency of her peers to detect a hidden vice behind every virtue. *Maxime* 61: "There is nothing which doesn't have some perfection. Happily, good taste finds it in everything. However, natural malignity often discovers a vice hidden among several virtues, in order to highlight and publish it. This is more a trait of congenital evil than an advantage of discernment, and it is quite wrong to pass one's life in the single-minded delight in another's imperfections."[63] In her theory of virtue and vice, as well as in her political and religious *praxis,* Mme de Sablé exhibits her characteristic moderation. The critique of the social counterfeits of virtue cannot obscure either the preeminent value of virtue itself or the authentic, if rare, instances of its exercise.

Mme de Sablé even argues that in the daily struggle between the virtuous and the vicious, the virtuous often win. *Maxime* 9: "Honesty and sincerity in action shake those who are cruel and make them lose the way by which they plot to arrive at their ends, because the cruel usually believe that one never does anything without artifice."[64] Not content with the defense of virtue, Mme de Sablé contends that even aristocratic vice is not without social utility. *Maxime* 71: "It is almost better that the great of this world seek glory and even vanity in good actions, rather than not being touched by it at all, because, although they do not act by principles of virtue, there is at least this advantage: that vanity makes them do what they otherwise would not."[65] Mme de Sablé's critique of human duplicity takes place in a universe notably more optimistic than that of La Rochefoucauld, one in which even vice can paradoxically serve the goals of virtue.

In one area, Mme de Sablé is particularly adamant on immunity from deceit: the personal experience of love. *Maxime* 80 encapsulates Mme de Sablé's position: "Love has a character so particular that one can neither hide where it is nor pretend where it is not."[66] The particular veracity of the sentiment of love is rooted in the unitive knowledge that distinguishes it. *Maxime* 79: "Love is to the soul of the one who loves what the soul is to the body of the one it animates."[67] Mme de Sablé's insistence on the veracity of the sentiment of love clarifies her disdain for the theater, which threatens to distort the one area where authentic interpersonal knowledge might emerge.

Mme de Sablé's defense of the value of human love emerges even more clearly in her small treatise, "Of Friendship." First published in the nineteenth century by Victor Cousin,[68] this treatise defends friendship as the most common example of virtuous relationships. Mme de Sablé argues that friendship represents a synthesis of the fundamental virtues of social intercourse. "Friendship is a species of virtue which can only be founded upon the esteem of the persons loved, i.e., upon the qualities of the soul, such as fidelity, generosity, and discretion, and on the good qualities of mind."[69] Mme de Sablé insists that authentic friendship requires equality, a basic reciprocity between the partners. "It is also necessary that friendship be reciprocal, because in friendship one cannot, as in romantic love, love without being loved."[70] Another characteristic of authentic friendship is freedom. Friendship can only arise from an act of the will, not from affective inclinations. "One must not give the name 'friendship' to natural inclinations, because they depend neither on our will nor on our choice. Although they may make our friendships more pleasant, they must not be the foundation."[71] Mme de Sablé admits that certain "friendships" seem to be constructed upon mutual calculation, but she dismisses such unions as counterfeits of authentic friendship. Silent on the merits of family hierarchy, Mme de Sablé touts friendship as a privileged locus for the mutual, egalitarian pursuit of virtue.

Mme de Sablé's positive evaluation of friendship is clearly a riposte to her protégé, La Rochefoucauld. In his own *maximes*, La Rochefoucauld argues that all friendship is but a mask for egoistic interests. *Maxime* 83 of his is typical: "What humanity has named friendship is only a society, a reciprocal arrangement of interests, only an exchange of services; finally, it is only a commerce in which self-love always proposes something to win."[72]

The literary success of La Rochefoucauld has long obscured the role of a predominantly feminine salon in creating a new genre of moral reflection. In effect, Mme de Sablé pioneered an alternative to the academic philosopher's approach to ethics through the treatise, the sermon, and the metaphysical dialogue. As an ironic sentence, the *maxime* permitted the author to evoke rather than analyze the moral psychology of the aristocrat. Mme de Sablé's *maximes* constitute only the most extensive creation in moral theory developed by the women of her salon. Mme de Longueville and Mme de Lafayette each contributed to the baroque canon of *maximes*, deeply tinted by the dissidence of the Fronde and the Jansenists.

Madame de Sablé's contribution to moral theory is not limited to the creation of a new genre in her salon. Her own moral theory, elaborated through her corpus of *maximes* and letters, strikes an original balance between the skeptic's unmasking of vice and the sentimentalist's defense of authentic virtue through love. In Mme de Sablé's own work, the salon becomes the subject, not simply the milieu, of moral reflection. The evidence of human duplicity is the carefully observed script of salon conversation: the gap between word and gesture, the refusal to listen, the minute strategies of political conquest. Conversely, Mme de Sablé locates virtue in one specific place: in egalitarian friendship pursuing moral and religious reform. In other words, Mme de Sablé designates as "virtue" none other than the devout friendship that constitutes the *telos* of her Jansenist salon.

Notes

1. See Wendy Gibson, *Women in Seventeenth-Century France* (New York: St. Martin, 1989), pp. 175–92.

2. Ibid., pp. 17–40.

3. Ibid., pp. 38–39; see also Erica Harth, *Cartesian Women* (Ithaca: Cornell, 1992), pp. 64–122.

4. See René Descartes, "Lettre au Père Vatier" in *Correspondance, T. IV,* Adam-Mihaud, ed. (8 vols.) (Paris: Alcan, [1636–1656] 1936–1963), p. 134.

5. See Marie le Jars de Gournay, *Egalité des Hommes et des Femmes* (Paris: n.p., 1622). On currents of French feminism in the seventeenth century, see Ian Maclean, *Woman Triumphant* (Oxford: Clarendon, 1977).

6. See Gibson, ibid., pp. 30–34.

7. The main published work of Mme de Sablé is her *Maximes,* a posthumous collection of *maximes.* Victor Cousin published her essay "On Friendship" as well as substantial portions of her correspondence in *Madame de Sablé* (Paris: Didier, 1854). Valuable details on Mme de Sablé's salon are contained in the Archives of Conrart, preserved at the Bibliothèque de l'Arsenal in Paris, and the Archives of Valant, preserved at the Bibliothèque Nationale.

8. For a study of the evolution of the genre of the *maxime* among the salon's practitioners, see Christine Liebich, *La Rochefoucauld, Mme. de Sablé, et Jacques Esprit: De l'Inspiration commune à la Création personnelle* (Ann Arbor: Dissertation Abstracts, 1983), 43(9): 3006.

9. See Cousin, op. cit., pp. 9–33.

10. Ibid., pp. 61–63.

11. The salon was conducted by Catherine de Vivonne, marquise de Rambouillet (1588–1665). Strongly oriented toward literature and the theater, the salon served as a center for the dissidents of the Fronde.

12. Madeleine de Scudéry (1607–1701), author primarily known for *Artamène ou le Grand Cyrus* (1649–1653), a novelistic treatment of members of the Fronde. Her final works elaborate her moral theories: *Conversations morales* (1686), *Nouvelles considérations morales* (1688), *Entretiens sur la Morale* (1692).

13. Anne-Marie-Louise d'Orléans, duchesse de Montpensier, Fronde leader, disgraced in 1652, author, and head of a literary salon at the Palais du Luxembourg. Principal works: *Retour de l'Ile invisible* (1659), *Divers Portraits* (1659), *Mémoires* (1735).

14. For a study of Scudéry's salon, see Jean Mesnard, "Mademoiselle de Scudéry et la société du Marais" in *Mélanges offerts à Georges Coton,* Jehasse, ed. (Lyon: PU-Lyon, 1981), pp. 169–88.

15. Marie-Catherine-Hortense, Mme de Villedieu (1632–1672), dramatist and essayist. Her works were published in ten volumes (1710–1711).

16. See Cousin, op. cit., pp. 33–39.

17. Valentin Conrart (1603–1675), author and cofounder of the *Académie française.* Principal work: *Mémoires sur l'histoire de son temps* (Paris: Monmergué, 1825), useful for its accounts of the Parisian salons of the period.

18. Marie de Rabutin-Chantal, marquise de Sévigné (1626–1696), author of letters, successively shaped into collections: *Mémoires de Bussy* (1696), *Lettres* (1697), *Nouvelles lettres* (1709).

19. Marie-Madeleine Pioche de la Vergne, comtesse de la Fayette (1634–1692), novelist and author of letters. Principal works: *La Princesse de Clèves* (1678) and *Histoire de Mme Henriette d'Angleterre* (1700).

20. François IV, duc de la Rochefoucauld (1613–1680), Fronde leader, author of *Réflexions ou sentences et Maximes morales* (1655) and *Mémoires* (1662).

21. On the genesis of the literary "portrait" see Erica Harth, "The Ideological Value of the Portrait in Seventeenth-Century France" in *L'Esprit Créateur* (Fall, 1981), 21(3): 15–25.

22. See Cousin, op. cit., p. 50.

23. Jean Regnauld de Segrais (1624–1701), poet, secretary to Mlle de Montpensier and Mme de Lafayette. Editor of numerous "portrait" anthologies and certain works of Mme de Lafayette.

24. Antoine Arnauld (1612–1695), priest, Jansenist leader, and philosopher. Principal works: *La Logique de Port-Royal* (1662), dedicated to Mme de Sablé, and *Réflexions sur la Nature et la Grâce* (1685).

25. Pierre Nicole (1625–1695), moralist, professor at schools of Port-Royal. Coauthor (with Arnauld) of *Logique de Port-Royal*. In 1671, he published the first of thirteen volumes of *Essais morals*.

26. Jean Domat (1625–1696), legal scholar, editor of Pascal. Major works: *Les Lois civiles* (1689–1694), *Le Droit public* (1697).

27. Jacques Esprit (1611–1678), Oratorian priest and essayist. Principal works: *La Fausseté des vertus humaines* (1678) and *Maximes politiques mises en vers* (1669), both composed in Mme de Sablé's salon.

28. Blaise Pascal (1623–1663), philosopher and mathematician, entered the Port-Royal circle in 1654. A participant in Mme de Sablé's salon, Pascal in his *Provinciales* (1656–1657) and in his posthumous *Pensées* reflects the epigrammatic genres and Jansenist anthropology of the salon.

29. See Cousin, op. cit., p. 72.

30. Ibid.

31. Charlotte Saumaize de Chazon, comtesse de Brégy (1619–1696), poet and letter writer. Principal work: *Lettres et poésies* (Leyden: 1666).

32. See Cousin, op. cit., p. 73.

33. For a study of the genesis of the *Maximes,* see Susan Read Baker, *Collaboration et Originalité chez La Rochefoucauld* (Gainesville: University of Florida Press, 1980).

34. See Cousin, op. cit., pp. 132–43.

35. La Rochefoucauld, *Oeuvres III.I* (Paris: Hachette, 1919), p. 147.

36. See Cousin, op. cit., p. 94.

37. Nicholas, Abbé d'Ailly (1640–1712), priest and author. He edited Mme de Sablé's *Maximes* (1678), to which he added his own *maximes* under the pseudonym "M.L.D." Principal work: *Sentiments et maximes sur ce qui se passe dans la société civile* (1697).

38. See Mme de Sablé, *Maximes de Madame la Marquise de Sablé; suivies de Pensées de M.L.D.,* d'Ailly ed. (Paris: Mabre-Cramoisy, 1678). A partial reedition, *Maximes de Mme de Sablé* (Paris: Jouart, 1870), was published in 322 copies. Unless otherwise noted, references in this article are to the Jouart edition. The translations from the French text are those of the author of this article.

39. Mme de Sablé (Jouart), p. 14.

40. Ibid., p. 23.

41. Ibid., p. 28.

42. Ibid.

43. Ibid., p. 27.

44. Ibid., p. 29.

45. Ibid., p. 16.

46. Ibid., p. 15.

47. Ibid.

48. Ibid., p. 24.

49. Ibid., p. 25.

50. Ibid., p. 40.

51. Ibid., p. 26.

52. Ibid., p. 43.

53. Ibid., p. 46.

54. See Pierre Nicole, "De la Comédie" in *Les Essais de Morale* (1671).

55. On the Christian critique of the dramatic profession, see Herbert Thurston, "Theatre" in *The Catholic Encyclopedia* vol. XIV (New York: Appleton, 1912), pp. 559–61.

56. See Blaise Pascal, "Divertissements" in *Oeuvres complètes,* Lafuma, ed. (Paris: Seuil, 1963), pp. 516–8.

57. Mme de Sablé, op. cit., p. 46.

58. Ibid., p. 20.

59. Ibid.

60. Ibid., p. 21.

61. Ibid., p. 22.

62. Ibid., p. 42.

63. Ibid., p. 38.

64. Ibid., p. 16.

65. Ibid., p. 42.

66. Ibid., p. 46.

67. Ibid., p. 45.

68. See Cousin, op. cit., pp. 79–80.

69. Mme de Sablé, op. cit., p. 58.

70. Ibid., p. 59.

71. Ibid.

72. La Rochefoucauld, *Oeuvres* I, Gilbert-Gourdault, ed. (Paris: Hachette, 1923), p. 66.

Ann Willeford

20 A Woman-Centered Philosophy: An Alternative to Enlightenment Thought (1700–1750)

When we speak of philosophy in eighteenth-century France, we almost always think of the Enlightenment and its well-known proponents, the *philosophes*. In this paper I wish to bring to light another powerful philosophical influence that, in the first half of the century, also deeply affected social, intellectual, and political life in France. Like the Enlightenment, it offered an alternative to the traditional Christian ethic, but in a very different way that eventually threatened the Enlightenment enterprise itself.

I am referring to a philosophy that I will call "woman-centered" because it differs essentially from mainstream Enlightenment thought in deriving its model of human excellence from a concept of woman prevalent in seventeenth- and eighteenth-century France. Mainstream Enlightenment thought, as others have observed, draws its inspiration from an eighteenth-century concept of man.[1] This lesser-known philosophy, which I will presently describe in greater detail, built on a concept of woman as the essence of civilization and refinement, and glorified faculties that were perceived in the eighteenth century as mainly feminine: imagination, taste, feeling, and sensitivity. This concept has roots in the medieval period and the court of François Ier, but it had been most recently articulated in France in the salons of the seventeenth century.[2]

The woman-centered philosophy differed from that of the Enlightenment not only in content but also in form. Enlightenment thought was articulated in discursive works, within the context of established philosophical tradition, by formally educated men who expended great effort to propagate their views. The woman-centered philosophy was usually expressed in letters, personal essays not intended for publication, or novels, all "marginal" forms of literature, by self-educated women or men writing anonymously. Its creators made no claim to a place in the philosophical establishment; some of them even avoided recognition.[3]

Their philosophy is nevertheless developed and coherent. While some of its principles are not stated explicitly and must be inferred from information we have about the salon culture, we do also have excellent spokesmen and spokeswomen among members of the salon culture. In particular, Madame de Lambert, center of the first important intellectual salon of the century, advanced a woman-centered view of life in her writings. Many novelists, among them Madame de Tencin, Marivaux, and Prévost, imbued their fiction with the values of such a philosophy. Of course there were salon-goers, among them many *philosophes*, who did not share these views. And while Georges May has established the link between feminism and the novel—a link so apparent even to contemporaries that one disgruntled male complained that the apotheosis of women in novels lacked only temples and altars[4]—there were "anti-novels" such as those of Voltaire and Diderot that exhibit a poor opinion of women. In addition to these eighteenth-century writings, we have modern accounts of salon life. Carolyn Lougee's *Le Paradis des Femmes* is particularly helpful.

This "other" philosophy has gone relatively unnoticed, perhaps because at the beginning of the century it was so closely associated with its eventual rival. We are accustomed to associating the *philosophes* with the salons and the *"idées nouvelles"* ("new ideas") with the novel. And rightly so, for through the period in question their similarities seemed to outweigh their differences. *Philosophes*, salons, and the novel were all three subversive of the *ancien régime*. It is worth repeating that society women contributed greatly to the development of *"honnêteté,"* the secular morality that weakened the authority of the Church. They further relaxed the class structure not only by inviting to the same gatherings artists and intellectuals as well as society folk, but also by advancing the careers of their intellectual and artistic *protégés*, many of whom were *philosophes*. The salons had transferred the center of intellectual life from the court to the city, and they provided an important means of dissemination of the new ideas. Likewise, novels, often through the depiction of women, love, and sexual license, threatened the bases of traditional authority to the point that they were banned outright for some twelve years starting around 1738.[5] But when, later in this paper, we examine the profound differences separating the woman-centered philosophy from Enlightenment thought, we will see that, despite the common cause they initially shared, the two were bound to part company.

Before reviewing those differences, I would like to pause over the concept of sexual difference as conceived in the period, because it lies at the base of these divergent philosophies. Eighteenth-century society rarely questioned whether women and men were different, and it is thus not surprising to see visions of the world that are widely different depending on whether they take either man or woman as point of reference. It is important to note, however, that the term "different" had divergent connotations for the *philosophes* and for the proponents of the woman-centered philosophy. For the latter, "different" did not necessarily mean "inferior." Women's difference gave them superiority in some domains, such as the love relationship, which in this context was a valued part of human experience. And the woman-centered view also integrated some supposedly masculine traits. In the salons, men were urged to cultivate their refinement and sensitivity, and women were exhorted to cultivate their reason.[6] In the novels, we witness a blurring of the usual sexual "differences." To cite an early (1713) and influential example, the heroines of *Les Illustres Françaises*[7] are stunningly active and enterprising in contrast to their male counterparts, who tend to be overly conventional, somewhat dull, and curiously passive in the love relationship. The novel, in fact, positively glorified difference, consistently emphasizing the singularity of the heroine that almost always was indicative of her moral superiority. (Prévost's *Manon* is an exception, but I believe it is because in this novel Prévost is more interested in des Grieux's fantasies about Manon than in the woman herself.[8]) For the woman-centered philosophers, it was woman's difference from man—man who had for centuries been the object of study of the seemingly worn-out Christian moral philosophy—that seemed to offer a new perspective on human nature in general.[9] Thus their "feminine" model was open to men as well as to women, and to study the "different" nature of woman was in effect to make new discoveries about human nature that would then be integrated into a model valuable for both sexes. I am not saying that woman-centered philosophers wished for the elimination of difference. It is clear, however, that they thought each sex would profit from emulating the other, and that they considered no attribute to be the exclusive province of either sex.

"Difference" for the *philosophes,* however, carried quite another set of associations. Concerned with restructuring society, they sought a uniform standard for human behavior, one that was "conceived as universal, uncomplicated, immutable . . . for every rational being."[10] Or in Paul Hazard's words, "The individual as such, that is to say whatever was unique and incommunicable about him, might be left for subsequent ages to consider."[11] As Condorcet wryly observed towards the end of the century, the *philosophes* were "a class of men less concerned with discovering or deepening their understanding of truth than they were in spreading it" ("une classe d'hommes moins occupés encore de découvrir ou d'approfondir la vérité que de la répandre"[12]); there was a strong reductionist tendency to their thought. In contrast to the proponents of the woman-centered philosophy who wished to expand the definition of human nature, the *philosophes* were intent on defining it more narrowly. They almost always had in mind a loosening of the authority of the Church and thus wished to define their position very clearly in opposition to the religious view. They perceived their struggle with traditional thought as an ideological war, as Voltaire's repeated war cry attests: "Ecrasons l'infâme!" (usually translated as "Let us crush the Beast!", "the Beast" being the intolerant practices of the Church). Diderot expressed delight at being delivered from powerful "enemies" when the Jesuits were expelled. To them, difference was not interesting but threatening, and what was different was usually inferior and to be excluded or overpowered. Their belief that women were different should be seen in that light. Most of them accepted the old assumption that women lacked reason,[13] and they proposed reason as the informing principle of a new society. Quite simply, the *philosophes* made no attempt to integrate either the traditional or the "rehabilitated" concept of woman into their model of human excellence.

This use of difference as an exclusionary tactic was by no means limited to women; the *philosophes* were likely to exclude from their ranks anyone who did not share their views. Diderot's inability to understand Rousseau's need for conformity of inner and outer (we might also say private and public) states that made Rousseau refuse a royal pension, or Rousseau's preference for solitude over the society of others, led Diderot to write the remark that Jean-Jacques claimed ended the friendship, "Only the wicked live alone" ("Il n'y a que le méchant qui vit seul"[14]).

In this short paper I can only sketch the outlines of this woman-centered philosophy and suggest for purposes of comparison the basic premises of Enlightenment thought. When writing about various Enlightenment positions, I am aware that writers like Voltaire and Diderot in the course of their lives changed their own attitudes on such essential questions as free will and the validity of the whole Enlightenment enterprise. The period under study was one of powerful ferment and of furious, ceaseless debate concerning human nature and ethics, with shifting grounds and arguments. I am concerned with the first half of the century because it is the period immediately preceding the shift of social power from women to the *philosophes*, a shift I believe was related to the differences between these two philosophies. In the second half of the century, the position of the writer-*philosophe* became secure[15]; he was no longer heavily dependent upon society women for the advancement of his career. Diderot was sought out by Catherine the Great; Voltaire was named Chamberlain by Frederick II. It was actually possible for a writer to make a living by his (rarely her) pen. Enlightenment philosophy eclipsed that of the salons, and novels, although widely read, were not appreciated for their philosophical content.

In the following pages I will compare woman-centered and Enlightenment philosophies in four ways: according to the general approach each had to the study of human nature, the mental faculty to which each attributed superiority and the role of determining value and purveying knowledge, the conception of human nature each had with regard to teleology, and the position of each regarding the source of authority.

One can note first of all that the two groups approached the study of human nature with different interests and assumptions. The *philosophes* were eager to clarify what men had in common[16]; they were interested in public life, and in psychological analysis only insofar as it could be applied to public life.[17] They wanted a simple model of human nature, having had enough of the notion of *homo duplex* and Pascal's conflicting souls, and they wanted nothing to do with innate ideas or innate knowledge. Furthermore, the Enlightenment model of human nature was drawn from beliefs and observations concerning the male sex. That is to say, the *philosophes* valued those qualities and activities most often associated in their culture with men and they tended to denigrate or even deny the existence of qualities associated with women. They prized reason, distrusted imagination, and refused to recognize as authentic literature the novelistic genre because, they said, it had been corrupted by women's frivolity, bad taste, and obsession with love.[18] (The genre also included far more women authors than any other genre of the time did.) In praising reason, Diderot said that women had less of it than men; Voltaire compared women to weather vanes in their inability to make up their minds for themselves; and both writers bestowed on their chosen female companions—whose intellects they admired—the compliment that they were fine men.[19]

Adherents of the salon culture and readers and writers of novels, however, found the singularity of the individual fascinating, delighted in the private life—as well as the public—and were interested in psychological analysis for its own sake. The complexity of human motivation intrigued them, and they took pleasure in identifying what they believed were the innate qualities of individuals and watching or encouraging their development. This attention is evident in one of the functions of salon society, the advancement of unknown artists. The novel, through its fascination with the singularity of its characters, also attests to these interests. Even the *philosophes* agreed that women were mysterious and complex, but this supposed complexity and ambiguity of women's motivation was cause for scorn in their eyes as well as in those of traditional Church moralists. In contrast, the woman-centered philosophic vision of human nature was drawn from a concept of the nature of woman. This concept had most recently been developed in the salons of the seventeenth century around the feminine attributes of beauty, refinement, and taste, and the Neo-Platonist interpretation of love and woman's role in the love relationship. In this context women's traditional defects were transformed into assets, and women were considered the superior civilizing force. Proponents of this view denigrated some traditionally masculine characteristics, such as brute force, but they were in general more apt to praise feminine qualities than to criticize masculine ones.[20]

Each "school" had a different conception of the basis of human nature. For the *philosophes*, it was a blank slate. Following Locke and Voltaire, they denied, even attacked, the notions of individual essence and innate ideas or innate knowledge. They had great faith in the malleability of human beings, upon which their vision of progress depended. The woman-centered philosophy, through its appreciation of qualities most often associated with women, offered quite a different model. Far from adopting the view of the blank slate, it accepted the notion of innate qualities such as beauty, taste, sensitivity, prized them above all others, and emphasized that, being inborn, they were impossible to acquire—although it was possible to cultivate them further. For the woman-centered philosophy, the basis of human nature was an essence that had to be developed and fulfilled. For the proponents of this view, human nature was thus in important aspects fixed, not malleable.

Each "school" also singled out as most valuable one of the three mental faculties that both recognized: reason, memory, and imagination. The *philosophes* chose reason. "Reason is to the *philosophe* what grace is to the Christian. Grace impels the Christian to act; reason impels the *philosophe*" ("La raison est à l'égard du *philosophe* ce que la grâce est à l'égard du chrétien. La grâce détermine le chrétien à agir; la raison détermine le *philosophe*"[21]). And according to Diderot and d'Alembert's tree of knowledge in the *Encyclopédie*, reason was the source of philosophy, subsuming knowledge of man, ethics, and nature.[22] While writings of the *philosophes* often coupled "imagination" with adjectives such as "disordered" and "unbridled," defenders of the woman-centered view praised the merits of imagination as a faculty much more likely to be laudable in women rather than in men. Madame de Lambert, citing Malebranche, attributed to women "all the pleasing qualities of the imagination" ("tous les agréments de l'imagination"[23]). Taste and sensitivity were subsumed under this faculty.

The role of the primary faculty was critical in each view, for it determined value and was the purveyor of knowledge. In the words of one *philosophe*, "reason is nothing other than an accurate discernment between the good and the bad and between the true and the false" ("la raison n'est autre chose qu'un discernement juste de ce qui est bon d'avec ce qui est mauvais et de ce qui est vrai d'avec ce qui est faux"[24]). Moreover, whether an action was considered "good" or "bad" depended upon the results it had. For the *philosophes*, value was relative, and to the terms "good" and "bad" they preferred "doing good" ("*bienfaisance*") and "doing harm" ("*malfaisance*"). Reason was also assigned the task of governing action: "The *philosophe*, even in his passions, acts only after reflection; he walks at night, but he carries a torch. . . . The *philosophe* is thus a decent man who acts in everything in accordance with reason" ("[L]e *philosophe*, dans ses passions mêmes, n'agit qu'après la réflexion; il marche la nuit, mais il est précédé d'un flambeau. . . . Le *philosophe* est donc un honnête homme qui agit en tout par raison"[25]). Reason was again critical in the acquisition of knowledge. Following Bacon and Locke, the *philosophes* recognized only knowledge having an empirical base, that is, information that had come through the senses and had been processed by reason. "The *philosophe* forms his principles on an infinity of individual observations" ("Le *philosophe* forme ses principes sur une infinité d'observations particulières"[26]). In the *Discours préliminaire* of the *Encyclopédie*, d'Alembert praises Newton for having restricted philosophy to the study of observed phenomena. In the words of Robert Darnton, "non-empirical knowledge . . . was out of bounds" and the *philosophes* were the "boundary keepers."[27]

In the woman-centered view, imagination and its adjuncts, taste, feeling, and sensitivity, determine value, govern conduct, and purvey knowledge. Emphasizing the nonrational, nonempirical, and innate character of taste, Madame de Lambert writes: "Taste refines the mind and makes you notice, quickly and keenly, and without making any demands on reason, everything there is to see in each object" ("Le goût met de la finesse dans l'esprit, et vous fait apercevoir d'une manière vive et prompte, sans qu'il en coûte rien à la raison, tout ce qu'il y a à voir dans chaque chose"[28]). (Although we may translate "*le goût*" as "taste," the French word, especially in its eighteenth-century context, has a wider range of meaning than its modern English equivalent.) She insists that we must distinguish between qualities meriting our esteem and those that are merely pleasant. "Those worthy of esteem are real and intrinsic to the object and, by the laws of justice, have a natural claim on our esteem," whereas "pleasant qualities, which stir the soul and which give such sweet impressions, are neither real, nor specific to the object; they have their source in our [sensory] organs and in the power of our imagination" ("Les estimables sont réelles et sont intrinsèques aux choses, et, par les lois de la justice, ont un droit naturel sur notre estime" . . . "les qualités agréables, qui ébranlent l'âme et qui donnent de si douces impressions, ne sont point réelles, ni propres à l'objet; elles se doivent à la disposition de nos organes et à la puissance de notre imagination"[29]). In other words, value is intrinsic, not relative, and sensory information is not really reliable. Marivaux, her close friend, declared: "As for me, I believe that our mind is only a poor dreamer every time, in such an instance, that it disagrees with the heart" ("Pour moi, je crois que notre esprit n'est qu'un mauvais rêveur toutes les fois qu'en pareil cas il n'est pas de l'avis du coeur"[30]). His case in point concerns a man criticizing a play he has just seen and describing the play's flaws, "weeping while he criticized it in such a way that his heart was doing the critique of his mind" ("pendant qu'il larmoyait en la critiquant: de sorte que son coeur faisait la critique de son esprit"[31]).

The woman-centered view also holds that feeling ("*le sentiment*") best determines our behavior. The novels are full of examples. The hero of Prévost's *Cleveland*, for example, who professes to govern himself by reason,[32] is forced to recognize its limits when divorced from feeling. Once in great despair, he planned to kill himself and his children (in order to spare them the pain of losing their father). But when he drew his sword to execute the plan, the boys ran away terrified. It was reason, he explained in recounting this episode, that led him to form the plan: "I do not think that I ever in my life followed more methodical reasoning than that which led me to the edge of the most horrible precipice" ("je ne crois pas que j'aie fait dans toute ma vie de raisonnements plus méthodiques que ceux qui me conduisirent jusqu'au bord du plus affreux précipice"[33]). Lambert expresses herself similarly: "Conviction of the heart is above that of the mind, since our conduct often depends on it: it is to our imagination and to our heart that nature has entrusted the governance of our actions and of its movements" ("La persuasion du coeur est au-dessus de celle de l'esprit, puisque souvent notre conduite en dépend: c'est à notre imagination et à notre coeur que la nature a remis la conduite de nos actions et de ses mouvements"[34]). Imagination also made available to women nonempirical knowledge, the kind most prized within the salon culture. Women were appreciated for their possession of it and, as Lougee relates, in the seventeenth century had acquired new authority because of it.[35] Fauchery writes of "this facility women have at acquiring knowledge without having to learn it, this science which ridicules science" ("cette facilité des femmes à s'instruire sans apprendre, cette science qui ridiculise la science"[36]).

Taste and sensitivity, adjuncts of imagination, were the purveyors of nonempirical knowledge. "We go as surely to the truth by the force and the heat of the feelings as by the extent and exactitude of reasoning; and we always arrive more rapidly, through them, at the goal in question than through facts" ("Nous allons aussi sûrement à la vérité par la force et la chaleur des sentiments que par l'étendue et la justesse des raisonnements; et nous arrivons toujours par eux plus vite au but dont il s'agit que par les connaissances"[37]), writes Madame de Lambert. She contrasts this kind of knowledge, which she calls "*les goûts,*" with empirical knowledge, "*les opinions*" or "*les connaissances.*"

One cannot give a reason for one's tastes, because one doesn't know why one feels; but one can always explain one's opinions and the things one knows. . . . I thus believe that I can persuade any intelligent person to adopt my opinion. I am never sure of persuading a sensitive person to share my taste. . . . There is nevertheless a rightness of taste as there is a rightness of reasoning. . . . But, since one cannot give any reliable rule for it, one cannot convince those who make mistakes. If their feeling does not instruct them, you cannot teach them. . . . It is nature which gives it [rightness of taste]; it cannot be acquired ([O]n ne peut rendre raison de ses goûts, parce qu'on ne sait point pourquoi on sent; mais on rend toujours raison de ses opinions et de ses connaissances. . . . Je crois donc pouvoir amener toute personne intelligente à mon avis. Je ne suis jamais sûre d'amener une personne sensible à mon goût. . . . Il y a cependant une justesse de goût comme il y a une justesse de sens. . . . Mais, comme on n'en peut donner de règle assurée, on ne peut convaincre ceux qui y font des fautes. Dès que leur sentiment ne les avertit pas, vous ne pouvez les instruire. . . . C'est la nature qui le donne; il ne s'acquiert pas[38]).

Marivaux gives to Marianne, and indeed to many of his protagonists, the gift of knowing nonempirically through delicacy of feeling. And salon-goer Abbadie held that feeling was the surest and most direct way to truth.[39]

Proponents of Enlightenment and those of the woman-centered philosophy differed on another important point, whether human nature should be conceived teleologically or not. The *philosophes* refused a teleological view; they conceived of no pre-established purpose for humankind, whether personal or collective. They felt that Christian thought had proposed an impossible goal of perfection, and "man-as-he-is" with all his imperfections was good enough for them.[40] They held that one should be satisfied with one's nature, and that it would be relatively useless to attempt to improve upon it. They articulated their goal to be the creation of a smoothly-functioning society, but they did not imagine that it involved the fulfillment of individual or collective destiny.

The woman-centered philosophy, on the contrary, revealed a teleological view of human nature. One of the most important functions of the salons was the identification and cultivation of essence in unknown artists. And a recurring theme found in both the writings of Madame de Lambert and in novels is the striving towards perfection. Madame de Lambert advises her daughter, "The purpose of moral philosophy is not to destroy nature, but to perfect it" ("La morale n'a pas pour objet de détruire la nature, mais de la perfectionner"[41]). The discovery of personal destiny and its fulfillment is also a major theme in most of the novels of the period. Critic John Freccero points out that the autobiographical form of these novels entails the opposition of two narrators, the younger, unformed one and the older, wiser one who recounts his or her transformation for the better.[42]

It is clear from these observations that the two groups differed deeply in regard to the source of authority. The *philosophes*, despite their overt rejection of authority, in effect urged people to accept only a different external authority: the *philosophes* themselves. "How happy the people will be when kings are *philosophes*, or when *philosophes* are kings!" ("Que les peuples seront heureux quand les rois seront *philosophes*, ou quand les *philosophes* seront rois!"[43]). They asked people to look to reason, while presenting themselves as the embodiment of that faculty. "Other men are carried away by their passions, without ever thinking beforehand about their actions: these are men who walk in darkness; whereas the *philosophe,* in his very passions, acts only after reflection" ("Les autres hommes sont emportés par leurs passions sans que les actions qu'ils font soient précédées de la réflexion: ce sont des hommes qui marchent dans les ténèbres; au lieu que le *philosophe,* dans ses passions mêmes, n'agit qu'après la réflexion"[44]). It is ironic that, at the same time as the *philosophes* were claiming to be freeing morality from identification with any particular social group, they were in fact making it entirely dependent upon the people in power.[45] Their insistence on human nature as a blank slate and their refusal to recognize nonempirical knowledge implied that knowledge and authority were somehow outside the individual and had to be either conquered or submitted to.

The woman-centered philosophy, in contrast, counseled people to look inward. Madame de Lambert advised her son, "Your court of judgment is within yourself: why look for it elsewhere?" ("Votre tribunal est en vous-même: pourquoi le chercher ailleurs?"[46]). The heroines of the novels are not satisfied to meet their society's standards; they have their own. For the proponents of this view, the human slate was not blank, innate qualities formed the basis of human worth, and mastery of oneself, not others, was one's task in life. Inner reality took precedence over sensory experience, and the source of authority was within, not without, the individual.

It is also clear that the woman-centered culture threatened, both theoretically and practically, the bases of the new society envisioned by the *philosophes.* Theoretically, it held different goals and opposing views on human nature, the source of knowledge and authority, and the place of the individual in society. Practically, society women wielded power the *philosophes* desired for themselves. The Enlightenment was an ideological struggle, identifying itself with *"les idées nouvelles."* It is impossible to imagine that the *philosophes* were unaware of the values and principles of the woman-centered philosophy, and, indeed, it seems no accident that they hailed as one of the fathers of their movement Bacon, whose presiding metaphor was the domination of nature—cast as feminine—by knowledge—cast as masculine.[47]

The Enlightenment movement eventually triumphed over the woman-centered philosophy as well as over the *ancien régime.* Two hundred years of women's social dominance ceased when "la philosophie" drove out "l'amour" as the topic of conversation in the salons. And with the revolution, women lost almost all traces of their former power and influence. The victory of the *philosophes* is not surprising. They offered clarity, psychological and ethical simplicity, and uncomplicated happiness in a well-ordered society. And yet the woman-centered culture offered the more comprehensive, although perhaps less comforting view: it allowed room for ambiguity, psychological and ethical complexity, and nonutilitarian values.

Certainly it was an audacious enterprise to elucidate a world view centered on the sex that, according to classical and Christian tradition, lacked soul and reason. In a culture that wished to confine woman to an instinctual nature, it was not only audacious but a tour de force that the originators of this philosophy should manage to transform the would-be liability of innateness into the organizing principle of refined society. Through this philosophy, for at least two hundred years, women exerted great influence in social, political, and intellectual affairs, while advocating the integration of what were perceived as masculine and feminine qualities and values. Madame de Lambert's "model of perfection," for instance, would be a person combining "the reason of men" with "the graces of women" ("la saine raison des hommes" and "les agréments des femmes"[48]). She noted, citing Saint-Evremond, that it was "less impossible to find reason in women than graces in men" ("moins impossible de trouver dans les femmes la saine raison des hommes que dans les hommes les agréments des femmes"[49]).

Notes

1. See especially Genevieve Lloyd, *The Man of Reason: "Male" and "Female" in Western Philosophy* (Minneapolis: University of Minnesota Press, 1984).

2. See Carolyn Lougee, *Le Paradis des Femmes: Women, Salons, and Social Stratification in Seventeenth-Century France* (Princeton, N.J.: Princeton University Press, 1977).

3. Madame de Lambert paid to have destroyed an edition of her work that she had not authorized. See Jules Bertaut, *La Vie littéraire en France au XVIIIe siècle* (Paris: Edition Jules Tallandier, 1954), p. 30.

4. "Que manque-t-il, en effet, dans les romans, à l'apothéose des femmes, sinon des temples et des autels?" Quoted in Georges May, *Le Dilemme du roman au XVIIIe siècle* (New Haven, Conn.: Yale University Press, 1963), p. 215.

5. See May, pp. 78–84.

6. See Madame de Lambert, "Traité de la vieillesse" and "Réflexions sur les femmes" in *Oeuvres complètes* (Paris: Léopold Colin, 1808). In 1989, when I did most of the research for this article, the only editions of Madame de Lambert's work available to me were those published in the nineteenth century. After being widely read in the eighteenth and nineteenth centuries, Madame de Lambert's writings, like those of many other women writers of her century, fell into oblivion. In 1990, Robert Granderoute published a new edition of her writings: Anne Thérèse de Marguenat de Courcelles, marquise de Lambert, *Oeuvres* (Paris: Honoré Champion). And in 1991 Roger Marchal published a detailed biography of her: *Madame de Lambert et son milieu* in *Studies on Voltaire and the Eighteenth Century* 289. Subsequent quotations from Madame de Lambert in this article are taken from Granderoute's edition

7. Robert Chasles [Challe], *Les Illustres Françaises*, 2 vols., Frédéric Deloffre, ed. (Paris: "Les Belles Lettres", 1973).

8. Abbé Prévost, *Histoire du Chevalier Des Grieux et de Manon Lescaut* (Paris: Gallimard, 1972).

9. See Pierre Fauchery, *La Destinée féminine dans le roman européen du dix-huitième siècle: 1713–1807* (Paris: Armand Colin, 1972), p. 9.

10. Paul Hazard, *European Thought in the Eighteenth Century: From Montesquieu to Lessing*, J. Lewis May trans. (London: Hollis and Carter, 1954), p. 292.

11. Ibid., pp. 230–1.

12. Antoine Nicolas de Condorcet, *Esquisse d'un tableau historique des progrès de l'esprit humain*, O. H. Prior, ed. (Paris: Boivin, 1933), p. 159, quoted in Herbert Dieckmann, "Philosophy and Literature in Eighteenth-Century France," *Comparative Literature Studies* 8.1 (1971): 23.

13. For a blatant example see Diderot's *Essai sur les femmes* in *Oeuvres complètes*, 20 vols., J. Assézat, ed. (Paris: Garnier Frères, 1875–1877), Vol. 2.

14. See Ernst Cassirer, *Rousseau-Kant-Goethe* (Hamden, Connecticut: Archon Books, 1961), pp. 7–8.

15. See Robert Darnton, *The Literary Underground of the Old Regime* (Cambridge, Mass.: Harvard University Press, 1982), p. 12.

16. See Hazard, pp. 230–1.

17. See Lester G. Crocker, *An Age of Crisis: Man and World in Eighteenth-Century French Thought* (Baltimore: The Johns Hopkins Press, 1959), p. 322.

18. See May, p. 175.

19. Voltaire described Madame du Châtelet as "that lady whom I look upon as a great man," and on another occasion spoke of her and Caesar as "two great men"; Diderot called Sophie Volland "man and woman, when it so pleases him/her." Quoted in Roseann Runte, "Woman as Muse" in *French Women and the Age of Enlightenment*, Samia Spencer, ed. (Bloomington: Indiana University Press, 1984), p. 150.

20. See Lougee.

21. This definition comes from the essay *Philosophe*, the fifth in a collection titled *Nouvelles libertés de penser*, published in Paris in 1743. See Roger Mercier, *La Réhabilitation de la nature humaine (1700–1750)* (Villemonble/Seine, France: La Balance, 1960), p. 264. The essay appeared in abridged form as the article *Philosophe* in the *Encyclopédie*, from which I quote in this paper. Subsequent references to this article will be noted as *Philosophe*. See *Encyclopédie, ou Dictionnaire raisonné des sciences, des arts et des métiers, par une société de gens de lettres, 1751–1780* (Stuttgart-Bad Cannstatt: Friedrich Frommann Verlag, Günther Holzboog, 1967).

22. See Robert Darnton, *The Great Cat Massacre and Other Episodes in French Cultural History* (New York: Basic Books, Inc., 1984), pp. 210–1.

23. Madame de Lambert, p. 219.

24. Ira O. Wade, *The Clandestine Organization and Diffusion of Philosophic Ideas in France from 1700 to 1750* (New York: Octagon Books, 1967), p. 2.

25. *Philosophe*.

26. *Philosophe*.

27. Robert Darnton, *The Great Cat Massacre*, p. 209.

28. Madame de Lambert, p. 220.

29. Madame de Lambert, p. 223.

30. Marivaux, "Le Spectateur français: Seizième feuille" in *Journaux et Oeuvres diverses* (Paris: Garnier Frères, 1969), p. 205.

31. Ibid. For discussion see Mercier, pp. 198–9.

32. Prévost, *Le Philosophe anglais ou Histoire de Monsieur Cleveland* in *Oeuvres de Prévost*, 8 vols. (Grenoble, France: Presses Universitaires, 1978), Vol. II, p. 244.

33. Prévost, *Cleveland*, pp. 289–91.

34. Madame de Lambert, p. 221.

35. Lougee, pp. 31–32.

36. Fauchery, p. 169.

37. Madame de Lambert, p. 221.

38. Ibid.

39. Mercier, p. 89.

40. Alasdair MacIntyre, *After Virtue: A Study in Moral Theory* (Notre Dame, In.: Notre Dame University Press, 1984), p. 55.

41. Madame de Lambert, p. 119.

42. See John Freccero, "Autobiography and Narrative" in *Restructuring Individualism:*

Autonomy, Individuality, and the Self in Western Thought, Thomas C. Heller, Morton Sosna, and David E. Wellbery, eds. (Stanford, Calif.: Stanford University Press, 1986), pp. 16–17.

43. *Philosophe.*
44. *Philosophe.*
45. See MacIntyre, pp. 231–3.
46. Madame de Lambert, p. 75.
47. For discussion see Lloyd, pp. 10–17.
48. Madame de Lambert, p. 223.
49. Ibid.

Karin Brown

21   Madame de Condorcet's Letters on Sympathy

Introduction

Madame de Condorcet (1764–1822) translated Adam Smith's *Theory of Moral Sentiments* into French and added her eight letters on sympathy. Her translation was the third and best French translation of Smith's work. But more important, her letters on sympathy provide criticism and add depth to Smith's moral theory. The reviewer Boijoslin suggested that the letters added an important dimension to Smith's somewhat superficial analysis of sympathy.[1] Her criticism is addressed to Smith's lack of attention to the origin of sympathy. Although sympathy is at the heart and base of his moral theory, Smith took the existence of this disposition for granted and did not try to provide an argument for its existence or explain its origin. Mme Condorcet took the challenge of tracing sympathy to its first causes and found them to lie in our first physical sensations of pleasure and pain. In her work, physical experience plays a major role in explaining how sympathy arises in the first place and how it is provoked throughout one's life. Her brother-in-law Cabanis, to whom she addressed the letters, wrote in his book, *On the Relation between the Physical and Moral Aspects of Man:*

> Smith carries out an analysis that was full of wisdom, though incomplete for his lack of success in relating it to physical laws; and which Mme Condorcet by simple yet rational considerations has been able in great part to draw out of the vagueness in which the *Theory of Moral Sentiments* had left it.[2]

The view that one can find the origin of morality in physical experience was quite prevalent in the French literature of the eighteenth century. John Locke was very influential in France at that time, and his view that passions or moral ideas originate in sensations of pleasure and pain was further developed and can be found in writers such as Helévitius, Condillac, and Vauvenargues.[3] Cabanis in *On the Relation between the Physical and Moral Aspects of Man* argued that man is reducible to the physical aspect; he rejected dualistic or mental properties. Sympathy, he thought, originates in instincts.

While the French concentrated their efforts in establishing the physical basis for a moral tendency, the Scottish developed their views on moral sentiments, on feelings that have a moral content. The idea that people possess natural social affections that constitute the basis of morality can be found as common denominator among Shaftesbury, Hutcheson, Hume, and Smith. Hume and Smith accepted sympathy as a natural moral sentiment and proceeded to construct their moral theories based on this assumption. In Mme Condorcet's writing we see a culmination of the two traditions. She writes on the physical origin of morality and she provides a moral theory based on sympathy. Picavet in his book *Les Idéologues,* a major work on the French *philosophes* written in 1891, noted:

> It is in reading the chapters of Smith that Mme Condorcet wrote her own to trace the line which separated the two traditions, French and Scottish, or perhaps unite them.[4]

Her work is original as she adds a new dimension to the theories developed by those two traditions, Scottish and French.

In what follows I will develop three themes: one on physical pain and the origin of sympathy, a second on sympathy with moral pain, and a third on reason and sentiments.

Physical Pain and the Origin of Sympathy

Mme Condorcet opens her letters by stating that it is regrettable that Smith did not pursue his analysis of sympathy further to show what its first causes are and how people come to possess it.

> You know that the subject of the first few chapters is sympathy. Smith contented himself with noting its existence and exhibiting its chief effects. I regretted that he had not dared to go further, penetrating up to its first causes and showing finally how it must belong to every sentient being capable of reflection. You will see that I had the foolhardiness to fill in his omissions.[5]

She goes on to fill this lack in his thought with her analysis of the physical origin of sympathy. Mme Condorcet provides an empirical account of the origin of sympathy, claiming that sympathy originates in sensations of pleasure and pain. Since she finds that pain is more intense than pleasure, she asks, what then is the connection between sympathy and physical pain? Upon observing the phenomenon of pain, Mme Condorcet notices that any physical pain produces a composite sensation, that is, we first feel a local pain where the cause of the suffering is, and then a general impression of pain on all our organs follows, a general feeling of sickness (*un sentiment général de mal-aise*).[6] The general impression of pain is distinct from the local pain and can continue to exist even after the local pain ceases. The idea that any pain gives rise to a general impression of pain has an important role in the explanation of sympathy.

According to Mme Condorcet, a general impression of pain can be renewed from memory or from merely the sight of pain. Thus when we remember a past pain, we feel pain again or have a painful memory; likewise, seeing another person suffer will renew the impression of pain as well. Sympathy then consists in feeling pain upon seeing another person suffer. This conception of sympathy is unique to Mme Condorcet. With her analysis of sympathy and pain, she can explain how it is that sympathy entails actually feeling pain when someone else suffers. Hume expresses a similar view of sympathy. According to him one feels a feeling analogous to what the sufferer feels. Hume's argument, however, is mechanical and simple; he claims that we perceive an idea of a passion that turns into a lively impression that resembles the original passion.[7] For Mme Condorcet it is the fact that we are able to recall our *own* pain that creates the similarity of feeling between the sufferer and the spectator. She writes:

> In the same way as the memory of harm which we have experienced reproduces in us the painful impression which all of our organs have suffered, and which was a part of the local pain caused by harm, so too we feel again this painful impression when, whilst discerning the signs of pain, we see a sentient being suffer, or know that he suffers.[8]

We see then that by the renewal of pain upon witnessing it, sympathy is created. Note that both memory and the sight of pain produce a painful impression in the same way. It follows that to remember our own suffering and to see another person suffer produces the same effect. Sympathy is as strong a reaction as remembering our own pain. Repeated experiences of feeling pain produce an abstract idea of pain, and eventually a painful impression can be produced from the abstract idea of pain as well. Sympathy no longer has to be specific; we can sympathize with general suffering as well. For example, we can learn of the suffering of an entire group of people; this too will evoke sympathy—some feeling of pain. Notice the contrast to Smith who writes:

> Nothing is so soon forgot as pain, the moment it is gone the whole agony of it is over, and the thought of it can no longer give us any sort of disturbance. We ourselves cannot then enter into the anxiety and anguish which we had before conceived.[9]

According to Smith we do not recall our own pain and consequently we do not sympathize with pain. Smith distinguishes between the passions that originate from the body and the passions that originate from the imagination. Bodily harm such as injury or hunger excites very little sympathy according to Smith. On the other hand, harm perceived through the imagination, such as a loss of fortune or dignity, provokes our deepest sympathies. This is so, Smith explains, "because our imaginations can more readily mould themselves upon his imagination, than our bodies can mould themselves upon his body."[10] Smith treats physical pain and emotional pain as two separate phenomena. Sympathy for physical pain is negligible and hard to achieve. In overlooking the significance of physical pain and the sympathy we have for it, Mme Condorcet claims, Smith was unable to account for the causes of sympathy.

In addition Mme Condorcet identifies the ability of a painful impression to be renewed from the sight and memory of pain as the moral presence of pain, since it is this ability of a general impression of pain to be recalled and felt again that enables us to sympathize. Pain then has a moral presence, since it produces a moral reaction—sympathy. Furthermore, although not explicit in the text, it follows that the painful sensation that accompanies sympathy motivates us to relieve pain in others and thus it affects our action. We are capable of sympathizing with physical pains first, but then the idea of a moral pain (for which she uses throughout the text the terms *douleur moral, peines morales, mal moral* as denoting any kind of emotional or mental pain) can also produce the same effect as a physical pain. Thus there are two kinds of sympathy: physical and moral. When we sympathize, whether it is sympathy with physical or moral pain, a painful sensation is present. She writes:

> Here is an effect of pain which equally follows its physical presence and its moral presence. One understands here by its moral presence either the ideas which our memories give us of it or the one which we can have by the sight or knowledge of another's pain. The cause of sympathy towards physical pains thus comes from the fact that the sensation which produces all physical pains in us is a composite sensation, a part of which can renew itself from the sole idea of pain.[11]

The moral presence of pain, the general impression pain leaves on us and its ability to be recalled, enables sympathy to exist. Sympathy includes both a physical sensation and an emotional reaction. Moral suffering includes a bodily reaction; that is, physical sensations accompany moral sympathy as well.

> It is thus obvious that what we have said of physical pains is also true of moral pains, seeing that we are capable of them. The sight and memory of the moral pains of another affect us like the sight and memory of physical pains.[12]

To elucidate what she means, one might think of a time of a great loss. Surely no one experiences it as a pure thought. Upon the hearing of bad news one has a physical reaction as well—it could be trembling, a fast heartbeat, feeling faint, or losing one's appetite. Notice how, in tracing the origin of sympathy in physical experience and in finding the necessary accompaniment of sympathy with sensations of pleasure and pain, we discover a complex sympathetic experience.

Sympathy with Moral Pain

Sympathy with moral pain, like sympathy with physical pain, begins with our first sensations of pleasure and pain, particularly with sensations of pleasure felt at the hands of our caretakers. Here Mme Condorcet relates the phenomenon of physical pleasure and the human contact between a parent and a child. A child would recipro-cate with care to those who care for him/her. In addition to caring for our caretakers, Mme Condorcet notes, we also depend on them. Specific dependency begins in the crib; it is our first tie to another human being (*cette dépendance particulière de quelques individus commence au berceau; elle est le premier lien qui nous attache à nos semblables*).[13] This dependency begins in infancy and remains throughout one's life. Each individual depends on many others for necessities. Dependency and care yield a disposition of sympathy. We feel for those we depend on. We have an emotional disposition to feel for their pleasure and pain. A person cannot be indifferent towards those who contribute to his or her existence and happiness.

> The force of our sensitivity . . . and the idea of the persons to whom we owe the greater part of our welfare being sufficient alone to make us feel a sentiment, we are thus predisposed toward emotion (*d'avance à l'émotion*) for all that may happen to them: their pleasures or pains must therefore affect us more intensely than the pleasures and pains of other people.[14]

We are tied to those who care for us, and we care for them out of this emotional tie. The sympathy that we first feel for those who give us care is a capacity that develops and expands to other people throughout one's life.

We see then that moral sympathy, like physical sympathy, starts with our experiences of pleasure and pain, but is actually formed by the ties we have towards the people who caused those experiences in us. Dependency on other people is a strong aspect of our moral development. It is notable that Mme Condorcet sees in the first ties we have to other human beings an explanation of the development or origin of our moral faculties.

In treating sympathy as a disposition that develops out of our own experience, Mme Condorcet can explain how we can easily relate to other people's experiences. For Smith, as we will see shortly, relating to other people's experiences will not be achieved with the same ease that it is achieved for Mme Condorcet. The following is Smith's formulation of sympathy:

> As we have no immediate experience of what other men feel, we can form no idea of the manner in which they are affected, but by conceiving what we ourselves should feel in the like situation . . . our senses will never inform us of what he suffers. They never did, and never can, carry us beyond our own person, and it is by the imagination only that we can form any conception of what are his sensations. . . . By the imagination we place ourselves in his situation, we conceive ourselves enduring all the same torments, we enter as it were into his body, and become in some measure the same person with him, and thence form some idea of his sensations, and even feel something which, though weaker in degree, is not altogether unlike them. His agonies, when they are brought home to ourselves, when we have thus adopted and made them our own, begin at last to affect us, and we then tremble and shudder at the thought of what he feels.[15]

Note that Smith does recognize a physical reaction—"we tremble and shudder"— yet he again dismisses sensation in his account of the development of sympathy, as he only mentions the occurrence of a physical phenomenon but does not describe its complexity. Smith then claims that we have no immediate experience of what another person feels. We have to think how we would feel in his situation and we do so through the imagination. The result is that we feel something that is similar but weaker. What gives rise to sympathy then, or what sympathy depends on, is our ability to imagine ourselves in another person's situation. Smith realizes that sympathy is an interactive process, inasmuch as we too have to feel something that has to relate to our own experience, but he does not account for sympathy as a disposition that develops out of physical and familial experience. We imagine our own experience—how we would feel in another person's situation—but we do not immediately feel with the other who is in pain. Hence, for Smith, it seems that we relate to another person only through *possible* experience, whereas for Mme Condorcet we relate through *actual* experience; we recall our own experience directly and immediately. Mme Condorcet nonetheless does recognize that imagination is very important for sympathy. Apart from the value of imagining another's circumstances, imagination is important, for not every experience we sympathize with is one we have experienced ourselves. Smith claims that imagination is the sole basis for sympathy, whereas for Mme Condorcet the basis of sympathy is the general impression of pleasure and pain that is actively renewed at the sight of suffering. Thus for her we are able to sympathize immediately.

Furthermore, Smith treats sympathy as a conditional sentiment. When we sympathize we imagine ourselves in another person's situation, consider how we would feel, and judge his/her reaction accordingly. We consider the cause of the person's grief or joy, and we judge whether a person's reaction is justified. According to the judgment we form we might or might not sympathize with him/her. Hence Smith concludes: "Sympathy, therefore, does not arise so much from the view of the passions, as from that of the situation which excites it."[16] Here sympathy is conditional: before we sympathize we judge whether or not we should sympathize. For Mme Condorcet we sympathize immediately, as soon as the object of sympathy is offered to our senses (*Les premiers mouvemens de cette sympathie naissent à l'instant même où les objets qui peuvent l'exciter s'offrent à nos regards*).[17] As I already mentioned, sympathy in Mme Condorcet's sense means relating directly to another through recalling our own experiences. She starts with the assumption that we are similar and connected first. Smith instead assumes a certain separation and therefore requires imagination to bridge the gap.

Reason and Sentiments

Sympathy depends not only on imagination, but on sensitivity and reflection as well. Our sensitivity determines how strongly we are affected. It is a capacity that is improved the more it is exercised. Through the imagination we can develop a more accurate picture of how another person feels. In spending more time reflecting we increase our feelings and create more sympathy. While sensation can present an idea to our mind, it is reflection that prolongs it and sustains it. Thus we can witness a person suffer for a moment, and yet think about it for much longer. For Mme Condorcet it is reflection that provides thoughts and images that motivate us to alleviate pain in others and perform morally good actions. Reflection gives rise to compassion by sustaining ideas of suffering. Sympathy then, which begins with a sentiment, increases through the exercise of sensitivity in reflection. Reason works here to enhance the sentiments.

> The sympathy of which we are capable for physical pains, and which is a part of what we understand by the name of humanity, would be a sentiment too brief to be often useful, my dear C***, were we not so capable of reflection as we are of sensitivity. . . . The sentiment for humanity is thus in some manner a seed lodged at the bottom of man's heart by nature and which the faculty of reflection will nurture and develop.[18]

The sentiment of humanity, our moral capacity, is born out of sympathy, and it needs to be cultivated. We are responsible for developing sensitivity in our children and enabling their moral capacity to grow. Mme Condorcet does not treat sympathy as Smith does, merely as a static disposition that just exists. Sympathy is rather a dynamic faculty that improves and needs to be exercised. Mme Condorcet draws an analogy between physical exercise and mental exercise, and she points both to the necessity of exercising and the pleasure we get from improving our physical and mental faculties. Sympathy, although clearly a human capacity, does not exist or develop on its own without our attention. We need to reflect on the well-being of others; their pleasure makes us feel pleasure and their misery makes us feel pain.

Our ability to feel pleasure and pain in sympathizing with other people extends itself in our help or harm to those people. From our ability to feel the pleasure or pain of others, it follows that we also feel pleasure in contributing to their happiness and feel pain in harming them. Furthermore, in addition to the pleasure of doing good, we also feel a pleasure of having done good, which remains in us as an *abstract sentiment*. In the same way that a general impression that follows a local pain can exist after the local pain ceases, the pleasure of having done good remains as a general impression no longer connected to the specific action that gave rise to it.

> Thus, to the pleasure of doing the good is joined the long duration of the satisfaction of having done good; a sentiment which becomes, in some way, general and abstract since we feel it anew at the sole memory of good actions, without recalling their particular circumstances.[19]

Just as having done good produces a pleasant sentiment, having done wrong produces a painful one, a feeling of regret and remorse. Moral sentiments thus arise from abstract feelings of pleasure and pain that accompany our actions. As general and abstract sentiments, they constitute a tendency to do good and avoid harm. They become permanent and active powers. For Mme Condorcet, feelings of regret, remorse, fear, or happiness that accompany our actions serve as moral motivation or deterrence. Out of the pleasure and pain we feel for helping or hurting someone, a moral conscience is born.

> The satisfaction attached to good actions, and the terror of the memory of bad ones, are two effective motives for the determination of all our actions. These two sentiments are universal: they constitute the principle and the ground of morality of the human genre.[20]

We see then that these moral sentiments are born out of sympathy that both arises from pleasure and pain and is accompanied by feelings of pleasure and pain that serve as a primary nonreflective moral tendency.

Mme Condorcet wrote at a time when the question whether morality is a matter of reason or of sentiments was a current issue.[21] The rationalists saw reason as discerning moral truths, as the faculty through which we perceive concepts such as good or evil and discover objective and universal moral concepts. To them the dictates of reason are obligatory, and it is because we rationally see a possible act as moral that we choose to perform it. The rationalists usually see the passion or sentiments as erratic and in need of correction by reason. The sentimentalists, on the other hand, hold that our moral motivation is primarily nonrational. Whether through moral sense or moral sentiments, we already possess a moral disposition through which we perceive moral concepts and by which we are motivated. Reason is viewed as instrumental only, as it is indifferent to a moral goal. One has to have certain feelings, has to care about a goal, in order to be motivated to achieve it.

For Mme Condorcet feeling is neither limited to the perception of particular ideas, nor is it context specific. Generality and abstraction, usually seen only as assets of reason, belong to the sentiments as well. As mentioned above, the pleasure of having done good and the pain of having caused harm remain in us as general and abstract sentiments not necessarily connected to the specific action that gave rise to these sentiments. In accompanying our actions the general sentiments produce feelings such as satisfaction, regret, and remorse that act in us as a moral motivation or deterrence. Thus, these sentiments are moral insofar as some discerning of moral concepts is necessarily embedded in them. They can function as a general moral rule does, in being referred to an action to determine if it is a moral one. For Mme Condorcet one can obey a general sentiment in the same way one obeys a general rule; both can be applied to an action, the former to indicate if the action feels morally wrong and the latter to indicate if the action seems rationally wrong (*De même, on obéit à des sentiments généraux, sans penser à la manière dont ils se sont formés et à tout ce qui les justifie*).[22] Therefore, the requirement of the rationalists that moral concepts should be general and abstract is fulfilled by the general and abstract sentiments.

Moral sentiments are very powerful to Mme Condorcet. But the question remains: if we have a primary nonreflective moral tendency, so that some moral distinctions have already been made through the sentiments before we reflect on them, what then is the role of reason? The pleasure that we feel from doing a good action is still a vital and important sign that the action is a moral one. But sentiments are also modified by reflection.

> There is then, my dear C***, a distinction between our actions already established by sentiment alone, since some of them are accompanied by pleasure and followed by an internal satisfaction, whilst the others are accompanied by pains and followed by a disagreeable and often painful sentiment. But this more enduring sentiment of satisfaction or pain, which is attached to the memory of the good or wrong we have done to others, is necessarily modified by reflection. And it is the modification which reflection brings to them which leads us to the idea of the moral good and evil. . . .[23]

A good action would be one that gives others pleasure as approved by reason, whereas an evil action is one that gives pain as condemned by reason. It is the activity of reason, when reflecting on the moral sentiments, that gives rise to ideas of good and evil. Mme Condorcet makes a fine distinction here in explaining the roles of both reason and sentiment. When we perform a good or evil act, certain sentiments accompany it. When we reflect on those sentiments, we get abstract ideas of good and evil. Without the sentiments, reason cannot give rise to these concepts.

> You have seen, my dear C***, that the sentiments which are awakened in ourselves when we perform some good or evil to others give us, when reflection accompanies them, the abstract idea of moral good and evil.[24]

It is important to remember Mme Condorcet's view on the existence of abstract sentiments that allow us to feel the presence or the consequences of good actions and of evil actions. It follows that there is a difference between feeling good and evil and having a rational idea of good and evil. Yet both are equally important to the constitution of a moral agent.

Apart from rational ideas of good and evil, moral concepts such as rights and justice also stem from reason. Mme Condorcet defines a right as a preference of reason in favor of an individual or an interest that is made into a general law. Ideas of good and evil, combined with ideas of rights, give rise to ideas of justice and injustice. Concepts such as justice have to be a product of reason since justice is founded on the concepts of rights and requires a thought process that takes into consideration personal interests and the general good. Unfortunately, Mme Condorcet is very brief when she gets to this important section.

For Mme Condorcet, justice arises from reason, yet justice is also founded on sentiments, since the effects of injustice are emotionally unbearable. Having sentiments that make primary moral distinctions, we submit them to the guidance of reason. In this way we lose neither the importance of the sentiments nor the contributions reason can make. She writes:

> It was necessary to show that the origin of our moral sentiments lies in the natural and unreflective sympathy for the physical pains of another, and that the origin of our moral ideas lies in reflection . . . yet one cannot say that morality is founded on sentiment alone, since it is reason which shows us what is just or unjust. But one can even less maintain that it is founded uniquely on reason, since the judgment of reason is nearly always preceded and followed by a sentiment which announces it and confirms it, and since it is even originally from sentiment that reason acquires moral ideas and forms principles out of them.[25]

The origin of our morals and our moral motivation is thus embedded in the sentiments. Sympathy is a sentiment that can move us not only to amend evil that affects our personal interest but also to oppose passions that oppress the weak and to avenge any kind of injustice. The sentiments also accompany any rational decision we make, and in doing so they approve or disapprove of the rational decision. Reason enhances our natural moral tendency by directing the sentiments through rules of justice and rights. Reason and sentiments work in conjunction in moral action.

Mme Condorcet indicates that assent to moral truths is different from assent to mathematical proofs, for moral thinking is unlike any other rational thinking in the sense that we are not indifferent to it. This is an important distinction. If we stop to think about it for a moment, we might realize that whether light consists of particles or waves might leave us indifferent, whereas to the question of abortion, for instance, we have an emotional reaction. In encountering moral truths there is thus both an emotional desire to fulfill a goal and a fear of avoiding it. Moral truths are accompanied by feelings that motivate us to act accordingly. Again, rather than creating a division between reason and sentiments, Mme Condorcet employs both. I regret, however, that she did not spend more time explaining the role of reason. Although she thinks that reason and sentiments equally constitute our morality, she does not give them equal treatment in her text.

Conclusion

We see how Mme Condorcet, building on the inadequacy of Smith's theory, provides a theory of the origin of sympathy. In doing so she makes an important contribution to moral theory. Her view that a specific experience of pain gives rise to a general impression of pain that can be renewed from the sight and memory of pain entails two moral implications. First, when we see someone suffer, a painful sensation is renewed in us and enables us to sympathize. Second, general impressions of pain that accompany our actions create abstract moral sentiments that serve as a moral motivation or deterrence. Sympathy then grows in the recalling of general impressions of pleasure and pain, and moral sentiments develop from the general impressions of pleasure and pain that accompany our actions. Moral ideas arise in reflection on the sentiments. In this way moral ideas are traceable to our first sensations of pleasure and pain. Mme Condorcet provides a valuable empirical account of moral ideas that not only improves on Smith's but also bridges the gap between the rationalists and the sentimentalists of her time.

I maintain that the general sentiments of regret and remorse are strong moral concepts. Remorse is something we feel, not something we merely rationalize. It has an important function in moral theory, for it shows how morality is for the most part embedded in feelings. A moral action should feel right in addition to seeming rationally correct. Indeed I wonder, can one really be a moral agent without ever feeling regret and remorse? By introducing such feelings and by showing how they can become general and abstract, and so function as a moral conscience, Mme Condorcet not only points to the importance of these sentiments but also shows how they serve in building and creating our moral behavior.

The strength and depth of Mme Condorcet's moral theory lie therefore not only in her seeing that both reason and sentiments are necessary to form a moral action but also in her showing how in and of themselves neither reason nor sentiment is sufficient to generate moral action. Mme Condorcet shows how both have an indispensable role. She does not reduce morality to either one. Instead, she shows how both reason and sentiments are complementary and how they enhance each other, and so she provides an improvement to Smith's moral theory. In affirming to the rationalists the importance of emotional experience while affirming to the sentimentalists the role of reason, she bridges the gap between them.

Biographical Note

Sophie de Grouchy, Marquise de Condorcet (1764–1822) was born to a noble family in a *château* outside of Paris. Her mother took a special interest in her education and provided her with a very good and well-rounded one. In 1786 she married Marie Jean-Antoine-Nicholas Caritat, Marquis de Condorcet (1743–1794). At the time he was the secretary of the Academy of Science in Paris. He was a mathematician, a political theorist, and a philosopher. He was an encyclopedist along with Diderot and D'Alembert, and was one of the youngest. Quite surprisingly he was a feminist ahead of his time, for he argued for complete equality between the sexes. As difficult as it is to evaluate a person's influence, there is no doubt that Sophie was a source of inspiration; she contributed to his ideas and writings throughout their marriage. Boissel Thierry, her most recent biographer, suggests that Sophie was more enthusiastic about reform and more extreme in her political views than was her husband, and that she pushed him in expressing his views and engaging in political activities that eventually led to his arrest.[26] Mme Condorcet was a beautiful, intelligent, and vivacious woman. Her husband admired her and was very much in love with her. They were an intellectually and politically active couple. They befriended Thomas Paine, and Sophie translated into French both Paine's written correspondence and his speeches to the National Assembly.

Their salon at the Hôtel des Monnaies in Paris flourished. Keith Michael Baker, M. Condorcet's biographer, called it the most influential salon in the pre-revolutionary period.[27] It was an international intellectual center about which it was said that English was spoken half of the time. Among the foreigners who visited the salon were Adam Smith, Charles Mackintosh, Thomas Jefferson, Benjamin Franklin, and Thomas Paine. In 1794, M. Condorcet was arrested and imprisoned. In order to survive the revolution and save some of the property for herself and her only daughter, Sophie on her own initiative divorced her husband while he was in prison.

M. Condorcet committed suicide in prison. Sophie edited his collected works and published them posthumously, with her introduction, as *Oeuvres complètes de Condorcet, Publiées par Mme Condorcet avec le concours de Cabanis et de Garat, 1801–1804*, 21 vols. She also reedited and published separately M. Condorcet's book *Esquisse d'un Tableau Historique des Progrès de L'esprit Humain*, which he wrote—with her encouragement—while in hiding. Mme Condorcet also wrote a book to her daughter about education, but it remained in manuscript form and is lost today. In 1798 she published her translation of Adam Smith's *Theory of Moral Sentiments* in French and added a translation of Smith's *Dissertation on the Origin of Language* to the end of the second volume. She then attached the 150 pages of her eight letters on sympathy.

The letters were written to Pierre-George Cabanis, her brother-in-law, who was a physician and a philosopher. Towards the end of her life she was not in good health and died in September 1822. After the time in which the letters of Mme Condorcet were originally published, references to this work are brief and are found either in histories or biographies. Today the book is rare and the work is almost unknown.

Notes

I would like to thank Maxime La Fantasie at the Fales Library in New York University for allowing me to handle Mme Condorcet's translation of Adam Smith's book. It is a rare book, and the Fales Library owns an original copy from 1798. Naturally, the book cannot be subjected to a microfilm procedure or to a copy machine for fear of damaging the spine. With Ms. La Fantasie's permission and with her help in gently prompting the book open, I photographed each page and then developed the film into 4x6 photos. I then enlarged the photos on a copy machine to 8½x11 paper. The copy came out nice and clear. I further would like to thank Eileen O'Neill for informing me on Mme Condorcet's work on sympathy, and Virginia Held, Charles Landesman, Sue Weinberg, and Lisa Dolling for their valuable comments.

1. See Barbara Brooks, *Studies on Voltaire and the Eighteenth Century,* Haydn Mason, ed. (Oxford: The Voltaire Foundation at the Taylor Institution, 1980), p. 354.

2. Pierre-Jean George Cabanis, *On the Relations between the Physical and Moral Aspects of Man,* Margarit Duggan Said, tr. (Baltimore and London: Johns Hopkins University Press, 1981), p. 598.

3. For more on this issue see Lester G. Crocker, *Nature, Culture and Ethical Thought in the French Enlightenment* (Baltimore: Johns Hopkins Press, 1963).

4. François Joseph Picavet, *Les Idéologues* (Paris: F. Alcan, 1891; New York: Arno Press Inc., 1975), p. 116. My translation.

5. Sophie de Grouchy, Marquise de Condorcet in *Théorie des sentimens moraux, . . .* Suivi d'une Dissertation sur l'Origine des Langues; Par Adam Smith; Traduit de l'Anglais, sur la septième et dernière Édition, Par S. Grouchy Ve. Condorcet. Elle y a joint huit Lettres sur la Sympathie (Paris: F. Buisson, Imprim.-Lib., 1798), p. 357. My translation.

6. Mme Condorcet, p. 358.

7. See David Hume, *A Treatise of Human Nature,* vol. III, iii, section 1.

8. Mme Condorcet, p. 359.

9. Adam Smith, *Theory of Moral Sentiments* (Indianapolis: Liberty Fund, 1982), p. 29.

10. Ibid., p. 29.

11. Mme Condorcet, p. 360.

12. Ibid., p. 405.

13. Ibid., p. 376.

14. Ibid.

15. Smith, p. 9.

16. Ibid., p. 12.

17. Mme Condorcet, p. 386.

18. Ibid., p. 370.

19. Ibid., p. 435.

20. Ibid., p. 438.

21. D. D. Raphael divides the participants along this line: Shaftesbury, Hutcheson, Hume, and Smith are on the side of sense, sentiment, or feeling, while Samuel Clarke, Wallaston, Balguy,

Richard Price, and Thomas Reid are on the side of rationality, reason, or knowledge. See D. D. Raphael, *The Moral Sense* (London: Oxford University Press, 1947).

22. Mme Condorcet, p. 444.

23. Ibid., pp. 439–40.

24. Ibid., p. 452.

25. Ibid., p. 463.

26. Boissel Thierry, *Sophie de Condorcet* (Paris: Presse de la Renaissance, 1988).

27. Keith Michael Baker, *Condorcet: From Natural Philosophy to Social Mathematics* (Chicago: Chicago University Press, 1975).

Patricia J. O'Connor

22   Iris Murdoch: Love and *The Bell*

> *We can only learn to love by loving. Remember that all our failures are ultimately failures in love. Imperfect love must not be condemned and rejected, but made perfect. The way is always forward, never back.*
>
> ——Iris Murdoch, *The Bell*

Love, in Iris Murdoch's (1919–1999) theory of ethics, can take four forms: attention to realities that are themselves excellent or valuable, attention directed upon an intellectual discipline, purified emotion, and purified imagination. In this essay I will restrict myself to a discussion of one of these: love as purified imagination.[1] Considering love as purified imagination allows me to explain two features that are constitutive of all four forms of love: attention and imagination. This variety of love is also directly connected with most of our interactions with others, since one cannot act virtuously with respect to other human beings unless one perceives them justly and compassionately.

Murdoch's understanding of human nature builds in part on Freud's account of the psyche. Like Freud, she thinks that human beings are strongly attached to their own egos and that the self is "an egocentric system of quasi-mechanical energy" in which "fantasy is a stronger force than reason."[2] On this view, the deep attachment of human beings to their own egos makes objectivity—in both the sense of detachment from self and the sense of seeing the world accurately—very difficult. We therefore live in worlds constituted, to a greater or lesser degree, by fantasy.

According to Murdoch, fantasy is "a powerful system of energy" and the chief enemy of excellence in morality.[3] Fantasy is a manifestation of immersion in self. Such immersion not only gives rise to self-centered images, dreams, and aims, but is also a grave impediment to the perception of reality. It prevents us from seeing, from attending to, human beings.

In its most extreme manifestation, fantasy leads to the objectification of others: to the transformation of human subjects into mere things or objects for use. One can think here of what Marilyn Frye calls the "arrogant eye," the possessors of which "organize everything [and everyone] seen with reference to themselves and their own interests," an organization that falsifies the reality of others and often leads to coercion, of a greater or lesser degree of subtlety, of the other.[4] One immersed in fantasy sees with an arrogant eye: other human beings appear as objects, as "things" that either have instrumental value for the achievement of one's aims, or lack it, or are merely impediments to the achievement of those aims.

One can find philosophical accounts of the self according to which others cannot *but* be regarded as objects.[5] Murdoch, however, regards objectification as a deeply inaccurate perception that is both pathological and inimical to morality. It is a result of immersion in fantasy, and fantasy is a manifestation of immersion in ego. Thus, the first step to health and virtue is to become less egocentric. Becoming less egocentric in turn allows us to begin to perceive reality accurately, instead of through the falsifying lens of self-absorption.

To achieve what Murdoch calls "a kind of intellectual ability to perceive what is true," we require an extended discipline.[6] We do not escape from self-absorption and fantasy through a single and simple act of will. Indeed, Murdoch thinks that "most of what is often called 'will' or 'willing' belongs to the system of energy which is fantasy," so that will itself needs discipline.[7] Moreover, Murdoch thinks that the moral life is praxis, "something that goes on continually, not something that is switched off between occurrences of explicit moral choices."[8] To be moral, then, requires a sustained discipline or practice. Furthermore, many psychologists and moral philosophers, as well as our own experience, tell us that human beings are creatures of habit, and that habits are hard to break. It seems unlikely that we could escape from habitual egocentrism by a special effort on some particular occasion. Conversely, it seems plausible that "what happens in between . . . choices is indeed what is crucial," and that we will therefore need a discipline if we are to see with other than arrogant eyes.[9]

Murdoch calls the process that goes on between the choices "attention." It is a "just and loving gaze directed upon an individual reality."[10] It is the effort to develop true rather than fantastic perceptions of the world; the attempt to reach out toward what is real; the striving, in particular, to perceive persons not as objects but as subjects. Attention is a continuing process, not only because it takes place between the choices, but also because there is always more to be known. Exercising "some continual slight control over the direction and focus of our vision,"[11] we can learn to look outward, away from self, toward other realities—and to allow those realities to remain "other," distinct from ourselves. Exercising this discipline, we need not remain rapt in the fantasy that impedes accurate perception and objectifies others. To borrow Frye's language, we can learn not to "annex" the other; we can learn not to create "vacuum molds" of self-serving expectations and aims "into which the other is sucked and held."[12] When we direct our attention outward we should, Murdoch says, not merely employ a "just" gaze (the cool glance of the "impartial observer" who, like Dickens's Gradgrind, perceives "the facts"), but also seek a compassionate, sustained, and imaginative engagement with reality.

In order truly to attend to the reality of human beings, we must employ our imaginations. Unlike fantasy, which is reductive and destructive, egocentric and pathological, imagination is constructive. It is, Murdoch writes, a kind of active, creative, nonscientific perception or "reflection on people, events, etc., which builds detail, adds colour, conjures up possibilities in ways which go beyond what could be said to be strictly factual."[13] Since people are not objects, but rather subjects, one's vision of them will at best be incomplete if it is limited to a set of current or historical "objective facts." The reality of a human being is not captured in a mere collection of facts of this sort. We must also reach out toward that reality with sympathetic imagination.

Moreover, in attempting to perceive another person, we are faced with the difficulty that others are, as Murdoch says, "to an extent we never cease discovering, different from ourselves."[14] Imagination enables us to perceive—and thereby prepares us to accept—particular differences. It does so by providing for "the non-violent apprehension" of difference, the "recognition of, that is respect for" other persons as irreducibly dissimilar subjects.[15] Imaginative reaching out toward the reality of others leads "the direction of attention . . . outward, away from self which reduces all to a false unity, toward the great surprising *variety* of the world."[16]

Thus, the process of overcoming egocentrism is a moral discipline involving both attention and imagination. Attention is the continuing process of reaching out toward reality; imagination is required when we attend to human beings, because the kind of "reality" humans are as particular individual subjects means that our reaching out cannot be done by means of universalizing reason alone. What we ordinarily think of as "reason" cannot adequately capture the growing, changing, elusive reality of the dissimilar individuals with whom we are in relation. But even less adequately can fantasy—the fantasy that Freud saw as a stronger force than reason—enable us to perceive the reality of others. Thus, we need sustained, compassionate, imaginative attention to achieve clear perception of distinct, particular human beings.

One who practices the moral discipline composed of attention and imagination begins to free herself from fantasy and self-absorption. She begins to achieve the clear eye, the just *and* compassionate gaze. To the focused attention of this eye and the reaching imagination that directs its vision, persons appear not as objects but as mysterious, elusive subjects.

Love, in this sense of purified imagination, is a necessary condition of moral action in the "central area" of morals[17]: our interaction with other human beings. One cannot act virtuously toward subjects if one perceives them as objects. By disciplining oneself to use attention and imagination to reach for reality, rather than remaining in consoling fantasy, one begins to prepare oneself for virtuous public interaction. As Murdoch says, "The more the separateness and differentness of other people is realised, and the fact seen that another man has needs and wishes as demanding as one's own, the harder it becomes to treat a person as a thing."[18] Insofar as one practices the discipline of purified imagination, one is able to treat others as subjects—to take their particular needs and desires into account when making a moral decision.

Accordingly, one might say Murdoch's account begins from a recognition that Kant is correct in asserting that human beings are not appropriately treated merely as means. Murdoch adds to Kant's assertion a description of a moral discipline that will not only enable us to avoid objectifying others and treating them merely as means to our ends, but also, more positively, will help us to see them accurately, justly, and compassionately as subjects. When our vision is cleared of exclusive concern with our own aims and desires, it can focus instead on irreducibly dissimilar others with projects, passions, and intentions of their own. We are then prepared to begin to treat others virtuously.

With this understanding of purified, attentive imagination as crucial to virtuous action in the central area of morals, we need only establish that Murdoch's philosophy and fiction are complementary in order to perceive how love transforms a character in *The Bell* and may direct the reaching imagination of readers of the novel. Alasdair MacIntyre has simply asserted that "Iris Murdoch's novels are philosophy."[19] I do not agree with this reductive claim of identity. Instead, I find that Murdoch's works in these two genres are related via parallels in Murdoch's literary and ethical theories. Read against the background of her philosophy, Murdoch's literary criticism makes it clear that the good novelist is required to resemble, in respect of her work, the virtuous moral agent. First, Murdoch's literary theory places on novelists demands similar to those that her ethical theory places on moral agents. Second, given that the novelist is, according to Murdoch, at least potentially "the greatest truth-teller of them all,"[20] and that she believes it is essential that ethical truths be communicated, we should expect Murdoch's own fiction to provide opportunities to exercise the discipline of purified imagination.

The virtuous person eschews the consolations of fantasy, attends to the reality of others, and acts on the basis of that attention. Murdoch's literary theory tells us that we can properly demand of novelists, just as we can of moral agents, that they attend to the reality of individuals—in the case of the novelist, to the reality of characters. Characters are to be persons—neither things, truths, objects, nor symbols. They are individual realities in a way very similar, perhaps even identical, to the way in which persons are individual realities.

As the ordinary moral agent is to use moral discipline to overcome fantasy, thus providing for the perception of reality and for the possibility of virtuous behavior, the author is to eschew fantasy. The most important truth the novel can reveal is that other people really exist.[21] The most significant area of the characters' activity is their effort to apprehend the reality of others.[22] The virtuous moral agent must recognize the truth that human beings are irreducibly dissimilar. The best novelist will not only recognize this dissimilarity but will also portray the often irreconcilable conflict of these individual realities.

Murdoch's parallel demands of the virtuous moral agent and of the good novelist strongly suggest that in relation to her creation the novelist should be virtuous. She is virtuous if and only if her characters are presented as subjects. The good novelist must give us a truthful depiction of the central area of morals. She must show us not only characters who are individual realities but also characters whose most significant activity is attending to—or failing to attend to—other such realities. Murdoch's theory of literature demands that a good novel should depict what her ethical theory identifies as the central area of morals.

Another crucial implication concerns the relationship a novelist has, through her work, with her readers. We saw above the moral import of a continuing effort to use our imagination in the right way. The novelist is writing for an audience, for readers who suspend disbelief and use their imaginations to enter the world of the novel. If taken as prescriptive, Murdoch's view would seem to require that good novelists, through their work, provide the opportunity for readers to exercise their moral imaginations. To the degree that Murdoch is prescribing for herself as well as for others, we should expect her novels to both depict the central area of morals and provide opportunity for the disciplined exercise of purified imagination.

Given the parallels between Murdoch's ethical and literary theories, her philosophy and her fiction should be seen as complementary: they can be expected to embody the same truth in different forms. Philosophy and literature, Murdoch says, are both truth-revealing activities. In general, the truths they reveal are not exactly the same, in part because philosophy attempts to reveal universal truths, literature particular ones. In Murdoch, however, we have not only a moral philosopher who tells us that love—endlessly still-to-be-attained knowledge of individual realities—is a virtue and the prerequisite for other virtuous behaviors. We also have a literary critic (and author of twenty-six novels) who claims that the best novels both reveal that other people really exist and show characters who attend to the reality of others.

Given Murdoch's ethical concept of love, then, we see that the central area of morals is our relations with other human beings. The most important ethical truth is that other people are independent realities. Without purified imagination, virtuous action is impossible. Accordingly, Murdoch's ethical theory gives a discursive account of how to achieve realism, how to avoid the dangers of fantasy. It gives us precepts, ways of thinking about virtue and value. Murdoch's novel *The Bell* reveals this central area of morals *in a particular way*. It *shows* us, concretely and in particular, what the ethical theory tells us abstractly and in general. It shows us in detail how difficult and valuable it is to attend to the reality of other people, not by theoretical assertion but by suggestive eloquence—by creating a large imaginative space that both serves the needs of the characters and engages the attention and the unconscious mind of the reader.[23]

The Bell leads to virtue not by precept but by example and by exercise. Murdoch thinks that stories and metaphors are morally indispensable; good literature enables us to make moral progress by providing us with a realistic depiction, not only of what human beings are like, but also of what real virtuous activity is like.

Like any good teacher with an important truth to convey, Murdoch has found several ways of expressing it. She thus conveys her philosophical views explicitly and directly in her ethical theory, and implicitly and indirectly in her fiction. The advantage of this is that one form primarily engages the reader's reason while the other requires the reader's imaginative attention—two modes, conveying the same truth, to reach and teach as many as possible. Murdoch considers this teaching an urgent, imperative task if we are to have a "good quality of human life."[24]

Having argued that Murdoch's fiction should be seen as complementary to her philosophy, I can now show how Murdoch's ethical concept of love drives the growth of a character in *The Bell* and may encourage moral growth on the part of a reader of the novel. Along the way, we will see that *The Bell* allows for a substantive response to certain criticisms of Murdoch's ethical theory, in particular one brought by Basil Mitchell. Mitchell objects that Murdoch's account of fantasy does not explain why the effort to perceive reality should be so difficult. He remarks in passing that her expression of her views is marred by "the absence, surprising in a novelist, of all discussion of the particular case, all attempt at illustration."[25] One can of course simply reply that if the view of human nature Murdoch shares with Freud is correct, the puzzle is not "Why is it so difficult to perceive reality?" but rather "How do people manage to do it at all?". An examination of *The Bell* is a better reply, for the novel shows us why it is so difficult to perceive the reality of other human beings even as it provides specific illustrations of both fantasy and purified imagination. Best of all, *The Bell* explores the connection between love and virtuous behavior in human interaction, the central area of morals.

A plot *précis* is in order; I will keep it brief and focused on Dora Greenfield, the character who learns to direct her attention outward and who thereby achieves a qualified success in loving in a problematic relationship. As the novel opens, Dora is returning to her husband Paul after having left him for six months to carry on an affair. At the time of her return, Paul is staying at Imber, a lay community connected with an Abbey across a lake. Paul tells Dora the legend of the old Abbey bell: sometime in the fourteenth century, the bell flew out of the bell tower into the lake when one of the nuns was discovered to be having an affair.

Dora's stay at Imber is difficult for her, not least because Paul is hostile, judgmental, and scornful. At one point, in an effort to gain perspective, Dora flees to London. While there, she begins to emerge from fantasy and to use her imagination properly. After she returns from London, Dora and another visitor to the lay community, Toby Gashe, discover the old bell in the lake and raise it. They plan to substitute the old bell for a new one that is soon to be installed at the Abbey. When another member of the community discovers their plan, Dora responds by ringing the old bell to summon everyone to see it. As the novel ends, Dora, while recognizing that she still loves Paul, refuses to return to London with him. Instead, she makes plans to complete art school, which she had abandoned years earlier in order to marry Paul.

We do not need to know Murdoch's ethical theory to realize that *The Bell* is about love, since we are given several details that tell us this. For example, Imber has, above two of its doors, stone medallions that read *"Amor via mea"* ("Love is my way"). Then there is the bell that Toby and Dora raise from the lake. It seems clear to me that the title of the novel refers to the old bell, named "Gabriel" and inscribed *"Vox ego sum Amoris"* ("I am the voice of Love"), rather than to the new one. The name of the old bell means "strong man of God" and links it with Gabriel, the angel of the Annunciation. Its inscription proclaims it to be the voice of love, as the angel was the voice of Love to Mary.[26] It seems to me that both the setting and the central metaphor of this work justify reading it as a novel primarily about love. I will limit my discussion of love to episodes in which Dora is central.

Dora, though in many ways an ignorant, foolish young woman, is richly endowed with the faculty of imagination. We are told: "Dora had a powerful imagination, at least in what concerned herself. She had long since recognized it as dangerous, and her talent was to send it, as she could her memory, to sleep."[27] Although she sometimes succumbs to consoling fantasy, Dora makes progress throughout the novel in learning to use her imagination correctly. In Dora we see how imaginative attention to reality can lead to virtuous behavior. Early in the novel, there are many examples of Dora succumbing to fantasy; I will relate only one. As Dora becomes more able to use her imagination to attend to reality, the occasions on which she does so multiply; two of the most important are given here.

The episode in which Dora indulges in a consoling fantasy occurs early in the novel. Dora and the head of the lay community, a man named Michael, come upon Toby, who is swimming nude. As they turn to leave, Dora notes that "Michael's face was . . . troubled as he looked upon the boy."[28] Dora considers the episode and she thinks:

> their strange experience had created between them a tremulous beam of physical desire which had not been present before. This secret homage was tender and welcome . . . she smiled to herself . . . apprehending in her companion a new consciousness of herself as incarnate, a potentially desirable, potentially naked woman, very close beside him in the warmth of the afternoon.[29]

The afternoon is certainly warm; Michael's face is certainly troubled. The remainder of the passage, however, is pure fantasy. Michael is a homosexual. We are told that he finds "all women unattractive and a trifle obscene."[30] He does not desire Dora. But Dora has, in general, a powerful need to be desired; at the time of the particular episode just recounted, she is uncertain, unhappy, exhausted, and seeking comfort.

Here Dora's immersion in self results in a failure to perceive reality. She does not perceive Michael as a particular individual; she perceives him only as a member of a category. To Dora, Michael is merely a male, present merely as an object for her pleasure or her use. Dora looks at Michael with arrogant eyes. What she does perceive is true, but it is not all that is true of Michael, and it is just this failure to perceive more than what suits her that allows Dora to use Michael in a fantasy that—because it soothes her battered self-esteem—consoles her. We can now answer Basil Mitchell's question (mentioned earlier) about why seeing reality is so difficult. Through this example we can see that the "obvious facts" about someone may not be all that is real, and that when we are focused on ourselves rather than on others, we are inclined to perceive no more than what suits us—especially when doing so advances our own conscious or unconscious purposes or needs.

Dora, however, also uses her imagination properly. When she goes to London, she does so not only because she is deeply disturbed by Imber, but also because she is haunted by a feeling that everything is "subjective" in the narrow relativist sense of "private and arbitrary." Among the things she does in London is to visit the National Gallery, where she looks at the masterpieces with the eye of an artist and with a familiarity born of hours of studying them on other occasions: "She could look, as one can at last when one knows a great thing very well, confronting it with a dignity which it has itself conferred."[31] Her looking leads to an epiphany:

> [H]er heart was filled with love for the pictures. . . . It occurred to her that here at last was something real and something perfect. . . . Here was something which her consciousness could not wretchedly devour, and by making it part of her fantasy make it worthless. . . . [T]he pictures were something real outside herself, which spoke to her kindly and yet in sovereign tones, something superior and good whose presence destroyed the dreary trance-like solipsism of her earlier mood.[32]

The important point to notice is that Dora, by attention to a work of art, is brought out of what she now recognizes as the fantasy of solipsism. Moreover, this outbreak of clarity resolves her underlying concern about whether she should stay with Paul at Imber. As she leaves the gallery she discovers that her questions have been answered "without her thinking about it."[33] She reflects:

> She must go back to Imber at once. Her real life, her real problems, were at Imber; and since, somewhere, something good existed, it might be that her problems would be solved after all. There was a connexion; obscurely she felt, without yet understanding it, she must hang onto that idea: there was a connexion.[34]

This moment of revelation alone does not, of course, solve all Dora's problems. One instance of using one's imagination does not resolve all difficulties. In directing her attention toward the artwork, however, Dora not only exercises her imagination but also gains energy to act more virtuously toward Paul. She does not, despite her difficulties at Imber, return to her lover; she returns to her husband.

Yet Paul and Dora continue to quarrel. Moreover, Dora embarks on what she later comes to realize is a thoroughly misguided plan to substitute the old bell, raised from the bottom of the lake, for the new. At first this plan attracts her because of its "triumphant, witch-like quality,"[35] because it will allow her to exercise power by bringing about a "miraculous" resurrection of the old bell. What Dora initially fails to realize is that effecting the substitution—playing out her fantasy—will make the bell, as well as the lay community and the Abbey itself, objects of ridicule when the supposed "miracle" is revealed as a hoax.

When Dora is forced to confront this fact she feels remorse for having constructed the plan, which "now seemed as cheap to her as it would shortly seem to the readers of the sensational press: at best funny in a vulgar way, at worst thoroughly nasty."[36] She cannot, however, immediately see how to negotiate the difficulty. In another instance of imaginative attention, she turns to the bell itself for help. She considers it as if it were an individual and tries to perceive it clearly. As she does so Dora feels "reverence, almost love."[37] She realizes that she cannot "leave the bell to be ambiguously the subject of malicious and untrue stories."[38] She "cannot" because, in attending to the bell, she has come to feel respect for it, in itself. To her, it is no longer simply an object to be used in her fantasy.

At this point Dora remembers one of the sermons she heard while at Imber, in which the bell that is about to be installed at the Abbey was characterized as "the truth-telling voice that must not be silenced."[39] She then rings the old bell, lending her energy, her life, to the voice of love, which is heard not only at Imber but "at the Abbey, in the village, and along the road, as the story was told later, for many many miles in either direction."[40] Dora's recognition of both the consequences of her fantasy and her responsibility for the bell draws her out of egocentric, solipsistic fantasy and into imaginative attention. This use of purified imagination in turn allows her to act virtuously.

Dora's two vital moments of vision permit her a qualified success in her attempt to relate justly and lovingly to Paul. The sense she gains in the National Gallery of "something real outside herself," no matter how obscured it may later become, sends her back to Imber. It enables her to continue in a difficult situation; it gives her energy and hope. Dora's reverence for the bell, her attention to it, leads her to sound and announce the voice of truth and love in a most public way—"for many many miles." We can read this action as indicating Dora's movement from immersion in fantasy to a genuine perception of the reality of another, and to a newly developed ability to respond to that reality. Moreover, her epiphany here also has consequences for her relationship with Paul. Partly because of her ringing the bell, Paul returns to London without Dora, thus giving her physical and psychological space in which to decide how to deal with him.

Dora then discusses her situation with Michael, revealing what is now a clearer imaginative understanding of both Paul's reality and her own:

> It was inevitable that Paul should bully her and that she should vacillate between submitting through fear and resisting through resentment. . . . As things were, she felt that she would never manage to live with Paul until she could treat with him, in some sense, as an equal. . . . She felt intensely the need and somehow now the capacity to live and work on her own and become, what she had never been, an independent grown-up person.[41]

The result of this conversation is that as the novel ends, Dora goes to Bath to complete her art degree. She does not divorce Paul, whom she still loves, but neither does she put herself back into his power. She has at last perceived more realistically both her incapacities and his rage and violence.

That there is yet hope for Paul and Dora's marriage is due to Dora's having learned, throughout the course of the novel, not to put her imagination to sleep, but rather to direct it outward—to purify it from something concerned with herself into something that can allow her to see others. In a difficult situation, Dora has qualified success because she slowly learns, through more events than I have been able to recount in detail here, to attend to reality rather than to her own ego. There is a morally significant difference between Dora's early fantasy that Michael is attracted to her and her later vivid imaginative understanding of her relationship with Paul: a difference generated by repeated efforts to attend to the reality of others.

This exposition of the novel shows how the ethical concept of love informs *The Bell*. It also replies to Basil Mitchell's question about why the perception of reality is so difficult, and answers his criticism that Murdoch does not provide particular cases to illustrate her moral theory. As we have seen, *The Bell* provides many such concrete illustrations of Murdoch's ethics. The novel shows us why it is so difficult to perceive the reality of other people. People can, like Paul, be violent, judgmental, and filled with rage and the desire to dominate. People can, like Dora, be ignorant and foolish, or be arrogant perceivers, immersed in delightful self-serving fantasies that console them or that enable them to triumph over those who have hurt them. Perceiving other human beings justly and compassionately, as subjects possessing their own reality, is not easy. It is sometimes difficult because their reality repels rather than attracts us. It is difficult because we ourselves are not perfect. And it is difficult because we are irreducibly dissimilar from one another.

As author of *The Bell*, Murdoch follows her own prescription for good novelists. First, she gives a truthful depiction of the central area of morals by depicting a character who comes to use purified imagination. Love of the painting rescues Dora from solipsism and sends her back to Imber to deal with Paul. Love of the bell enables Dora to rescue it from the peril in which she herself has placed it through her immersion in fantasy. That rescue is virtuous in itself; it also has consequences for Dora's relationship with Paul. Applying her imagination both to Paul's reality and to her own, in the context of the new situation she has helped to establish, Dora chooses a course that comes closer to meeting her needs than living with Paul would have. At the same time, she respects Paul's needs more than she did in having an affair. In this final development we see an excellent example of the connection between purified imagination and virtuous behavior in the central area of morals.

Murdoch also follows her prescription for good novelists by providing exercise for the moral imagination of her readers. In my view, *The Bell* succeeds very well in engaging the attention of "the common reader" (to use Virginia Woolf's term), who is also the ordinary moral agent. The novel fixes its moral vision on a complex imaginary world, and it successfully engages the reader-agent's imaginative attention to this world.

There are three ways in which this novel may be helpful to the reader as moral agent, even if she is not reading the novel as complementary to Murdoch's ethical theory. First, the novel gives the reader practice in attending to individual realities. Fictional individuals are often easier to perceive than real ones. They are less complex, less vulnerable to our efforts to use them instrumentally, and less threatening to our egos than are live human beings. Hence, we can begin to access the characters in a novel more easily than we can living people—and so begin exercising our moral imaginations.

Second, the novel directs the reader's attention toward the attempts of individuals to perceive the reality of others and to act virtuously toward them. We are not only given particular examples of fantasy, imagination, and the acts that result from them, but we are also allowed insight into the minds of characters as they maneuver within the central area of morals. Thus, we can come to share in the novel, more fully perhaps than we can in real life, another's effort to perceive reality.

Finally, the novel shows readers that virtue begins in overcoming attachment to our own egos through the moral discipline of directing imaginative attention toward individual realities outside ourselves. *The Bell* depicts a character who begins to develop the moral discipline that Murdoch's ethical theory commends. Through the transformations in Dora, we perceive that purified imagination—love—can make a vast moral difference in our lives. At the beginning of the novel Dora is an arrogant perceiver, rapt in consoling fantasy. By the novel's end her moral discipline, while still far from perfect, does have her sufficiently detached from ego to perceive reality better than she did when the novel opens. Other people now exist in her life not simply as objects—as instruments for the achievement of her aims or as obstacles impeding the movement of her will—but as subjects, as distinct individuals with pressing needs of their own. Seeing these individuals more clearly at last, Dora is better able to act virtuously toward them. Imaginatively engaging with Dora, the reader is also drawn along this path of moral development.

Independently of her fiction, Murdoch's ethical theory tells us how we can escape from fantasy and attain one of the prerequisites for virtuous interactions with other people. *The Bell* offers us practice in doing exactly this. Presented for our attention are examples of fantasy, of imagination reaching for reality, and of the connection between love and virtuous behavior. Here there is indeed work for the moral imagination—in the individual realities of the characters, which we can engage; in their attempts to perceive the reality of others, which we can share; and in the moral development of Dora, who shows us what love can achieve in the moral life.

Biographical Note

Critic, dramatist, librettist, literary theorist, novelist, pamphleteer, philosopher, poet: to refer to Dame Iris Murdoch as a "woman of letters" seems somehow to understate the case. Born in Dublin in 1919, she was raised in London; read Greats at Somerville College, Oxford, where she received a First; and later held a studentship in philosophy at Newnham College, Cambridge, where she studied with Elizabeth Anscombe. During World War II she worked briefly in the Treasury of Great Britain. In 1946, unable to accept a scholarship to the United States because of having been briefly a member of the Communist Party as a student, she worked for the United Nations Relief and Rehabilitation Administration in London, Belgium, and Austria. Between 1948 and 1963 she taught philosophy at St. Anne's College, Oxford. She lived near Oxford with her husband, the critic John Bayley. She died in 1999.

Murdoch is the author of twenty-six novels. The first is *Under the Net* (1954); the most recent is *Jackson's Dilemma* (1996). Three of her plays are adapted from her novels. Among these adaptations is *A Severed Head*, which was rewritten for the stage in collaboration with J. B. Priestly. If one counts her books *Acastos: Two Platonic Dialogues* and *Sartre: Romantic Rationalist,* Murdoch has written five volumes of philosophy; the others are *The Sovereignty of Good* (among philosophers, the best known of her works), *The Fire and the Sun: Why Plato Banished the Artists,* and—published most recently— *Metaphysics as a Guide to Morals* (1993).

Notes

1. Readers interested in a fuller discussion of Murdoch's ethical concepts of imagination, attention, and love may see Patricia J. O'Connor, *To Love the Good: The Moral Philosophy of Iris Murdoch* (New York: Peter Lang, 1996).

2. Iris Murdoch, *The Sovereignty of Good* (London: Ark-Routledge and Kegan Paul, Ltd., 1986) p. 51.

3. Ibid., p. 67.

4. Marilyn Frye, "In and Out of Harm's Way" in *The Politics of Reality* (Freedom, CA: Crossing Press, 1983), pp. 66–67.

5. See, for example, Stuart Hampshire's account of the self in *Thought and Action* (Notre Dame, In.: University of Notre Dame Press, 1959 and 1983), p. 125. Our wills here are "the centre, from which *everything* else can be regarded as an object"; they are like flashlights or lighthouses that "illuminate resisting objects" in their paths (emphasis added).

6. Murdoch, *Sovereignty,* p. 66.

7. Ibid., p. 67.

8. Ibid., p. 37.

9. Ibid.

10. Ibid., p. 34.

11. Ibid., p. 40. There are parallels to be found here with the views of Peirce and James, among others.

12. Frye, p. 69.

13. Murdoch, "The Darkness of Practical Reason," *Encounter* (July 27, 1966), p. 48.

14. Murdoch, "The Sublime and the Good," *Chicago Review* XII (Autumn 1959), p. 52.

15. Ibid., p. 54, p. 52.

16. Murdoch, *Sovereignty,* p. 66. Emphasis Murdoch's.

17. Ibid., pp. 91–92.

18. Ibid., p. 66.

19. Alasdair MacIntyre, "Good for Nothing" (review of *Iris Murdoch: Work for the Spirit,* by Elizabeth Dipple), *London Review of Books,* 4:10 (June 3–16, 1982), p. 15.

20. Murdoch, "Existentialists and Mystics," *Essays and Poems Presented to Lord David Cecil,* W. W. Robson, ed. (London: Constable, 1970), p. 231.

21. Murdoch, "The Sublime and the Beautiful Revisited," *Yale Review* XLIX (December 1959), p. 267.

22. Ibid., p. 270.

23. The concept of "suggestive eloquence" appears in "The Sublime and the Beautiful Revisited," p. 271. It has its origin in a passage from a letter by Henry James. The idea that a good novel provides space, both for the characters who inhabit it and for the reader, is present in a number of Murdoch's publications; it receives what is arguably its fullest expression in Murdoch's interview with Bryan Magee in *Men of Ideas: Some Creators of Contemporary Philosophy* (London: British Broadcasting Company, 1978), pp. 264–84.

24. Murdoch, "Existentialists and Mystics," p. 221.

25. Basil Mitchell, *Morality: Religious and Secular* (Oxford: Clarendon Press, 1980), p. 67.

26. My thanks to Cecile Tougas for suggesting that I include mention of the Annunciation, and for attentive and sensitive editing of the paper as a whole.

27. Murdoch, *The Bell* (London: Penguin, 1958 and 1988), p. 22.

28. Ibid., p. 77.

29. Ibid.

30. Ibid., p. 110.

31. Ibid., p. 190.

32. Ibid., pp. 190–1.

33. Ibid., p. 191.

34. Ibid.

35. Ibid., p. 265.

36. Ibid.

37. Ibid., p. 266.

38. Ibid., p. 267.

39. Ibid.

40. Ibid., p. 268.

41. Ibid., p. 301.

23 Why I Have Worked on This Book for Several Years

March, 1996. While I was composing parts of this essay, I received a postcard from a male friend from Japan who is a philosophical colleague (I will refer to it later). I had recently read a paper he had written for presentation at a conference in the United States in April 1996. I read this paper for him as a native English—or at least, American English—speaker trying to help make it easily understandable to his audience. In reading it, however, I became very upset. He was criticizing an important philosopher on the basis of a misunderstanding of that philosopher. He was joining a group of people whom he defended in this attack. It pained me physically and mentally to see an important philosopher so terribly misrepresented and dismissed. So I left the attitude of detached observer "helping" the English and explicitly recognized my involvement in the situation. I realized: I am looking at a friend's expression with a grammatical eye, but the eyes I see with grammatically are also personal—they are *my* eyes, inseparable from my heart. And so I briefly wrote my friend about what I was feeling and included my letter with the edited manuscript.

I realize now that I was responding with indignation to an injustice. My friend was being duped by an inferior philosopher who was belittling a superior one and was changing what the better one said, tragically and substantially "making it over" into what it is not and so neglecting its genuine import. While attack is a tone of philosophical argument that has often found favor, misrepresentation has not. I felt it was important for me to tell my friend that there is another way to understand the attacked philosopher. In doing this I was, of course, implying that my friend was at least partially wrong in his interpretation. Telling a male philosopher he is wrong, however, is not easy.

Still, among true friends and family I feel you can tell someone he or she is wrong and expect that you will continue to be heard. The same week I wrote my friend the letter, I happened to see *Les Misérables* in a 1995 movie version adapted and directed by Claude Lelouch. In one of the beginning scenes, an illiterate prisoner who was wrongly convicted of murder on the basis of a misunderstanding is having supper with a literate prisoner who helped build the Eiffel Tower but cheated Gustave Eiffel out of the money for a whole floor. (His friend replies that, well, he gets nauseous after the third floor anyway.) They are in a dark cellar, a common room with only little windows, and they are eating soup with unshelled seafood in it. As they warm up in the conversation and tell each other their crimes, the illiterate one is asking the other to write a letter to his wife saying that he loves her. He loves her passionately, enormously, to all folly. All he wants to say in the letter is "I love you"—three pages of "I love you." Now the other, the literate "Tour-Eiffel" as he is nicknamed, responds by giving advice: women get bored by the same thing over and over, and so you must say other things and tell her your love in different, roundabout ways so that the letter will be interesting, and then she will put the letter under her pillow or in her clothes. In effect "Tour-Eiffel" is telling his friend he is wrong to say "I love you" for three pages. But the friend answers, no, that is exactly what he wants to say, she can put the letter wherever she wants, and how does the other know—he who cheated Gustave Eiffel out of a whole floor? Despite the friction between them, they continue to eat and are still friends. In the next scene, the wife, who is also illiterate, is hearing someone read her a letter that is three pages of "I love you" and she insists on hearing every word. She is completely moved, her impoverished face lights up, and she begins to cry. The man reading her the letter himself gets excited and tries to seduce her, but she runs away. These are among my favorite scenes in the whole movie.

I got to musing about these scenes and my philosophical friend. When I wrote and told him indirectly but kindly that he was wrong, I expected he would continue to hear me. But he did not receive my words in a friendly way. He took offense at my being philosophical in a letter. In response he sent me a postcard saying he did not expect my critique of content and could not understand why I was "so excited, because of the difference of opinion." He thought that since I liked his conclusion, I must "respect its procedure, too." He ended by saying that he did not want to continue "such a primitive exercise" that to him seemed "like a black joke!" I had liked his conclusion because in the last page he speaks in his own voice. I then wrote him further saying that the end does not justify the means and that, while I continue always to have great respect for him, I nevertheless find something wrong in his procedure, his means, even though I like the last page. I explained to him how it is that I cannot keep the attitude of detached observer but rather must in this case say something philosophical about the content of his paper. My involvement is not merely a matter of a "difference of opinion" or a "primitive exercise"—not to mention a "black joke"—but rather a matter of informing my friend about an injustice that I believe he is part of, somewhat unwittingly. After all, he is my friend, and can't friends tell each other the truth?

In this particular instance I was encountering an impasse that occurs rather often, for male philosophers do not like to hear women philosophize in a frank, intimate, friendly way. The response of my Japanese friend is not an isolated event. Several weeks ago an American colleague mailed me (without my requesting it) an essay he was planning to present before an important philosophical society. I read it and then wrote him, as a friend whom I had known and worked with over many years, that his essay on community and environment disturbed me greatly because I couldn't find him—or indeed, anybody—in it. What I did find, rather, was his saying that community is expressed through "polyvalent semiotic networks" and that effective networks of shared meaning help us grow morally. He concluded that the concepts of community and experience can be restored within the tradition of the systematic thinking of American metaphysics.

My friend's essay pained me. With his "polyvalent semiotic networks" he was ignoring the reality of people in the immediate feeling we have for one another. He was affirming that community and morality can be made through a "pragmatic efficacy" of thoughts, words, and symbols in a metaphysical system—at the expense of his recognizing that community has been here all along and that the problem is we ourselves who have mistreated one another. I felt he was ashamed of subjectivity and too embarrassed to mention individual responsibility. He had wonderful-sounding words that I imagined everyone at the meeting would applaud, but he did not bear witness to the bad and terrible things we do to others and suffer from others. He showed no grief about our actual failure and misery in living communally.

In dealing with community only in an abstract way, my friend left out what to me as a philosopher is most important: a vivid, urgent, personal relation of one's words and abstract distinctions to oneself, one's feeling, and one's actual situation in one's community. To me the close, the intimate, and the frank are crucially fundamental in philosophizing; individual decision and action are the necessary ground for genuine cultural change. In writing back to my friend, I took great pains to tell him gently what I found drastically missing in his essay. I told him that I knew what it was like to receive criticism and that it hurt me every time I was given it, but that after a while I got over it and realized that it improved my writing. But in his return letter, he dismissed my criticism as though it were trivial. He avoided what, in effect, I was asking him to do: to have a living experiential relation to his abstractions—actually to feel grief and pain. Like my Japanese friend, he too took offense at my philosophizing when it was not simply praise of his work.

I wish we could have talked like the friends in prison eating supper together. Even though I have talked closely over meals with both my American friend and my Japanese friend at different times, I still find that I cannot be frank with them about philosophical matters without their recoiling in displeasure. While I continue to esteem, accept, and even like them, I have a fundamental perspective different from theirs to which they do not want to pay serious attention. I speak as the woman I am and do not forget my subjective relation to the abstract distinctions I am making. I do not consider feeling to be a hindrance to the truth. Rather, as Madame de Lambert says and Ann Willeford quotes in her essay: "Nous allons aussi sûrement à la vérité par la force et la chaleur des sentiments que par l'étendue et la justesse des raisonnements; et nous arrivons toujours par eux plus vite au but dont il s'agit que par les connaissances." ("We go as surely to the truth by the force and the heat of the feelings as by the extent and exactitude of reasoning; and we always arrive more rapidly, through them, at the goal in question than through facts.")

For several years I have worked intently on this book with Sara Ebenreck and twenty contributors who were writing about women philosophers, in order to make present some women's ways of philosophizing. Women have grieved over the way a great number of men have philosophized without the presence of women; these men have left out much that is crucial to a search for wisdom. Traditional male philosophers have often excluded feeling as a means of arriving at truth, while women have included both feeling and reasoning reflection. Many men seem to me to believe they can—and must—philosophize in detachment from the close relationship and unabashed viewing that many women value. They don't talk philosophically in an intimate, personal, subjective way but rather suppose that philosophical discourse must be universal, impersonal, and objective without any necessary relation to subjectivity. Like the two male philosophical friends who have just written to me, many intellectual men act as though truth consisted chiefly in abstraction and occasionally in concrete factual listing, but rarely if ever in a reciprocal relation between abstraction and their own lives.

It saddens me, and tends to make me silent, when men strongly believe that argument is a battle in which one person wins and the other loses. They then identify an evident conclusion with winning and a winner with being right. To them loss and failure are wrong of themselves. In their eyes, erring or even being vulnerable means losing an argument and philosophizing badly. Since showing affection or feeling necessarily involves some tenderness and vulnerability, men tend to avoid it in rigorous philosophical argument, for fear of losing a battle. When women bring feelings into a discussion, men seldom pay serious attention and often avoid conversing with them—thereby breaking themselves off from a large part of our human condition.

Thus, men come to have only their logical abstractions and metaphysical systems by which to see themselves. They are not fully themselves in their philosophizing, for being oneself inevitably involves loss, weakness, and failure. I have seen women accepting the inevitability of failure in being human, and recognizing it in their thinking, much more often than I have seen men doing so. The kind of mistake we women philosophers tend to make, however, is to idolize great men thinkers. We fall for them because their words and sentences sound so wonderful. What woman has not been overwhelmed—or at least charmed—by a sublime expression of vast intention? Such expression powerfully calls up and brings into focus what we have felt intuitively and wondered about intensely for a long time. We have known life has deep inexorable meaning; when a man speaks logically and metaphysically, he allows us to enjoy this meaning with a degree of clarity and force we did not have before. Oh, this is just what we needed! Our disastrous error then occurs when we fail to distinguish the man from the awesome meaning at which his words are aiming. He goes along with the error, too, for he would much rather pretend that he is one with his words than fully be himself in relation to them.

It takes a long time and a great deal of sobriety for us to get over our gullibility and realize that a man is not the same thing as his thought is. It is yet harder to realize that the man may not even feel the need to make a relation between his impressive metaphysical concepts and his everyday living. If he did feel the need to make such a relation, he would have to recognize his losses and endure the degradation that suffering our human condition often brings. It is indeed difficult for anyone to exist in concrete, ever-flowing relation to one's philosophical thought. Still, one day the woman wakes up to the fact that the sublime expression is not the man. On this day she can nonetheless speak to him with compassionate respect, as one struggling human philosopher to another. She all too often comes to find, however, that the man then breaks off the conversation and sometimes even the friendship. He does not like to be told, even indirectly, that he is wrong, even by a woman who loves him as a friend and esteems him unwaveringly; he thinks he must be a loser if he is open to basic criticism. In this way, like my Japanese colleague who saw my candor as "a black joke," he loses his sense of humor along with his friend.

Women philosophers have attempted to address men's reluctance to be themselves in their philosophizing. We are at present still trying to draw forth some feeling response from them. We do not look forward to being silenced by a statement that what we are doing is not genuine philosophy. At the same time, we are not pretending that women are never wrong. As Mary Astell says, as quoted by Jane Duran in her essay: "But do the Women never chuse amiss? Are the Men only in fault? that is not pretended; for he who will be just, must be forc'd to acknowledge, that neither Sex are always in the right." Like individual women over the many centuries past, we are not so much interested in winning a battle as we are in being listened to with seriousness, respect, and patience.

I have worked on this book for several years because its authors philosophize in ways that are different from the ways of men who have left both women and them-selves out of their thinking. There is something terribly wrong with such exclusion, and this book gives us a chance to get beyond it and perhaps even become friends who can eat together and tell each other frankly what is wrong.

Perhaps we might have been more effective had we said "I love you" at least once in some way on every page, giving the reader some assurance that friendship is something we have long wanted. Perhaps we, like "Tour-Eiffel" the literate prisoner, have been wrong to want to use many different words. Still, we have written for literate people who were expecting to find some distinctions made and a variety of perspectives given. At the level of feeling, though, we are indeed saying the same thing over and over again: we hope that you the reader, who may put this book wherever you want, continue to reread it and take it to heart.

Contributors

TRACY ADAMS is assistant professor of French at the University of Maryland, University College, Schwäbisch Gmünd, Germany. She has published on the medieval French and English romances and on Diderot.

LISA A. BERGIN received her Ph.D. in philosophy from the University of Minnesota. Her dissertation topic was "The Communication of Knowledge across Difference." She is visiting assistant professor of philosophy at Michigan State University in East Lansing.

KARIN BROWN is visiting lecturer at the Stevens Institute of Technology in Hoboken, New Jersey, and holds a postdoctoral fellowship in ethics at Mount Sinai School of Medicine.

KATIE GENEVA CANNON is associate professor of Christian Ethics at Temple University. She has received numerous awards and is the author or coeditor of numerous books, including *Black Womanist Ethics* and *Katie's Canon*.

VEDA A. COBB-STEVENS was professor of philosophy at the University of Massachusetts Lowell. She was the founder of the Society for the Study of Women Philosophers.

JOHN J. CONLEY is associate professor of philosophy at Fordham University in New York City. He has published articles on ethics and aesthetics in *Cahiers, Inquiry, Society,* and *Philosophy and Theology*.

JANE DURAN is lecturer in the humanities at the University of California in Santa Barbara, where she is also visiting fellow in the Department of Philosophy. She is the author of *Toward a Feminist Epistemology* and numerous journal articles on feminist theory.

THERESE B. DYKEMAN is editor of the anthology *American Women Philosophers 1650–1930: Six Exemplary Thinkers* and has published articles in rhetoric and philosophy. An independent scholar, she is an adjunct professor of philosophy at Fairfield University in Connecticut.

SARA EBENRECK is assistant professor of philosophy at St. Mary's College of Maryland. She was the founding editor of *Earth Ethics* and executive editor of *American Land Forum*, and has published numerous articles in environmental philosophy.

MARILYN FISCHER is associate professor of philosophy at the University of Dayton. She has published articles in the areas of political philosophy, philosophy and philanthropy, and philosophy of music.

JO ELLEN JACOBS is the Griswold Distinguished Professor of Philosophy and chair of the Philosophy Department at Millikin University. She has two books with Indiana University Press: *The Complete Works of Harriet Taylor Mill* (1998) and *Harriet Taylor Mill: Portrait of a Victorian Radical* (forthcoming).

HELEN J. JOHN, S.N.D., is Professor of Philosophy Emerita at Trinity College, Washington, D.C., and the author of several earlier articles about Hildegard of Bingen.

GERDA LERNER is Robinson-Edwards Professor of History Emerita at the University of Wisconsin-Madison. She is a former president of the Organization of American Historians and the author of numerous books in women's history, including the pathbreaking volumes *The Creation of Patriarchy* and *The Creation of Feminist Consciousness*.

ELIZABETH KAMARCH MINNICH is the author of *Transforming Knowledge*. She is professor of philosophy and women's studies at the Graduate School of the Union Institute; she also writes, speaks, and consults widely on issues of diversity, democracy, and education. During her graduate study, she was teaching assistant for her mentor, Hannah Arendt, at the Graduate Faculty of the New School, New York.

BEATRICE K. NELSON has been a student of the work of Susanne K. Langer for over a decade. She has been a member of the Philosophy Department and of the Critical and Creative Thinking Program at the University of Massachusetts at Boston more semesters than not since 1967 and now consults to Fortune 500 companies in the area of new product development.

ANDREA NYE teaches philosophy and feminist theory at the University of Wisconsin—Whitewater. Her most recent books are *Philosophy and Feminism: At the Border* and her translation of and commentary on Elisabeth's letters to Descartes, *The Princess and the Philosopher*.

PATRICIA J. O'CONNOR began working on Iris Murdoch's philosophy in 1988 while a graduate student at the University of Exeter in the United Kingdom. She is currently associate provost at Queens College of the City University of New York. Her book *To Love the Good: The Moral Philosophy of Iris Murdoch* is published by Peter Lang.

SHERI STONE-MEDIATORE is an assistant professor of philosophy at Ohio Wesleyan University. She is working on a book, *The Power of Stories: Hannah Arendt, Storytelling, Feminist Politics*.

CECILE T. TOUGAS teaches Latin and algebra at Ben Franklin Academy in Atlanta, Georgia, and has written a book entitled *Dreaming as Intentional.* She taught philosophy for over ten years in New England.

MARY ELLEN WAITHE is the editor of the four-volume *A History of Women Philosophers* and the author of numerous studies of women philosophers in that history. She is professor of philosophy at Cleveland State University.

MARY HELEN WASHINGTON is professor of English at the University of Maryland at College Park. Her numerous books include *Memory of Kin* and *Invented Lives: Narratives of Black Women, 1860–1960.* She has received many awards, including the Lyndhurst Prize, 1994–1996.

ANN WILLEFORD received her doctorate in French literature from the University of Washington at Seattle and taught for several years at the University of New Hampshire. She is now teaching French at the Atlanta International School.

Index